# Psychiatry

*FIFTH EDITION*

# Psychiatry

## FIFTH EDITION

### David A. Tomb, M.D.

*Associate Professor*
*Department of Psychiatry*
*University of Utah School of Medicine*
*Salt Lake City, Utah*

## Williams & Wilkins

BALTIMORE • PHILADELPHIA • HONG KONG
LONDON • MUNICH • SYDNEY • TOKYO

A WAVERLY COMPANY

*Editor:* Charles W. Mitchell
*Managing Editor:* Linda S. Napora
*Copy Editor:* Ann Howard
*Designer:* Dan Pfisterer
*Illustration Planner:* Ray Lowman
*Production Coordinator:* Charles E. Zeller

Copyright © 1995
Williams & Wilkins
428 East Preston Street
Baltimore, Maryland 21202, USA

*Printed in the United States of America*

First Edition 1980
Second Edition 1984
Third Edition 1988
Fourth Edition 1992

**Library of Congress Cataloging in Publication Data**

Tomb, David A.
   Psychiatry / David A. Tomb.—5th ed.
     p.   cm.—(House officer series)
   Includes bibliographical references and index.
   ISBN 0-683-08343-0
   1. Psychiatry—Handbooks, manuals, etc.  2. Mental illness—Handbooks, manuals, etc.  3. Psychological manifestations of general diseases—Handbooks, manuals, etc.  I. Title.  II. Series.
   [DNLM: 1. Mental Disorders—handbooks.  WM 34 T656pa 1995]
RC456.T64   1995
616.89—dc20
DNLM/DLC
for Library of Congress
                                      94-31117
                                         CIP

94   95   96   97   98   99
1  2  3  4  5  6  7  8  9  10

To Jane, Collin, and Ian
for time lost

# *Preface*

I would like to believe that an edition of a book such as this would last more than 3 or 4 years, but that never seems to be the case. Basic science and clinical knowledge race ahead of all but the most determined professional's ability to keep up. The changes in this latest edition are numerous—not just because it must adapt itself to DSM-IV, but more importantly because the field has changed in its outline and its details.

In spite of these changes, however, some things remain constant: respect for, interest in, and conviction to help our patients. It's not always easy or straightforward, but it's what we are about.

**David A. Tomb, M.D.**

# Contents

# Chapter 1

# Psychiatric Classification

## DSM-IV

Psychiatric diagnosis has long been criticized as ambiguous and unreliable. Some diagnoses have been based on subjective, unverifiable intrapsychic phenomena, whereas others have been heterogeneously broad.

Modern diagnosis attempts to avoid these pitfalls through the use of the 4th edition of the Diagnostic and Statistical Manual of Mental Disorders (DSM-IV) that identifies each disorder by a unique, specific collection of symptoms. It defines a limited number of identifiable (although possibly overlapping) psychiatric disorders and contains specific diagnostic criteria for each diagnosis. One matches facts from a particular patient's history and clinical presentation with criteria from a likely diagnosis and, if an adequate number are met, that diagnosis should be made. Each disorder has a unique set of these "operationally defined" diagnostic criteria. Multiple diagnoses are permitted and each general group of disorders has one disorder "Not Otherwise Specified" (NOS) which allows for placement of the (often many) patients who have unusual presentations. In addition, some disorders have **subtypes,** which are mutually exclusive, and/or **specifiers** which are not (eg, mild, moderate, and severe; or in full remission). Finally, it's okay to make a **provisional** (you are not sure) or a **deferred** (not enough information) diagnosis.

For example: A patient who (A) has been having delusions and auditory hallucinations that (B) have impaired his social relations and functioning at work (C) for at least 6 months and

1

who is without evidence of (D) a general medical condition or (E) prominent symptoms of a major mood disorder must be given the diagnosis of schizophrenia. It the patient also has (F) a flat, inappropriate, or silly affect and (G) disorganized speech and behavior, an additional diagnosis of disorganized subtype should be made.

DSM-IV has improved diagnostic **reliability** (the likelihood that different professionals would make the same diagnosis on the same patient) but has had only a modest impact on **validity** (the certainty that the diagnoses identify unique, meaningful conditions). Note also that DSM-IV makes no assumptions about what causes these disorders (it just describes and categorizes them), and in most cases the etiology is unknown. Although DSM-IV holds up well across cultures, its use in those settings requires special care in the interpretation of symptoms. For this reason, among others, DSM-IV allows the use of "clinical judgment" as well as strict application of the criteria in making a final diagnosis.

## MULTIAXIAL CLASSIFICATION

In addition to operationally defined criteria, DSM-IV also uses a multiaxial system of classification to capture other important information. A patient is not fully classified until he is coded on each of five axes (although only the first three axes are needed for an official diagnosis):

— Axis I: The clinical disorder(s) described above.
— Axis II: Personality disorders and/or mental retardation (none may be present).
— Axis III: Physical disorders relevant to the mental disorder.
— Axis IV: A listing of psychosocial and environmental problems, usually but not always during the preceding year, such as unemployment, divorce, financial problems, victim of child neglect, etc.
— Axis V: The Global Assessment of Functioning Scale (GAF; DSM-IV, pg 32) a measure of (A) current general functioning and (B) the highest functioning over the preceding year (scale of 1–100); used in treatment planning and predicting outcome.

### Suggested Readings

American Psychiatric Association Task Force on Nomenclature and Statistics: Diagnostic and Statistical Manual of Mental Disorders, 4th ed., (DSM-IV). Washington, D.C., American Psychiatric Association, 1994.

Bayer R, Spitzer RL: Neurosis, psychodynamics, and DSM-III. Arch Gen Psychiatry 42:187–196, 1985.

Fabrega H: Diagnosis interminable: toward a culturally sensitive DSM-IV. J Nerv Ment Dis 180:5–7, 1992.

Goldman HH, Skodol AE, Lave TR: Revising axis V for DSM-IV: A review of measures of social functioning. Am J Psychiatry 149:1148–1156, 1992.

Longabaugh R, Fowler DR, et al: Validation of a problem focused nomenclature. Arch Gen Psychiatry 40:453–461, 1983.

Pincus HA, Frances A, Davis WW, et al: DSM-IV and new diagnostic categories: holding the line on proliferation. Am J Psychiatry 149:112–117, 1992.

Williams JBW: The multiaxial system of DSM-III: where did it come from and where should it go? Arch Gen Psychiatry 42:175–186, 1985.

# Chapter 2

# Assessment

A psychiatric evaluation helps (1) make a diagnosis, (2) estimate the severity of the patient's condition, (3) decide on an initial course of action, (4) develop a relationship with the patient (therapeutic alliance), (5) assemble a dynamic understanding of the patient, and (6) engage the patient in psychotherapy. Some (primarily analytically oriented) psychiatrists argue that the most reliable understanding of a patient results from an open-ended interview in which the course of the interview is directed by the patient's conscious and unconscious concerns. An alternate form of interview, and one encouraged by the requirements of DSM-IV, uses a structured format that demands precise historical and descriptive information and the answers to specific questions. Which technique produces a more accurate and useful understanding of the patient remains unresolved, yet modern diagnosis requires the structured form described below.

A thorough evaluation of a psychiatric patient consists of a psychiatric history, mental status examination, complete physical examination, laboratory screening evaluation, and, when indicated, specific psychological and biological tests. The history and mental status are usually obtained during the initial interview.

More is required than merely collecting facts. The interviewer seeks useful information not only from the history and mental status examination, but also from the patient's interpersonal style and nonverbal communications and from the sequence and choice of issues raised by the patient. Because there is so much information available from the patient outside the formal part of the interview, it is essential to avoid structuring the interview too early. Initially, allow the patient to express his concerns and find out his reason for coming for help (Why now?). Be supportive, attentive, nonjudgmental, and encouraging, develop a rapport with the patient, and try to get an empathic understanding of his distress. Develop a qualitative sense for the patient's impairment. Help allay anxiety, if present. Be patient, friendly, and receptive if the patient is quiet. If he rambles, you may have to impose a structure early. If the patient is paranoid, progress slowly. Decide early if he is likely to be aggressive, suicidal, or in need of hospitalization.

If skillfully conducted, much of the information required by the history and mental status exam may be obtained unobtrusively. As the interview proceeds, you usually can identify and narrow missing data so that more formal questions are minimal. However, certain information is almost always required (e.g., data to satisfy DSM-IV diagnostic criteria, family psychiatric history, or mental status responses to rule out organicity or loss of abstracting ability). At times during the interview mentally review what is missing and save time toward the end to pursue it by direct questioning. The transition to a more formal style of interviewing can be smooth if rapport has been developed beforehand ("Now I need to ask you some very specific questions").

## PSYCHIATRIC HISTORY

### Identification of the Patient

1. Name, age, birth date, marital status, number of children, ethnic status, religion, occupation, education, social class, handicaps, etc;
2. Identification of informants (if not the patient). Mood and apparent biases of informants;
3. Estimate of the reliability of the information.

### Chief Complaint

Usually a verbatim statement of "the problem." Does it differ significantly from the reports of those who accompany the patient?

### Present Illness

Usually the focus of the interview. Get the patient's description of and feelings about his illness (problem). Establish the chronological order of symptoms and treatments. Has the patient noticed any other changes in himself? Have there been major life changes during this time or particular stresses and conflicts? Is any secondary gain identifiable? Any past psychiatric history—particularly diagnoses and severity of illnesses; types of treatment; drug use?

## Personal History

Birth and early development: Mother's pregnancy and delivery; Prematurity? Planned pregnancy? Get estimate of temperament and behavior problems. Any psychophysiological problems? (Relatives may be a source of information.)

Childhood: Personality traits, behavior problems, social relationships, school adjustment, family relationships, and family stability. Any abuse or family violence?

Social history: What kind of interpersonal relationships can the patient make? Has he been a loner? follower? leader? What kind of group activities has he had in the past and in the present? Who are the people important to him now? in the past? What was his premorbid personality? Military history?

Marriage: At what age? How many times? Relationship patterns within the marriage? Number of children and attitude toward them?

Education: Highest grade attained? Specific academic difficulties? Behavior problems? Social problems?

Occupational history: Concentrate on job changes, length of time jobs have been held, best job obtained and when—get details. Social relations on job; with boss? with workers? How does job compare with ambition? with family expectations?

Sexual history: Sexual orientation? Psychosexual problems or deviant behavior? Feelings about sex?

Current social situation: Personal living situation, income? Social environment? Estimated current marital and family stability and happiness?

## Family History

Who lives in the home?—patient should describe them and describe his relationship with them. Get description of patient's family of origin and his role in it. Upwardly mobile family? Get detailed description of psychiatric (and medical) illnesses in family members (family psychiatric history).

## Medical History

Current and past medical problems and treatments.

## MENTAL STATUS EXAMINATION

A mental status examination is a systematic documentation of the quality of mental functioning at the time of interview. It helps both with current diagnosis and treatment planning, and it serves as a baseline for future reference. Although much of the information sought in a mental status exam is obtained informally during other parts of the interview, it is usually necessary for the patient to answer a few formal questions if the interviewer is to learn the patient's abilities in each of the categories of mental functioning listed below. Upon concluding the mental status examination, estimate its reliability.

### General Presentation

Appearance: overall impression of the patient: attractive, unattractive, posture, clothes, grooming, healthy vs sickly, old looking vs young looking, angry, puzzled, frightened, ill-at-ease, apathetic, contemptuous, effeminate, masculine, etc.

General behavior: mannerisms, gestures, combative, psychomotor retardation, rigid, twitches, picking, clumsy, hand wringing, etc.

Attitude toward the examiner: cooperative, hostile, defensive, seductive, evasive, ingratiating, etc.

The psychotic patient may appear disheveled and bizarre with odd posturing (particularly catatonics) and grimacing. Some schizophrenics may stare and others look "blank." Paranoid patients may be hostile and suspicious, borderline patients hostile and angry, while histrionic patients often are seductive in manner and dress. Depressed patients may be nearly mute and display psychomotor retardation. Restlessness may suggest anxiety, withdrawal, mania, etc.

## State of Consciousness

Is the patient alert (eg, normally aware of both internal and external stimuli) or is he hyperalert? Is the patient lethargic, eg, does he "drift off" or do his thoughts wander? The patient needs to be reasonably alert for the remainder of the exam to be reliable. The causes for decreased alertness are usually organic.

## Attention

Can the patient pay attention for short periods of time (attend) without being distracted by minor stimuli? Can he attend for long periods of time (concentrate)? This ability is necessary if you are to assess higher level functions (ie, they may be intact, but the patient cannot demonstrate them due to lack of attention). Test attention by digit recall (digit span), eg, speak a series of numbers in a monotone and ask the patient to repeat them; begin with three numbers and increase by one with each successful trial; a normal maximum is seven numbers repeated. Have them repeat numbers backward: normal = 5. Test concentration by Random Letter Test, eg, tell patient to note (by raising his finger) each time a certain letter is mentioned and then read a long string of letters; most people make very few errors. Defects in attention usually are due to organic causes but may be caused by marked anxiety or psychotic interruption of thoughts.

## Speech

Listen to the patient's speech. Is it loud, soft, fast, slow, pressured, mute, etc? Does the patient speak spontaneously? with good vocabulary? Does the patient articulate with difficulty (dysarthria)? Is there a deficiency in language, eg, aphasia? This speech is usually identifiable by the experienced listener (eg, patient tries to communicate but incorrect words are chosen and grammatical errors made) but may be confused with rambling psychotic speech. Manic patients often speak loudly and rapidly; depressed patients are soft and slow. Bizarre speech usually suggests a psychotic and/or organic state.

## Orientation

Check for <u>person</u> (name? age? when born?), <u>place</u> (What place is this? What is your home address?), <u>time</u> (today's date? day of the week? time? season?), and <u>situation</u> (Why are you here?). Time sense is usually the first lost. Major disorientation suggests organicity. Minor loss may reflect temporary stress. If without problems, they are "oriented × 4."

## Mood and Affect

<u>Mood</u> is a sustained emotional state, eg, depressed, euphoric, elevated, anxious, angry, irritable.

<u>Affect</u> is the patient's current emotional state; it is the state the interviewer can <u>observe</u>. Common abnormal affects include flat, blunted, restricted, and inappropriate.

Note if the affect you observe is consistent with the patient's expressed mood and congruent with his thought content. Distinguish a depressed mood from an organically caused apathy. The affective disorders most commonly display alterations in mood but so do psychotic, anxiety (eg, panic), and organic (eg, drug use) disorders.

## Form of Thought

Does the patient's thinking make sense? Does one thought follow another logically, or does the patient display <u>circumstantiality</u> (take forever to make his point; many irrelevant details, over-inclusiveness), <u>flight of ideas</u> (rapidly jumping from idea to idea; usually stimulated by a previous word or thought, but with understandable associations), <u>evasiveness,</u> <u>loosening of associations</u> (tangentiality or derailment—thoughts are unrelated, but the patient seems unaware of this), <u>perseveration</u> (needless repetition of the same thought or phrase), or <u>blocking</u> (speech and train of thought is interrupted and picked up again a few moments or minutes later). Are answers to questions relevant? Ask the patient for his impressions of his own thoughts. Record quotes of abnormal speech—it adds clarity.

These abnormalities in thought processes are most commonly associated with schizophrenic or affective disorders.

None are pathognomonic, but any major abnormality suggests a psychotic process.

### Thought Content

Check for: abnormal preoccupations and obsessions, excessive suspiciousness, phobias, rituals, hypochondriacal symptoms, déjà vu experiences, depersonalization, delusions (fixed, false beliefs—characterize them as persecutory, of grandeur, of reference, of influence, unsystematized, etc). Always check for preoccupations concerning suicide or homicide.

Get at the presence of delusions by questions like: "Do you have any strong ideas other people don't share?" "Are there things you think about a lot?"

Delusions usually suggest a functional psychotic disorder (most commonly schizophrenia), but other conditions may display them (eg, poorly systematized delusions in delirium). Obsessions may occur with psychosis but also are typical of OCD. Phobias characterize phobic disorders.

Is the patient unaware that he is ill or has abnormal thinking (lacks insight)? Does he have a generalized loss of ability for abstract thinking (ie, concreteness)? Test for abstractive ability by:

1. Similarities: "What do these things have in common? "
                baseball—orange
                car—train
                desk—bookcase
                happy—sad
                horse—apple
2. Proverbs: "What do people mean when they say . . . ? "
                When the cat's away, the mice will play.
                The proof of the pudding is in the eating.
                A golden hammer breaks an iron door.
                The tongue is the enemy of the neck.
                The hot coal burns, the cold one blackens.

Always correlate abstract thinking with intelligence. Concreteness in the face of normal intelligence "suggests" a psychotic thought disorder. Note any bizarre responses to similarities or proverbs, Are the answers personalized? Are the answers vague because the patient is aware of failing (eg, delirium, early dementia) and is obfuscating?

## Perceptions

Does the patient display misperceptions (draw wrong conclusions from self-evident information)? Are there illusions (misinterpretations of sensory stimuli, eg, a shadow becomes a person) or hallucinations (totally imagined sensory perceptions: note whether auditory, visual, tactile, olfactory, etc)? Always determine if hallucinations are accusatory, threatening, or commanding. If not volunteered, detect the presence of hallucinations by questions such as: "Have you had the experience of walking down the street, hearing your name called, and finding no one there?" "Have you had any mystical or psychic experiences?"

Illusions are most common in delirium but may also occur in other psychoses. Hallucinations occur in a variety of conditions but most commonly in psychotic disorders. Schizophrenia usually has auditory hallucinations although visual hallucinations are more common in organic conditions. Tactile hallucinations are frequent in sedative-hypnotic and alcohol withdrawal states.

## Judgment

An estimate of the patient's real life problem solving skills is often difficult to make. Judgment is a complex mental function that depends on maturation of the nervous system (poor in children). The best indicator is usually the patient's behavior; therefore history is very important. Some sense of the patient's judgment can be obtained through hypothetical examples: "What should you do if you find a stamped, addressed letter?" "What should you do if you lose a book belonging to a library?"

Judgment is regularly impaired in delirium, dementia, psychosis, and some retardation. Its assessment helps determine the patient's capacity for independent functioning.

## Memory

Test all three types of memory: immediate (retention and recall), recent, and remote.

Immediate:
1. Digit repetition

2. Ask patient to remember three objects and three words—ask for them after 5 minutes (they should be recalled).
3. Ask the patient to count—stop him at 27—(wait 1 minute)—tell him to continue counting—stop at 42—(wait 3 minutes)—then continue counting.

Recent:

Ask questions about the past 24 hours, eg, "How did you travel here?" "What was on the television news last night?"

Remote:

Personal: born? school? work? etc. Historical: name four presidents in this century; the dates of WW II; etc.

Recent and remote memory usually can be tested inconspicuously during the interview. Is the patient aware of his deficit? What is his attitude toward it? Loss of memory usually indicates an organic process unless it has some of the characteristics of the dissociative disorders (Chapter 9).

Constructional ability is a sensitive test for early diffuse cortical damage. Draw a diamond and a three-dimensional cube and have the patient copy them. Ask the patient to draw a flowerpot with a flower, or the face of a clock set at 2:45. Incomplete or very poorly done responses are suggestive of early organicity.

## Intellectual Functioning

Intelligence is a global function that can be estimated from the general tone and content of the interview as well as by the patient's fund of information and ability to perform calculations.

### FUND OF KNOWLEDGE

How many weeks in a year?
Name the last six Presidents.
What does the liver do?
How far is it from Chicago to LA?
Why are light-colored clothes cool?
Who wrote Remembrance of Things Past?
What causes rust?
How many nickels in $1.15?

### CALCULATIONS

Serial 7's: "Take 100 and subtract 7 from it, then take 7 from that answer, etc";
Serial 3's: "Take 3 from 20, etc";
Simple calculations: $2 \times 3, 5 \times 3, 4 \times 9$.

Calculation relies on functions other than intelligence, including concentration and memory. If in doubt, ask for formal IQ testing. Organic conditions may produce a loss of intellectual functioning, but psychoses seldom do (as long as the patient can concentrate on the tests).

## PSYCHOLOGICAL TESTS

Psychological testing is occasionally requested for psychiatric patients and may provide a useful enlargement of the understanding of those patients. Although not essential for most patients, testing may:

1. Help identify organic syndromes;
2. Help localize organic pathology;
3. Contribute to the identification of borderline psychotic states;
4. Provide a baseline of general and specific functioning;
5. Generally help with differential diagnosis among psychiatric conditions.

Talk to the psychologist. Describe what you are looking for. Ask for recommendations. Although most patients receive a battery of tests, very specific questions may be answered by only one test. Carefully integrate the psychologist's report with your own evaluation but do not allow test results to supersede clinical judgment. Commonly used tests for adults include:

**Wechsler Adult Intelligence Scale (WAIS):** A very useful test. Although it does yield three separate IQ scores (full-scale, verbal, and performance), a careful evaluation of how the patient answered the 11 different subtests within the WAIS provides clues to the presence of a thought disorder, an attention or memory deficit, visual-motor impairment, etc.

**Minnesota Multiphasic Personality Inventory (MMPI-2):** This is a true-false, self-administered personality test of 567 items which takes little of the therapist's time, produces a general description of the patient's personality characteristics, and can even be computer scored. Although a useful global description of the patient, do not stretch it too far diagnostically.

**Bender-Gestalt Test:** This test is easily administered—the patient draws nine specific geometric figures on a blank sheet of paper. Its greatest application is in detecting visual-motor impairment and organic deficits.

**Rorschach Test:** This is an unstructured projective test that asks the patient to "describe what he sees" in a series of 10 standardized ink blots. Elaborate scoring systems exist that allow a skilled examiner to infer elements of the patient's personality functioning. It is used diagnostically to help identify psychoses and personality disorders. Its diagnostic validity, while not assured, is reasonably high using the standardized rating system devised by Exner.

**Thematic Apperception Test (TAT):** This is a projective test similar to the Rorschach that draws conclusions from stories a patient generates in response to a series of suggestive but ambiguous human figure drawings.

**Draw-a-Person Test:** The patient is asked to draw a picture of a "person" and then a picture of a person of the opposite sex. The results are then interpreted by the examiner, usually as a screen for brain damage.

**Mini-Mental State Exam:** A brief, formal, mental status screening exam devised by Folstein for "bedside" use which tests orientation to time and place, immediate and short-term memory, calculation, language, and constructive ability. Although widely used because of its simplicity, it is flawed and improved versions exist.

Psychiatric Rating Scales are a class of measures that rate emotional symptoms or disorders. They usually consist of lists of short questions that require brief numerical answers and typically are filled out by the patient or the therapist. They serve several purposes: (1) provide a baseline measure of a set of symptoms or diagnoses, (2) allow the severity of psychopathology to be followed longitudinally, (3) complement clinical judgment with an objective measure, (4) evaluate the effectiveness of treatment, (5) provide a uniform standard across evaluators, (6) help determine disposition, and (7) function as a standard measure of patients' symptoms in research trials. They assess differing psychopathology including general emotional problems (Global Assessment Scale or GAS; Brief Psychiatric Rating Scale or BPRS), organicity (such as the Folstein Mini-Mental State Exam, MMSE, mentioned above), the diagnosis of mood and psychotic disorders (Schedule for Affective Disorders and Schizophrenia; SADS), depression (Beck Depression Inventory; Hamilton Depression Rating Scale), and anxiety (Hamilton Anxiety Rating Scale; State-Trait Anxiety Scale). There are dozens of rating scales available and their use is growing rapidly both for their own sake and because managed care agencies increasingly demand objective measures of the severity and course of a patient's illness. Moreover, they are philosophically consistent with the concepts of psychiatric disease underlying DSM-IV.

## EEG

The EEG plays a useful, but only supportive, role in psychiatry. It is suggestive but not definitive in any psychiatric condition, but it does help rule in or out a diversity of conditions. Its primary use is in the differentiation between organic and functional conditions.

1. Epileptics (particularly temporal lobe epilepsy) often mimic "pseudoseizure" psychiatric patients—the EEG helps differentiate (although 30% of epileptics have a normal tracing between attacks).
2. The patient who is confused and disoriented (delirium) due to organic factors usually has diffuse EEG slowing. A major exception is Alcohol Withdrawal Delirium (delirium tremens) which shows increased fast activity as does confusion due to sedative-hypnotics. Major tranquilizers increase slow wave activity.
3. The patient who has dementia of the Alzheimer type (50% of demented patients) usually has a normal EEG early on, with abnormalities later (a help in staging). Most reversible forms of dementia produce abnormal tracings. The EEG of a person with pseudodementia (eg, depression that mimics dementia) is usually normal.
4. A variety of organic causes can produce bizarre behavior (eg, brain tumor, cerebral infarcts, cerebral trauma). A normal EEG does not rule out organic pathology, but an abnormal tracing is suspicious.

Several populations of psychiatric patients have a slightly increased frequency of nonspecific abnormalities on the EEG, eg, schizophrenics (particularly catatonics) and manic-depressives. Patients with antisocial personality disorder have perhaps the highest frequency of abnormal tracings—look for but don't overread organic pathology in these patients.

Brain electrical activity topographic mapping (quantitative EEG or QEEG) groups each wave length type and plots their positions over a map of the head. This new technology may extract more information from EEG data and increase its usefulness. Although still a research tool, it may help diagnose delirium, dementia, and intoxication as well as stroke, schizophrenia, depression, and OCD. A related EEG technique, visual and/or auditory evoked potentials (EPs), remain an (actively investigated) research tool in psychiatry.

## BRAIN IMAGING

### Structural Techniques

Both the CT scan and MRI supply brain structure information useful in psychiatric diagnosis. Because it is relatively inexpensive, the CT scan is used to screen for organic brain disease, particularly in older patients with sudden psychiatric symptoms and in patients with a history of head trauma. The more expensive MRI gives a better image and is much better able to differentiate between gray and white matter and so is used to look for subtle changes in CNS structures as well as to identify demyelinating disorders, dementia, infarctions, and neoplasms. CT or MRI may be combined with neuropsychological testing or functional imaging such as PET or SPECT scans for more information.

### Functional Techniques

PET and SPECT scans both measure brain metabolic activity. PET provides better resolution and can provide a direct measure of brain glucose metabolism but is very expensive and available in only a few centers. SPECT is now available in most major medical centers and at a "reasonable" cost but currently reflects brain blood flow and thus is a more indirect measure of metabolism. Both remain research techniques, even though they have provided many fascinating, but unproven, insights into psychiatric disorders (eg, parietal lobe hypofunction may occur in catatonic schizophrenia but not in other types of schizophrenia; inferior right frontal and temporal hypoperfusion is seen in some major depression; orbitofrontal and globus pallidus hyperactivity in OCD). SPECT now has clinical utility in the differential diagnosis of stroke, dementia, and epilepsy and may soon have use in schizophrenia, OCD, depression, and brain receptor imaging. It is likely that, in the near future, PET will teach us much more about the psychobiological functioning of the brain and SPECT will become a useful diagnostic tool for specific psychiatric conditions.

## AMYTAL INTERVIEW

The administration of amobarbital (Amytal), thiopental (Pentothal), or pentobarbital (Nembutal) during an interview to produce a sedated state has been used for many years both diagnostically (Amytal interview) and therapeutically (narcoanalysis). Despite a long history of use, the indications for and value of this technique are unclear.

The technique usually consists of administering a total of 200–500 mg (occasionally more) of sodium amobarbital IV at a rate of 25–50 mg/min. The interviewer talks with the patient throughout administration and halts the drug temporarily when the desired level of sedation is attained (eg, appearance of lateral nystagmus for light sedation; development of slurred speech for a deeper state). Additional Amytal may be given if the interview is lengthy.

In this sedated state some patients present a markedly altered clinical picture which may be of diagnostic value. Although opinion varies, diagnostic uses for the Amytal interview may include:

1. Evaluation of mute patients—Patients with catatonic schizophrenia often recover dramatically when sedated (although a thought disorder usually remains) but return to the full catatonic state when the Amytal wears off. This helps differentiate catatonia from marked psychomotor retardation in the depressed patient (they show little improvement). Patients mute for other reasons (eg, hysterical, acute stress) may begin to talk under sedation.
2. Acute panic states—Patients immobilized by severe stress may talk about their concerns when sedated and find some relief.

3. Organic vs functional differentiation—Patients who are confused, disoriented, or demented due to organic factors usually worsen with Amytal although clinically similar functional patients often clear temporarily.
4. Hysterical phenomena—Amnesias, fugues, and conversion disorders often are temporarily relieved by Amytal. Useful information may be obtained during this time, eg, the patient's name and address; the cause of the patient's anger.
5. The interview is less reliably useful with psychotic states (except for catatonic schizophrenia), although some patients may contribute information they would not have otherwise.

Although helpful in confirming some diagnoses, the Amytal interview also may contribute to the treatment of a few patients by allowing them to confront and deal with stressful or troubling experiences that they previously had been reluctant or unable to face. However, the validity of old memories in patients with a presumed past history of child abuse and/or a current dissociative disorder that are recalled under Amytal interview is uncertain (the "false memory" vs "repressed memory" controversy).

## Suggested Readings

American Psychiatric Association Task Force: Quantitative electroencephalography: A report on the present state of computerized EEG techniques. Am J Psychiatry 148:961–964, 1991.

Butcher JN, Williams CL: Essentials of MMPI2 and MMPIA Interpretation. Minneapolis, University of Minnesota Press, 1992.

Exner JE: The Rorschach: A Comprehensive System, vols 1, 2, 3. New York, John Wiley & Sons, 1982.

Fenton GW, Standage K: Clinical electroencephalography in a psychiatric service. Can J Psychiatry 38:333–338, 1993.

Folstein MF, Folstein SE, McHugh PR: "Mini-mental state"—a practical method for grading the cognitive state of patients for the clinician. J Psychiatr Res 12:189–198, 1975.

George MS, Ketter TA, Post RM: SPECT and PET imaging in mood disorders. J Clin Psychiatry 54(11, suppl):6–13, 1993.

Gur RC, Erwin RJ, Gur RE: Neurobehavioral probes for physiologic neuroimaging studies. Arch Gen Psychiatry 49:409–414, 1992.

Innis RB: Neuroreceptor imaging with SPECT. J Clin Psychiatry 53(11, suppl):29–34, 1992.

Kahn EM, Weiner RD, Coppola R, et al: Spectral and topographic analysis of EEG in schizophrenic patients. Biol Psychiatry 33:284–290, 1993.

MacKinnon RA, Michels R: The Psychiatric Interview in Clinical Practice. Philadelphia, WB Saunders, 1971.

MacKinnon RA, Yudofsky SC: The Psychiatric Evaluation in Clinical Practice. Philadelphia, JB Lippincott Co, 1986.

McGuire PK, Bench CJ, Frith CD, et al: Functional anatomy of obsessive-compulsive phenomena. Br J Psychiatry 164:459–468, 1994.

Molloy DW, Alemayehu E, Roberts R: Reliability of a standardized mini-mental state examination compared with the traditional mini-mental state examination. Am J Psychiatry 148:102–105, 1991.

Morrison J: The First Interview. New York, Guilford Press, 1993.

Perry JC, Jacobs D: Overview: clinical applications of the Amytal interview in psychiatric emergency settings. Am J Psychiatry 139:552–559, 1982.

Pollock VE, Schneider LS, Zemansky MF, et al: Topographic quantitative EEG amplitude in recovered alcoholics. Psychiatry Res: Neuroimaging 45:25–32, 1992.

Prichep LS, Mas F, Hollander E, et al: Quantitative electroencephalographic subtyping of obsessive-compulsive disorder. Psychiatry Res: Neuroimaging 50:25–32, 1993.

Rosse RB, Giese AA, Deutsch SI, et al: Laboratory and Diagnostic Testing in Psychiatry. Washington, D.C., American Psychiatric Press, 1989.

Satoh K, Suzuki T, Narita M, et al: Regional cerebral blood flow in catatonic schizophrenia. Psychiatry Res: Neuroimaging 50:203–216, 1993.

Spiegle D, Scheflin AW: Dissociated or fabricated? Psychiatric aspects of repressed memory in criminal and civil cases. Intern J Clin Exp Hypnosis 42:411–432, 1994.

Strub RL, Black FW: The Mental Status Examination in Neurology, 3rd Ed. Philadelphia, FA Davis Co, 1993.

Teng EL, Chui HC: The modified mini-mental state (3MS) examination. J Clin Psychiatry 48:314–318, 1987.

Warner MD, Boutros NN, Peabody CA: Usefulness of screening EEGs in a psychiatric inpatient population. J Clin Psychiatry 51:363–364, 1990.

# Chapter 3

# Schizophrenia and other Psychotic Disorders

"Psychosis" describes a degree of severity, not a specific disorder. A psychotic patient has a grossly impaired sense of reality, often coupled with emotional and cognitive disabilities, which severely compromises his ability to function. He is likely to talk and act in a bizarre fashion, have hallucinations, or strongly hold ideas that are contrary to fact (delusions). He may be confused and disoriented and typically is not aware of his impairment (lacks insight).

This chapter covers the major psychotic disorders, ie, conditions that must reach psychotic proportions at some time during their course (although the patients may be nonpsychotic most of the time). Recognize that these are descriptive groupings of clinical syndromes—not discrete diseases.

Schizophrenia:
  Disorganized type
  Catatonic type
  Paranoid type
  Undifferentiated type
  Residual type
Schizophreniform Disorder
Brief Psychotic Disorder
Schizoaffective Disorder
Shared Psychotic Disorder
Delusional (Paranoid) Disorder
Psychotic Disorder Due to a General Medical Condition

Substance-Induced Psychotic Disorder
Psychotic Disorder NOS (Not Otherwise Specified)

## Differential Diagnosis

The majority of psychotic disorders have no known organic basis; some do. Look for this basic dichotomy by identifying any underlying medical and neurological causes or psychoses due to substance intoxication or withdrawal. Obtain a complete history and physical on all psychotic patients. Most nonorganic conditions present with emotion and thinking disturbances in a patient with a clear sensorium while most organic psychoses have a degree of delirium (eg, clouding of consciousness, confusion, disorientation). Unfortunately, exceptions to either pattern are frequent. Possible organic causes of psychosis include almost any type of serious medical illness or drug abuse (see Chapters 5, 6, 14, and 15). Suspect an organic etiology if:

The patient presents with significant memory loss, confusion, disorientation, or clouding of consciousness.

There is no personal or family history of serious psychiatric illness.

The patient has a serious medical illness or a chronic medical condition with periodic relapses.

The psychosis has developed rapidly (eg, days) in a patient who previously had been functioning well.

Psychiatric conditions that may (but do not necessarily) reach psychotic proportions (addressed in other chapters) include:

1. Major Depressive Disorder or Bipolar Disorder (see Chapter 4)—look for the psychosis to coexist with and be dominated by an affective component (either manic or depressed) which preceded the development of the psychosis.
2. Brief psychotic disorders may occur with stress in patients with personality disorders of the histrionic, borderline, paranoid, and schizotypal types. Some obsessive-compulsive persons at times may develop a psychosis if they fail to control their environment.
3. Some acute panic or rage attacks may be of psychotic intensity, eg, acute homosexual panic; rage in the patient with an explosive disorder (see Chapter 7).
4. A few psychotic conditions develop in childhood and continue into the adult years—AUTISTIC DISORDER (DSM-IV p 66, 299.00) and

<u>PERVASIVE DEVELOPMENTAL DISORDER NOS</u> (DSM-IV p 77, 299.80).

5. Psychotic states occasionally may be mimicked unconsciously or even "faked"—Factitious Disorder with Predominantly Psychological Signs and Symptoms; Malingering.

## SCHIZOPHRENIA

Schizophrenia is the most common psychotic disorder—almost 1% of people worldwide develop it during their lifetime; more than 2 million persons are affected in the United States. It occurs more frequently in urban populations and in lower socio-economic groups—probably due to a "downward drift" (ie, poorly functional, unemployable persons end up in marginal settings). Poor environments do not "cause" the disorder, although they make it more intractable.

The diagnosis of schizophrenia has had a checkered history. There have been numerous different ways to make the diagnosis, which have thus represented numerous different populations of patients. The current diagnostic scheme (DSM-IV) uses specific objective criteria to define several forms of schizophrenia. Because there are no pathognomonic findings, "schizophrenia" is a <u>clinical</u> diagnosis that may represent a non-specific syndrome of heterogeneous etiologies. However, biological, genetic, and phenomenological information suggest that it is a valid disorder(s). The five identified subtypes are also based on clinical variables.

### Clinical Presentation

While the nature of schizophrenia is uncertain, the current clinical description and method of making the diagnosis are more clear (DSM-IV).

Most schizophrenics are psychotic for only a small part of their lives. Typically they spend many years in a <u>residual phase</u> during which time they display more minor features of their illness. During these residual periods the patients may be withdrawn, isolated, and "peculiar." They usually are noticeable to others and may lose their jobs or friends both because of their own lack of interest and ability to perform and because they are behaving oddly. Their thinking and speech are vague and are believed by others to be odd and to "not quite make sense." They may be convinced that they are different from others, feel that they have special powers and sensitivities, and have "mystical" or "psychic" experiences. Their personal appearance and manners deteriorate, and they may display affect that is blunted, flat, or inappropriate. Although they maintain close to normal intelligence, performance on most cognitive tests is modest. They are frequently anhedonic (unable to experience pleasure). Often this deterioration merely represents a gradual worsening of a condition the patient has displayed for many years—the first psychotic episode may have been preceded by a similar period of eccentric thinking and behavior (prodromal phase).

A "prepsychotic personality" is seen in some chronic schizophrenics and is characterized by social withdrawal, social awkwardness, and marked shyness in a youth who has difficulty in school despite a normal IQ. An equally common pattern is involvement in minor antisocial activities in the year or two prior to the initial psychotic episode. Many of these patients have been diagnosed previously as having a schizoid, borderline, antisocial, or schizotypal personality disorder. It is only when they develop their first psychotic episode (normally in their teens or early 20's (men) or 20's and early 30's (women); a first "breakdown" after age 40 is unusual) that the diagnosis is changed to schizophrenia. Often a presumed precipitating stress can be identified. The typical acute psychosis displays a variable mixture of several of the following symptoms.

**Disturbance of Thought Form:** These patients usually have a formal thought disorder, ie, their thinking is frequently incomprehensible to others and appears illogical. Characteristics include:

Loosening of associations (derailment or tangential associations)—Patient's ideas are disconnected. He may jump obliviously from topic to unconnected topic, confusing the listener. When this occurs frequently (eg, in midsentence), the speech is often incoherent.

Overinclusiveness—Patient continually may disrupt the flow of his thoughts by including irrelevant information.

Neologisms—Patient coins new words (which may have a symbolic meaning for him).

Blocking—Speech is halted (often in midsentence) and then picked up a moment (or minutes) later, usually at another place. This may represent the patient's ideas being interrupted by intrusive thoughts (eg, hallucinations). These patients are often very distractable and have a short attention span.

Clanging—The patient chooses his next words and themes based on the sound of the words he is using rather than the thought content. Usually he rhymes a primary word in one sentence with a word in the preceding sentence.

Echolalia—Patient repeats words or phrases in a musical or sing-song fashion but without an apparent effort to communicate.

Concreteness—Patient of normal or above average IQ thinks in abstract terms poorly.

Alogia—Patient may speak very little (but without being intentionally resistant; "poverty of speech") or may speak a normal amount but say very little ("poverty of speech content").

**Disturbance of Thought Content:** Delusions are fixed, false beliefs far beyond credibility that may be "bizarre" (eg, "my right eye is a computer that controls the world") or "nonbizarre" (just very unlikely; "the FBI follows me") and remain unmodified despite clear evidence to the contrary. They are common in most serious mental disorders, but some specific forms of delusional thought are particularly frequent in schizophrenia. The more acute the psychosis, the more likely the delusion is to be disorganized and nonsystematized.

Bizarre, confused delusions

Persecutory delusions—particularly nonsystematic types.

Grandiose delusions

Delusions of influence—patient believes that he can control events through telepathy.

Delusions of reference—patient is convinced that there are "meanings" behind events and people's actions which are directed specifically toward himself.

Delusions of thought broadcasting—the belief that others can hear the patient's thoughts.

Delusions of thought insertion—the belief that someone else's thoughts have been inserted into the patient's mind.

Many schizophrenic patients display lack of insight, ie, the patient is unaware of his own illness or of his need for treatment, even though his disorder is evident to others.

**Disturbance of Perception:** Most common are <u>hallucina-</u>
<u>tions,</u> usually auditory but also visual, olfactory, and tactile. The
auditory hallucinations (most often voices—one or several) may
include a running commentary about the patient and events,
derogatory or threatening comments made to the patient, or
direct orders to the patient (command hallucinations). The
voices usually (but not necessarily) are perceived as coming
from outside the patient's head and occasionally he may hear
his own thoughts spoken aloud (often to his shame or embar-
rassment). The voices are quite "real" to the patient, except in
the early phases of the psychosis.

These patients may also have illusions, depersonalizations
(feels like he is observing himself from the outside), derealiza-
tions (the world seems unreal), and a hallucinatory sense of
bodily change.

**Disturbance of Emotions:** Acutely psychotic patients may
display various emotions and may switch from one to another
in a surprisingly short span of time. Two frequent (but not
pathognomonic) underlying affects are:

<u>Blunted or flat affect</u>—The patient expresses very little emotion, even
when it is appropriate to do so. He appears to be without warmth.
<u>Inappropriate affect</u>—The affect may be intense, but it is inconsistent
with the patient's thoughts or speech.
<u>Labile affect</u>—Marked changes in affect over a short period of time.

**Disturbance of Behavior:** Many different bizarre and inappropriate behaviors may be seen including strange grimacing
and posturing, ritual behavior, excessive silliness, aggressiveness, and some sexual inappropriateness.

An acute psychotic attack can last weeks or months (occasionally years). Many patients have recurrences of the active
phase periodically throughout their lives, typically separated by
months or years. During the intervening periods, patients usually present residual symptoms (often with the degree of impairment gradually increasing over the years); however, a few patients are symptom-free between acute episodes. Many
schizophrenic patients in remission display early signs of a developing relapse—always look for them. These early signs include increasing restlessness and nervousness, loss of appetite,

mild depression and anhedonia, insomnia, and trouble concentrating.

## Classification

To be considered schizophrenic, a patient must (DSM-IV, p 285)

1. have had at least 6 months of
2. sufficiently deteriorated occupational, interpersonal, and self-supportive functioning,
3. must have been actively psychotic in a characteristic fashion during at least part of that period, and
4. must not be able to account for the symptoms by the presence of a Schizoaffective or Major Mood Disorder, Autism, or an organic condition.

The course of the illness should be classed as continuous, episodic with or without interepisode residual symptoms, or single episode in partial or full remission. Moreover, all schizophrenic patients should be classed as one of five recognized subtypes which describe the most frequently occurring behavioral manifestations of the illness. There have been numerous subclassifications of schizophrenia in the past, all unsatisfactory, and the current divisions share some of those deficiencies. Although genetic data suggest that schizophrenia is a stable diagnosis, there is no comparable information for the subtypes. Symptomatically, they tend to overlap, and the diagnosis can shift from one to another with time (either during one episode or in a subsequent episode). Finally, over the years, the clinical presentations of many patients tend to converge toward a common picture of interpersonal withdrawal, flattened affect, idiosyncratic thinking, and impaired social and personal functioning. (At the same time, the course becomes more stable, with fewer acute symptoms or episodes.)

**DISORGANIZED TYPE** (DSM-IV p 288, 295.10): The patient has (A) blunted, silly, or inappropriate affect, (B) frequent incoherence, and (C) no systematized delusions. Grimacing and bizarre mannerisms are common.

**CATATONIC TYPE** (DSM-IV p 289, 295.20): The patient may have any one (or a combination) of several forms of catatonia.

1. <u>Catatonic stupor or mutism</u>—Patient does not appreciably respond to his environment or to the people in it. Despite appearances, these patients are often thoroughly aware of what is going on around them.
2. <u>Catatonic negativism</u>—Patient resists all directions or physical attempts to move him.
3. <u>Catatonic rigidity</u>—Patient is physically rigid.
4. <u>Catatonic posturing</u>—Patient assumes bizarre or unusual postures.
5. <u>Catatonic excitement</u>—Patient is extremely (eg, wildly) active and excited. May be life-threatening (eg, due to exhaustion).

**PARANOID TYPE** (DSM-IV p 287, 295.30): This is the most stable subtype over time and usually develops later than other forms of schizophrenia. The patient must display consistent, often paranoid, delusions that he may or may not act on. These patients are often uncooperative and difficult to deal with and may be aggressive, angry, or fearful, but they rarely display disorganized, incoherent behavior.

**UNDIFFERENTIATED TYPE** (DSM-IV p 289, 295.90): The patient has prominent hallucinations, delusions, and other evidences of active psychosis (eg, confusion, incoherence) but without the more specific features of the preceding three categories.

**RESIDUAL TYPE** (DSM-IV p 290, 295.60): The patient is in remission from active psychosis but displays symptoms of the residual phase (eg, social withdrawal, flat or inappropriate affect, eccentric behavior, loosening of associations, and illogical thinking).

## Prognosis

Schizophrenia is a chronic disorder. A person gradually may become more withdrawn, "eccentric," and nonfunctional over many years. Some patients may experience low-level delusions and hallucinations indefinitely. Many of the more dramatic and acute symptoms disappear with time, but the patient ends up chronically needing sheltered living or spending years in mental hospitals. Involvement with the law for misdemeanors is common (eg, vagrancy, disturbing the peace) as is associated mixed drug abuse. A few patients become somewhat demented. Overall life expectancy is shortened—primarily due to accidents, suicide, and an inability of the patients to care for themselves.

This pattern has exceptions. Psychiatrists have long distinguished between <u>process</u> schizophrenia (slowly developing; chronic, deteriorating course) and <u>reactive</u> schizophrenia (rapid onset; somewhat better prognosis). Similarly, they have differentiated between <u>positive symptoms</u> (hallucinations, delusions, bizarre behavior, etc.) which frequently respond to usual antipsychotic medications and <u>negative symptoms</u> (flattened affect, poverty of speech, anhedonia, social withdrawal, etc.) which do not. Clinical characteristics associated with an improved prognosis include:

1. A rapid onset of the active psychotic symptoms.
2. An onset after age 30, particularly in women.
3. Good premorbid social and occupational functioning. Past performance remains the best predictor of future performance.
4. Marked confusion and emotional features during the acute episode (positive symptoms); some question this.
5. A probable precipitating stress to the acute psychosis and no evidence of CNS abnormalities.
6. No family history of schizophrenia.

It may be that process and reactive schizophrenia are two etiologically (and biologically?) distinct disorders. Although there is great variability, Disorganized Type generally has the worst prognosis while Paranoid Type (and some catatonics) have the best. The patient's prognosis is worsened if he abuses drugs or if he lives in a dysfunctional family setting.

Approximately 25–50% of patients recovering from an acute episode develop a major depression during the months after improvement (postpsychotic depression). Although treatment-resistant, psychotherapy and antidepressant medication may be useful (lithium may also help). Watch for it—suicide rate is increased in this population—but don't over diagnose since some of these patients may have a medication-induced akinesia mimicking depression.

## Biology of Schizophrenia

No pathognomonic structural or functional abnormality has been found in schizophrenics; however, numerous intriguing abnormalities exist (and have been replicated, as well as contested) in subpopulations of patients: frontal concentrations of neuropeptides, increased platelet MAO activity, CSF cytomegalovirus antibody, P-type (stimulated) atypical lymphocytes, cerebral ventricular enlargements, generalized loss of cortical gray matter, abnormal left hemisphere function, hippocampal pyramidal cell disarray, impaired transmission in and reduced size of the corpus callosum, a small cerebellar vermis, decreased frontal lobe blood flow and glucose metabolism (by PET scan), decreased prefrontal lobe size (by MRI), EEG and auditory P300 EP abnormalities (by QEEM), difficulty focusing attention, slowed reaction time, and pathologically demonstrated fibrillary gliosis in the basal forebrain, to name a few. Some of these measures can be correlated roughly with the specific symptoms and severity of the schizophrenia. Also, among individuals who develop schizophrenia there is an increased incidence of birth complications (prematurity, low birth weight), a greater likelihood to have been born in the late winter and early spring, and minor neurological abnormalities. Each of these changes is real in some patients, but their significance is unknown. However, taken together, they underscore (A) the biological nature and (B) the heterogeneity of schizophrenia.

## Biochemistry of Schizophrenia

The biochemical etiology of schizophrenia is unknown. Most of the major hypotheses implicate an abnormality of central neurotransmitters. The current predominant theory postulates excessive central dopamine (DA) activity (the Dopamine Hypothesis) and is based on two key findings:

1. The antipsychotic activity of neuroleptic medications (eg, phenothiazines) is derived in major part from their blockade of postsynaptic dopamine receptors (of the $D_2$ type).
2. Amphetamine psychosis often is clinically indistinguishable from an acute paranoid schizophrenic psychosis. Amphetamines release central dopamine. Also, amphetamines worsen schizophrenia.

These findings could reflect (A) a hypersensitivity of postsynaptic $D_2$ receptors, (B) an increased number of receptors, (C) an overactivity of presynaptic dopamine neurons, or (D) a relative deficiency of dopaminebetahydroxylase (the enzyme which converts DA to NE, forcing DA to become the active transmitter in the absence of NE). Other theories include elevated CNS serotonin and excessive limbic forebrain NE (occurs in some schizophrenics and decreases with medication and improved clinical state).

## Genetics of Schizophrenia

Schizophrenia has a significant inherited component—possibly polygenic.

Consanguinity studies: Schizophrenia is a familial disorder; ie, it "runs in families." The closer the relative, the greater the risk (see Table 3.1).

Twin studies: Monozygotic twins are 4–6 times more likely to develop illness than dizygotes.

Adoption studies: Children of schizophrenic parents adopted at birth into normal families have the same increased rate of illness as if they had been raised by their biological parents.

Although inadequately studied, several nonpsychotic disorders occur with increased frequency in the families of schizophrenics and may be related genetically: schizotypal and borderline personality disorders (the Schizophrenia Spectrum Disorders); obsessive-compulsive disorder; possibly antisocial and paranoid personality disorders.

**Table 3.1**
**Genetic Counseling—Lifetime Risk of Developing Schizophrenia**

| | |
|---|---|
| General population | 1% |
| Monozygotic twins[a] | 40–50% |
| Dizygotic twins | 10% |
| Sibling of schizophrenic | 10% |
| Parent of schizophrenic | 5% |
| Child of one schizophrenic parent | 10–15% |
| Child of two schizophrenic parents | 30–40% |

[a] Note that 50% of monozygotic twins do *not* both develop schizophrenia—thus clearly environment plays a role. Development of illness reflects nature *and* nurture.

## Family Processes

Family dynamics and family turbulence play a major role in producing a relapse or maintaining a remission. Patients who are discharged to home are more likely to relapse over the next year than are those who are placed in a residential setting. Most at risk are patients from hostile families or families that display excessive anxiety, overconcern, or overprotectiveness toward the patient (called expressed emotion or EE). Schizophrenic patients often do not "emancipate" from their families.

Some researchers have identified peculiar and pathological styles of communication in these families—typically, communications are vague and subtly illogical. Bateson (1956) described a characteristic "double bind" in which the patient is frequently required by a key family member to respond to an overt message that contradicts a covert message. The significance of this unpleasant bind in either maintaining or causing (as Bateson suggests) schizophrenia is unclear. Recent work suggests that these family communication patterns may be the effect of having a schizophrenic child, not the cause of it.

## Differential Diagnosis

Schizophrenia must be differentiated from all of those conditions that produce active psychoses (see above). Of all the possibilities, be particularly careful to eliminate schizoaffective disorder, the major affective disorders, and several organic conditions that may closely mimic schizophrenia, eg, early Huntington's chorea, early Wilson's disease, temporal lobe epilepsy, frontal or temporal lobe tumors, early MS, early SLE, porphyria, general paresis, chronic drug use, chronic alcoholic hallucinosis, and the adult form of metachromatic leukodystrophy. Carefully evaluate catatonia for medical/neurological conditions.

## Treatment

**Biological methods (see Chapter 23):** Treat acute psychoses with antipsychotics (equivalent dose range = chlorpromazine 300-600 mg/day; occasionally more). Low dose antipsychotic drug maintenance is the norm. Since noncompliance is common (particularly among substance abusers), long-acting depot fluphenazine or haloperidol may be the drug of choice for many patients. This medication is primarily useful in controlling the positive symptoms and not the negative symptoms, so don't expect too much long-term benefit from meds (except in preventing relapse). Be aware that a chronically excessive dose may chronically hinder patient functioning. A subgroup of schizophrenics may benefit from augmentation with either lithium or a benzodiazepine (particularly in agitated or anxious patients; eg, diazepam 15–30$^+$ mg/day or clonazepam 5–15 mg/day).

Clozapine (Clozaril) is a new, expensive, dangerous (unpredictable, potentially lethal agranulocytosis), effective antipsychotic which clinically improves and is better received (due to fewer side effects) by one-third or more of previously refractory chronic schizophrenics. It can be used safely with constant monitoring of WBCs—seriously consider a trial in such patients, but DO NOT FAIL TO MONITOR CLOSELY. An additional "second generation" antipsychotic, risperidone (Risperdal), is newly available and appears safe (in use and overdose), effective (on positive and negative sxs), and comparatively side effect free (insomnia, agitation, headache, anxiety, and mild extrapyramidal sxs at doses of more than 6 mg/day).

ECT may be useful for rapid control of a few acute psychotics. A very few chronic schizophrenics who respond poorly to medication may improve with ECT—unpredictable.

**Psychosocial methods:** The primary mode of treatment of schizophrenia is pharmacological. Long-term insight psychotherapy has a limited place. On the other hand, supportive, reality-oriented psychosocial methods are particularly useful in the long-term treatment of schizophrenia.

The acutely psychotic patient should be approached cautiously, but he should be approached. Keep a comfortable distance from the patient if he appears disturbed by your presence. It is essential to establish some communication with these patients.

1. Talk to the patient. Be relaxed, interested, and supportive. Give the impression that you believe the patient can respond appropriately to you.

2. Be specific. Ask pointed, factual questions. Try to identify the patient's major current fears and concerns but don't be led into a lengthy discussion of complex delusions and hallucinations.
3. Take your time during the interview. Don't rush the patient to respond to each question but do maintain some control over the direction of the conversation.
4. Make some specific observations of the patient's behavior (eg, "you look frightened; you look angry") but don't become involved in lengthy "interpretations." Don't draw incorrect conclusions about the patient's emotional state from inappropriate affect.
5. Explain to the patient what is being done to him, and why.
6. If the conversation is going nowhere (eg, the patient refuses to talk), break off the interview with a positive expectation eg, "I'll be back to see you in a little while when you are feeling better and able to talk."

If the acutely psychotic patient is delirious, suicidal, homicidal, and/or has no community support—hospitalize. It is usually better to avoid long-term hospitalization if alternate outpatient arrangements are possible: the deleterious effects of chronic hospitalization are real (regression and marked withdrawal, loss of skills, etc.). The recent trend has been toward short hospital stays during acute episodes with maintenance as outpatients in between.

When hospitalized, allow the patient as much independence as his behavior permits within the limits of a safe environment. Therapeutic milieus (eg, therapeutic community, token economy, etc.) all depend upon community support (staff and patients)—be aware of the patient's behavior and provide helpful "corrective feedback" to him. The milieu is a place for the patient to develop skills in maintaining interpersonal relationships and to learn new methods of coping. Behavior modification has been found clearly effective at eliminating specific unacceptable behaviors and in teaching low-level personal skills with some regressed, poorly functioning inpatients.

Most schizophrenics can be treated as outpatients. Several principles should be kept in mind.

— See the patient frequently enough to safely monitor medication and detect early deterioration (eg, weekly, monthly, or even every several months dependent upon the patient's course and reliability).
— Communicate with the patient clearly and unambiguously. Be factual and goal-oriented. Avoid extensive discussion of hallucinations

and delusions (although a recent study suggests that using cognitive therapy to change what the patient thinks of his voices may decrease their frequency). Help the patient with reality issues, eg, living arrangements, work. Help the patient avoid excessive stress. Recognize that the more productive and skillful the patient, the more likely he is to maintain a recovery—encourage the patient to hold an appropriate job. Provide social skills training.

— Talk about medication, eg, the need for it; the patient's feelings about taking it; etc.

— Develop a consistent, trusting relationship (often difficult). Be empathic over time, even when the patient is being "unreasonable," but also maintain a professional distance. Be a constant presence.

— Learn the patient's strengths and weaknesses. Teach him to identify an impending decompensation. What are the precipitants, if any? If the patient misses appointments, investigate (he may be relapsing). If the patient is decompensating, be ready to insist on hospitalization. Recognize that overstimulation and overdependence can precipitate a decompensation. These patients are at risk for suicide at times during their illnesses (particularly if they have self-destructive command hallucinations).

— Always evaluate the family. Have they contributed to the patient's decompensation? Can the members deal appropriately with the patient's illness? Are they hostile? Suspicious? Overprotective? Consider family therapy—reality-based, in-home, family/patient interventions may be particularly useful. Family members often need considerable support and understanding themselves. When worked with well, they can be a (the?) major help to the patient.

— Consider group therapy. The usual orientation is toward support and reality testing. It helps with resocialization, forces interpersonal interactions, and provides support. Several studies have shown it to be effective (in combination with medication) in preventing relapse in outpatients.

— Know and use community resources. Be alert to the devastating effect on the patient of a poor quality of life (eg, Does he live in a "psychiatric ghetto" or "on the street?").

— Do not expect too much. Many patients have chronic disability.

### SCHIZOPHRENIFORM DISORDER
### (DSM-IV p 291, 295.40)

This disorder is clinically indistinguishable from brief psychotic disorder and schizophrenia except that the symptoms last more than 1 month but less than 6 months. This population of patients seems to differ from schizophrenic patients in several important ways:

1. Symptoms begin and end more abruptly.
2. Symptoms are usually more turbulent and "acute."
3. There is good premorbid adjustment and higher functioning after recovery.
4. There is only a slightly increased prevalence of schizophrenia in the family. There may be a higher prevalence of affective disorder.

Thus, schizophreniform disorder appears to be a separate disease from schizophrenia. Recognize, however, that many schizophrenic patients pass through a period (ie, the first 6 months) when their diagnosis needs to be schizophreniform disorder. Also, don't miss an organic psychosis.

Treatment is similar to that of an acute schizophrenic episode, but the prognosis is better.

## BRIEF PSYCHOTIC DISORDER
### (DSM-IV p 304, 298.8)

This condition describes those patients who experience an acute psychotic episode lasting longer than 1 day but less than 1 month and that may ("with marked stressor(s)") or may not ("without marked stressor(s)") immediately follow an important life stress or a pregnancy ("with postpartum onset"). The illness comes as a surprise—there is usually no forewarning that the person is likely to "break down," although this disorder is more common in people with a preexisting personality disorder (particularly histrionic and borderline types).

The psychosis is typically very turbulent and dramatic with marked emotional lability, bizarre behavior, confused and incoherent speech, transient disorientation and memory loss, and/or brief but striking hallucinations and delusions. Thus, it mimics the acute psychotic onset of a major affective disorder, schizophreniform disorder, or psychosis with delirium. Always carefully rule out medical conditions and, particularly, substance-induced problems. The validity of this diagnosis as a separate category is debated.

Treat the acutely psychotic patient with understanding, a secure environment, and antipsychotic medication, if needed. The patient usually recovers completely in several days, and the long-term prognosis is good, although the patient may be at risk for future brief episodes when equivalently stressed.

## SCHIZOAFFECTIVE DISORDER
### (DSM-IV p 295, 295.70)

This is a vague and poorly defined disorder meant for patients who have evidence of <u>both</u> schizophrenia and major affective disorder with depressed mood. These patients may present with an affective disturbance that grades into a purely schizophrenic picture or may display symptoms of both conditions simultaneously, although the schizophrenic symptoms dominate. It is a genetically heterogeneous disorder—both schizophrenia and mood disorders occur with increased frequency in family members. Be cautious that you don't mistake for a substance-induced psychosis, eg, amphetamines, PCP, or exogenous steroids. Much work remains to be done to better define these patients.

Treat as one would the equivalent schizophrenic or affective patient. Antipsychotics are generally most useful but lithium has benefitted some patients. These patients seem to have a better prognosis than those with schizophrenia but a poorer outcome than those with a mood disorder.

## DELUSIONAL DISORDER
### (DSM-IV p 301, 297.1)

These patients <u>do not</u> display the pervasive disturbances of mood and thought found in other psychotic conditions. They do not have flat or inappropriate affect, prominent hallucinations, or markedly bizarre delusions. They <u>do</u> have one or more delusions, often of persecution but also of infidelity, grandiosity, somatic change, or erotomania that are:

1. Usually specific, eg, involve a certain person or group, a given place or time, or a particular activity.
2. Usually well organized, eg, the "culprits" have elaborate reasons for what they are doing, which the patient can detail.
3. Usually grandiose, eg, a powerful group is interested just in <u>him</u>.
4. Not bizarre enough to suggest schizophrenia.

These patients (who tend to be in their 40's) may be unrecognizable until their delusional system is pointed out by family or friends. Even then the diagnosis may be difficult because they may be too mistrustful to confide in the examiner and don't voluntarily seek treatment. They are frequently hypersensitive, argumentative, and litigious, and come to attention through ill-founded legal activities. Although they may perform well occupationally and in areas distant from their delusions, they tend to be social isolates either by preference or as a result of their interpersonal inhospitality (eg, spouses frequently abandon them). Social and occupational dysfunction, when it occurs, usually is in direct response to their delusions.

These conditions appear to form a clinical continuum with conditions such as paranoid personality disorder and paranoid schizophrenia; delineation of the limits of each syndrome awaits further research. Rule out an affective disorder—morbid jealousy and paranoid ideas are common in depression. Paranoia is common among the elderly (see Chapter 24) and among stimulant drug abusers. Acute paranoid reactions frequently are seen in patients with mild delirium and in patients who are bedridden (and sensory-deprived).

Etiology is unknown. No genetic or biological factors have been identified. There is a higher incidence among refugee and minority groups and among those with impaired hearing. There is a tendency for their family relationships to be characterized by turbulence, callousness, and coldness yet the significance of this pattern is unclear. Typical defense mechanisms seen in these patients include denial, projection, and regression.

### Treatment

Treatment is notoriously difficult. Individual psychotherapy is useful. Emphasis should be on developing a trusting relationship, with the patient seeing the therapist as neutral and accepting. Interfere with the patient's freedom of choice as little as possible. Gradually help the patient see his world from your perspective. These patients are very sensitive to criticism (overt or implied), so this kind of a relationship is extremely difficult to develop and maintain.

Antipsychotic medication may help a few—it may at least take the "energy" out of the delusion. Antidepressants appear promising—consider them.

## SHARED PSYCHOTIC DISORDER
### (DSM-IV p 306, 297.3)

An otherwise normal person may adopt the delusional system of someone else. Most commonly, a dependent, isolated wife will accept the delusional ideas of her (dominant) spouse (eg, both may come to believe that their children are attempting to murder them with poison gas). When two people share the same delusion, it is folie a deux. Separation of the partners with shared delusions often results in disappearance of the delusions in the healthier member.

## PSYCHOTIC DISORDER DUE TO A GENERAL MEDICAL CONDITION
### (DSM-IV p 309, 293.81 or 293.82)

These patients have a medical condition that causes prominent delusions (293.81) or hallucinations (293.82) about which they have no insight and cannot appreciate the symptom's connection to their medical illness. Of course, a careful medical workup is in order, and even then the relation between the psychosis and the medical condition is often uncertain. Look for medical symptoms that appear just after the onset or worsening of the medical problem, prominent visual or olfactory hallucinations, and/or the "wrong age" of onset for normal psychoses (eg, often in the elderly). Many conditions can produce an isolated psychosis (see Chapters 14 and 15): don't use this diagnosis if symptoms occur only in the presence of an illness-related delirium or dementia.

## SUBSTANCE-INDUCED PSYCHOTIC DISORDER
### (DSM-IV p 314)

Drugs of abuse, certain medication (see Chapter 13), and toxins all can occasionally produce flagrant psychoses, usually with marked organic features such as confusion and prominent visual, olfactory, or tactile hallucinations. Most drugs of abuse can produce temporary psychoses with intoxication, while a few (eg, alcohol and hypnotic-sedatives) produce them upon withdrawal in the dependent patient (see Chapters 16 and 17). Most intoxication psychoses resolve upon discontinuing the drug but occasionally may persist if caused by heavy use of stimulants, PCP, or LSD.

## PSYCHOTIC DISORDER NOS
### (DSM-IV p 315, 298.9)

If a psychotic patient does not have an affective disorder, an organic condition, or one of the disorders in this chapter and is not malingering, he has Psychotic Disorder NOS. The most common use of this classification is for patients for whom there is insufficient information to make a more specific diagnosis.

### Suggested Readings

Bateson G, Jackson DD, Haley J, Weakland JH: Towards a theory of schizophrenia. Behav Sci 1:251–264, 1956.

Becker RE, Singh MM, Meisler N, Shillcutt S: Clinical significance, evaluation and management or secondary depression in schizophrenia. J Clin Psychiatry 46 (11, Sec.2):26–32, 1985.

Breier A, Schreiber JL, Dyer J, et al: National institute of mental health longitudinal study of chronic schizophrenia. Arch Gen Psychiatry 48:239–246, 1991.

Chadwick P, Birchwood M: The omnipotence of voices. Br J Psychiatry 164:190–201, 1994.

Conrad AJ, Abebe T, Austin R, et al: Hippocampal pyramidal cell disarray in schizophrenia as a bilateral phenomenon. Arch Gen Psychiatry 48:413–417, 1991.

Dixon L, Haas G, Weiden PJ, et al: Drug abuse in schizophrenic patients: Clinical correlates and reasons for use. Am J Psychiatry 148:224–230, 1991.

Frank AF, Gunderson JG: The role of the therapeutic alliance in the treatment of schizophrenia. Arch Gen Psychiatry 47:228–236, 1990.

Glazer WM, Pino CD, Quinlan D: The reassessment of chronic patients previously diagnosed as schizophrenic. J Clin Psychiatry 48:430–434, 1987.

Heinrichs DW, Carpenter WT: Prospective study of prodromal symptoms in schizophrenic relapse. Am J Psychiatry 142:371–373, 1985.

Heinrichs DW, Buchanan RW: Significance and meaning of neurological signs in schizophrenia. Am J Psychiatry 145:11–18, 1988.

Hellerstein D, Frosch W, Koenigsberg HW: The clinical significance of command hallucinations. Am J Psychiatry 144:219–221, 1987.

Hogarty GE, Anderson CM, Reiss DJ, et al: Family psychoeducation, social skills training, and maintenance chemotherapy in the aftercare treatment of schizophrenia. Arch Gen Psychiatry 48:340–347, 1991.

Hyde TM, Nawroz S, Goldberg TE, et al: Is there cognitive decline in schizophrenia? Br J Psychiatry 164:494–500, 1994.

Kanter J, Lamb HR, Loeper C: Expressed emotion in families: A critical review. Hosp Commun Psychiatry 38:374–380, 1987.

Kendler KS, Gruenberg AM, Tsuang MT: A family study of the subtypes of schizophrenia. Am J Psychiatry 145:57–62, 1988.

Lane RD: Successful fluoxetine treatment of pathological jealousy. J Clin Psychiatry 51:345–346, 1990.

Levinson DF, Levitt MEM: Schizoaffective mania reconsidered. Am J Psychiatry 144:415–425, 1987.

Marder SR, Meibach RC: Risperidone in the treatment of schizophrenia. Am J Psychiatry 151:825–835, 1994.

McCarley RW, Shenton ME, O'Donnell BF, et al: Auditory P300 abnormalities and left posterior superior temporal gyrus volume reduction in schizophrenia. Arch Gen Psychiatry 50:190–197, 1993.

Munoz RA, Amado H, Hyatt S: Brief reactive psychosis. J Clin Psychiatry 48:324–327, 1987.

Perry W, Braff DL: Information-processing deficits and thought disorder in schizophrenia. Am J Psychiatry 151:363–367, 1994.

Raine A, Lencz T, Reynolds GP, et al: An evaluation of structural and functional prefrontal deficits in schizophrenia: MRI and neuropsychological measures. Psychiatry Res: Neuroimaging 45:123–137, 1992.

Randolph ET, Eth S, Glynn SM, et al: Behavioral family management in schizophrenia. Br J Psychiatry 164:501–506, 1994.

Schlaepfer TE, Harris GJ, Tien AY, et al: Decreased regional cortical gray matter volume in schizophrenia. Am J Psychiatry 151:842–848, 1994.

Schooler NR: Negative symptoms in schizophrenia: Assessment of the effect of risperidone. J Clin Psychiatry 55(5, suppl):22–28, 1994.

Siever LJ, Kalus OF, Keefe RS: The boundaries of schizophrenia. Psychiatr Clin North Am 16(2):217–244, 1993.

Stabenau JR, Pollin W: Heredity and environment in schizophrenia, revisited. J Nerv Ment Dis 181:290–297, 1993.

Tsuang MT, Gilbertson MW, Faraone SV: The genetics of schizophrenia: Current knowledge and future research. Schizophr Res 4:157–171, 1991.

Wolkin A, Angrist B, Wolf A, et al: Low frontal glucose utilization in chronic schizophrenia: A replication study. Am J Psychiatry 145:251–253, 1988.

Wolkowitz OM, Pickar D: Benzodiazepines in the treatment of schizophrenia: A review and reappraisal. Am J Psychiatry 148:714–726, 1991.

Woodruff PW, Pearlson GD, Geer MJ, et al: A computerized magnetic resonance imaging study of corpus callosum morphology in schizophrenia. Psychol Med 23:45–56, 1993.

Yassa R, Suranyi-Cadotte B: Clinical characteristics of late onset schizophrenia and delusional disorder. Schizophr Bull 19:701–707, 1993.

# Chapter 4

# Mood Disorders

Patients with disorders of mood are common (35% of the population at any one time) and are seen by all medical specialists. It is essential to identify them and either treat or refer appropriately.

Two basic abnormalities of mood are recognized: depression and mania. Both occur on a continuum from normal to the clearly pathological—symptoms in a few patients reach psychotic proportions. Although minor symptoms may be an extension of normal sadness or elation, more severe symptoms are associated with discrete syndromes (affective disorders) that appear to differ qualitatively from normal processes and that require specific therapies.

## CLASSIFICATION

DSM-IV has defined several different mood disorders that differ, among other things, in their clinical presentation, course, genetics, and treatment response. These conditions are distinguished from one another by (1) the presence or absence of mania (bipolar vs unipolar), (2) the severity of the illness (major vs minor), and (3) the role of medical or other psychiatric conditions in causing the disorder (1° vs 2°).

MAJOR MOOD DISORDERS—major depressive and/or manic signs and symptoms.
  Bipolar I Disorder (Manic Depression)—mania in past or present (with or without presence or history of depression). Major depression usually occurs sometime.
  Bipolar II Disorder—hypomania and major depression must be present or have been present sometime.
  Major Depressive Disorder—serious depression alone.

OTHER SPECIFIC MOOD DISORDER—minor depressive and/or manic signs and symptoms.

Dysthymic Disorder—depression alone.

Cyclothymic Disorder—depressive and hypomanic symptoms in the present or recent past (consistently over the past 2 years).

MOOD DISORDER DUE TO A GENERAL MEDICAL CONDITION and SUBSTANCE-INDUCED MOOD DISORDER—may be depressed, manic, or mixed; these are the 2° mood disorders.

ADJUSTMENT DISORDER WITH DEPRESSED MOOD—depression caused by stress.

The DSM-IV classification also requires the examiner to specify whether the current bipolar episode is manic, depressed, or mixed; whether the unipolar or bipolar disorder is a single episode or recurrent and/or shows psychotic features, catatonia, rapid cycling, complete clearing between episodes, a seasonal pattern, or a postpartum onset; and whether a major depressive episode is chronic (present at least 2 years), meets the criteria for melancholia (profound vegetative and cognitive symptoms including psychomotor retardation or agitation, sleep disturbance, anorexia or weight loss, and/or excessive guilt—see DSM-IV p 384), or is atypical. These characteristics are believed to be important in determining treatment and prognosis.

## CLINICAL PRESENTATION OF MOOD DISORDERS

Of the core clinical features common to affective disturbances, the Major Mood Disorders have the greater number and severity of symptoms and signs while dysthymia and cyclothymia have fewer. The most common symptoms and signs of mood disorders are listed in Tables 4.1 and 4.2.

A sufficient combination of these symptoms often clinches the diagnosis. However, particularly when the symptoms are mild, disorders of mood are frequently missed.

Although many depressed patients complain of depression, some do not. Moreover, other problems may obscure the diagnosis. Some patients present with alcohol or drug abuse or acting-out behavior. Others, particularly early on, present primarily with anxiety or agitation. Still others, instead of feeling sad, complain of fatigue, insomnia, dyspnea, tachycardia, and vague and/or chronic pains (usually GI, cardiac, headaches, or back-aches—all unrelieved by analgesics). People with such presentations (known as masked depressions) often have a personal or family history of depression and frequently respond to antidepressants. Suspect depression in the unimproved patient who has atypical medical symptoms.

Patients with mania often do not complain of their symptoms. A few feel too good and elated to complain; others feel agitated and unpleasant but fail to notice that their behavior is

**Table 4.1**
**Symptoms of Depression**

Emotional features
   depressed mood, "blue"
   irritability, anxiety
   anhedonia, loss of interest
   loss of zest
   diminished emotional bonds
   interpersonal withdrawal
   preoccupation with death
Cognitive features
   self-criticism, sense of worthlessness, guilt
   pessimism, hopelessness, despair
   distractible, poor concentration
   uncertain and indecisive
   variable obsessions
   somatic complaints (particularly in the elderly)
   memory impairment
   delusions and hallucinations
Vegetative features
   fatigability, no energy
   insomnia or hypersomnia
   anorexia or hyperrexia
   weight loss or gain
   psychomotor retardation
   psychomotor agitation
   impaired libido
   frequent diurnal variation
Signs of depression:
   stooped and slow moving
   tearful, sad facies
   dry mouth and skin
   constipation

**Table 4.2**
**Symptoms of Mania: (When Nonpsychotic and Not Severe Enough to Impair Social or Occupational Functioning = Hypomania)**

Emotional features
  excited, elevated mood, euphoria
  emotional lability
  rapid, temporary shifts to acute depression
  irritability, low frustration tolerance
  demanding, egocentric
Cognitive features
  elevated self-esteem, grandiosity
  speech disturbances
  loud, word rhyming (clanging)
  pressure of speech
  flight of ideas
  progression to incoherence
  poor judgment, disorganization
  paranoia
  delusions and/or hallucinations
Physiological features
  boundless energy
  insomnia, little need for sleep
  decreased appetite
Signs of mania
  psychomotor agitation

outrageous. Hypomanic patients can be irritable, or "full of life," or both.

Patient rating scales can help determine the severity of a depression and can be used to measure change over time: eg, the Beck Depression Inventory (21 questions—patient self-rates) and the Hamilton Rating Scale for Depression (17–21 questions—therapist rates).

## NORMAL AFFECTIVE PROCESSES

Sadness or simple unhappiness affect us all from time to time. The cause is often obvious, the reaction understandable, and improvement follows the disappearance of the cause. However, prolonged unhappiness in response to a chronic stress may be indistinguishable from a minor affective disorder and require treatment. Support and altered life circumstances are the keys to recovery.

Grief or BEREAVEMENT (DSM-IV p 684, V62.82) is a more profound sense of dysphoria which follows a severe loss or trauma and which may produce a full depressive syndrome but, as time distances the precipitating event, the symptoms disappear. This process often takes weeks or months and requires a "working through" which often includes disbelief, anger, intense mourning, and eventual resolution (see Chapter 10). Some bereavement grades into and, with time (eg, longer than 2 months), becomes a major depressive disorder.

There is no generally accepted equivalent nonpathological manic process, although some people do react to stress with hypomania.

## MINOR AFFECTIVE DISORDERS

### Depression

The common chronic nonpsychotic disorder of lowered mood and/or anhedonia is DYSTHYMIC DISORDER (DSM-IV p 349, 300.4). These patients feel depressed, have difficulty falling asleep, characteristically feel best in the morning and despondent in the afternoon and evening, and can display any of the nonpsychotic symptoms and signs of depression. Symptoms must have been present, at least intermittently, for 2 or more years. It is more common in women (W:M = 2-3:1), often develops for the first time in the late 20's or 30's, has a lifetime prevalence of 6%, and begins insidiously, frequently in a person predisposed to depression by:

— major loss in childhood; eg, parent (maybe)
— recent loss; eg, health, job, spouse.
— chronic stress; eg, medical disorder.
— psychiatric susceptibility; eg, personality disorders of histrionic, compulsive, and dependent types; alcohol and drug abuse; major depression in partial remission; obsessive-compulsive disorder. It frequently coexists with these conditions.

It is similar to but less severe than a Major Depressive Disorder, however, 20%+ of patients who experience major depression will clear incompletely, and chronically suffer a residue of Dysthymic Disorder ("double depression"). It tends to last for many years.

Dysthymia must be differentiated from ADJUSTMENT DIS-ORDER WITH DEPRESSED MOOD (DSM-IV p 623, 309.0). This disorder occurs in an adequately functioning individual shortly after a readily identifiable, causative stress, results in impaired functioning, and resolves as the stress disappears. These patients present a depressive syndrome midway between normal sadness and major depression. If feelings of anxiety commingle with those of depression, the patient may have ADJUSTMENT DISORDER WITH MIXED ANXIETY AND DEPRESSED MOOD (DSM-IV p 624, 309.28).

### Mania

CYCLOTHYMIC DISORDER (DSM-IV p 365, 301.13) requires the presence of mild depression <u>and</u> hypomania, separately or intermixed, continuously or intermittently over at least a 2-year period. It usually begins in the 20's in patients (F:M = 1:1) with a family history of major affective disorder and forms a chronically disabling pattern that yields troubled interpersonal relationships, job instability, occasional suicide attempts and short hospitalizations, and a markedly increased risk of drug and alcohol abuse.

### MAJOR MOOD DISORDERS

Patients with major mood disorders are profoundly depressed or excited. Clinical presentations and genetic studies support two distinct groups, MAJOR DEPRESSIVE DISORDER (unipolar) (DSM-IV p 344, 296.2x.3x) and two types of bipolar disorders: BIPOLAR I DISORDER (DSM-IV p 355, 296.0x and 296.4x.7x and BIPOLAR II DISORDER (DSM-IV p 362, 296.89); yet some question this dichotomy (eg, bipolar disorder <u>may</u> be a more severe form of recurrent unipolar disorder). The lifetime risk in the general population for a major depression is about 12%[+]: 10 times the frequency of bipolar disorder. Fifteen percent of patients kill themselves eventually.

### Major Depression

These patients have many serious symptoms and signs of depression, yet their clinical presentations can vary markedly—

from profound retardation and withdrawal to irritable, unrelieved agitation. A presumed precipitating event occurs in 25% (50% among the elderly). A diurnal variation is common, with the most severe symptoms early in the day. Some fail to recognize their depression, complaining instead of their "insides rotting out" or their "minds going crazy," yet the profound affective disturbance is usually recognizable to the observer.

A thought disorder is occasionally present. Delusions are usually affect-laden and mood congruent, but need not be. Hallucinations are uncommon, auditory, and usually have a self-condemning or paranoid content. These "psychotic depressions" may represent a separate disorder or may simply be a more severe form of depression (M.D., or B.D., With Psychotic Features). Depressed elderly patients may present primarily with retardation, memory impairment, and mild disorientation (pseudodementia).

The disorder can occur at any age (median age of onset is late 20s; 10% occur after age 60) with the majority of cases spread evenly throughout the adult years and with females affected 2:1. (However, increasing numbers of teenagers and young adults seem to be afflicted.) Unlike schizophrenia, it occurs frequently in the higher social strata. Family and twin studies strongly suggest a genetic factor—increased incidence of major depression, alcoholism, and possibly antisocial personality disorder in relatives (the "depressive spectrum" disorders). The prevalence of affective illness in first degree relatives is 13% contrasted with 1-3% in the general population. Thirty to forty percent of identical twins are concordant for unipolar depression. Alcoholism and chronic stress may predispose to the development of the illness.

Less than 50% of patients will have only one episode (M.D., Single Episode, 296.2x); 50%-60% have two or more attacks (M.D., Recurrent, 296.3x). Some patients clear between episodes; others remain mildly depressed (20%); and 10% are chronically, severely depressed. Most attacks begin gradually over 13 weeks and, untreated, last from 38 months or longer. Relapse shortly after recovery from an acute episode is common but may be partly avoidable. These patients are often incapacitated during an episode and are at great risk of suicide. About half of patients with recurrent illness will recover over 12 decades, while the rest will be chronically affected, although most at the level of dysthymia with infrequent relapses into major depression.

Postpartum depression is a severe depression usually beginning 1-2, and certainly by 4, weeks after delivery, usually of the second or third child. Affected women are at risk for repeated episodes with future births.

Seasonal affective disorder (SAD) is characterized by the development of major depression with a seasonal pattern: symptoms appear each fall/winter and return to normal (or even hypomania) during the spring/summer. It afflicts predominantly younger women (F:M = 2–4:1), displays many features of "atypical" depression (hypersomnia, weight gain, hyperphagia), and is often treated successfully with bright, artificial light (2–6 hours/day—response in 2–3 days, occasionally hypomania occurs) with or without antidepressants. Its relationship to more classical major depression is unclear.

The apparent biological nature of many serious depressions is reflected in the recent development of several putative biological tests for depression: the dexamethasone suppression test (DST—positive test is the failure of normal suppression of plasma cortisol 6-24 hours after an oral dose of dexamethasone); elevated serum cortisol (30% of patients have adrenal hypertrophy); urinary MHPG (3-methoxy-4-hydroxyphenyleneglycol—a catabolite of norepinephrine, low in some depressions); CSF 5-HIAA (a metabolite of serotonin, low in some depression); TRH stimulation test (low TSH and blunted TSH and GH responses to exogenous TRH suggest unipolar depression); sleep abnormalities (short REM latency—time from falling asleep to start of REM sleep; frequent awakenings; early morning awakenings; decreased NREM sleep; increased REM density—frequency of rapid eye movements in REM sleep (all may be a trait in people prone to depression)); and the stimulant challenge tests (some depressed patients briefly improve when given 10 mg of amphetamine). Unfortunately, these tests have little routine clinical utility (the best seem to be (1) abnormal sleep studies, (2) abnormal TSH levels and TRH responses, and (3) a posttreatment positive DST as a measure of poor outcome). They all suffer from inadequate sensitivity and specificity (too many false positives and negatives). However, each further emphasizes that biology plays a role in many depressions. (Still, environment also plays a role since 25% of patients with serious medical conditions and others under marked psychosocial stress will develop a major depression.)

## Bipolar Disorders

Mania, at some time severe enough to produce compromised functioning, is necessary to diagnose Bipolar I Disorder, but $90\%^+$ of patients also have periods of depression (B.D., Depressed, 296.5x). The manic episode typically develops over days and may become uncontrolled and psychotic (B.D., Manic, 296.4x). A total of $20\%^+$ of manics have hallucinations and/or delusions. A severe mania may be indistinguishable from an organic delirium (sudden onset, anorexia, insomnia, disorientation, paranoia, hallucinations, and delusions) or schizophrenia. When the bipolar patient is depressed, the depression is usually profound but may present as a mild depressive syndrome. Attacks are usually separated by months or years but the patient occasionally may cycle from one to the other over days or weeks (With Rapid Cycling—four or more mood episodes in a year; $10\%^+$ of pts, F:M = 4:1, younger, poorer prognosis, but the pattern may disappear) or actually present contrasting symptoms simultaneously (eg, spirited singing intermixed with crying) (B.D., Mixed, 296.6x). This is a recurrent illness—single attacks are rare. Pure manic syndromes (patients who have had only mania—unipolar mania) occur clinically but are unusual and are probably not a separate entity.

Bipolar II Disorder occurs when a patient who has had a major depression also experiences an hypomanic episode (usually around the time of the depression), but never gets fully manic. It occurs more frequently in women who have a family history of mood disorder; $10\%^+$ go on to develop Bipolar I Disorder by later having a manic episode.

The lifetime risk for developing bipolar disorder is approximately $1.0\%^+$. This is a genetic disorder. First-degree relatives are at risk for bipolar disorder (5-10% develop it), major depression ($10\%^+$), and cyclothymia. There is a $70\%^+$ concordance for bipolar illness in identical twins. In contrast with major depression, M:F = 1:1. The type of inheritance is uncertain—probably polygenic, although recent linkage studies suggest several possibly aberrant genes (eg, on chromosome 11 in one large Amish family—but with failure to confirm on re-study).

The first manic episode is often before age 30, begins quickly, and resolves in 24 months if untreated. One or more episodes of depression usually have already occurred. Most patients go on to have a majority of depressive episodes. Suicide is the major risk during periods of depression. Legal difficulties and drug and alcohol abuse (as well as suicide) occur during manic periods.

## MOOD DISORDER DUE TO A GENERAL MEDICAL CONDITION

Various medical conditions can directly produce major depressive and/or manic syndromes (DSM-IV p 369, 293.83), although who will develop such a syndrome is unpredictable. Some illnesses have a high likelihood of producing a mood disturbance (eg, depression in 50%$^+$ of patients with stroke, pancreatic carcinoma, and Cushing's syndrome) although it is much less common, but no less direct, with other illnesses. This disorder is not meant for those medical conditions that produce depression or mania as a reaction to having the illness nor for those patients who only show a mood disturbance when delirious. Likely medical diseases include (see Chapters 14 and 15):

**Depression**

    Tumors—particularly of brain and lung, carcinoma of pancreas (50% develop psychiatric symptoms before the diagnosis is made).

    Infections—influenza, mononucleosis, "flu-fatigue" syndrome (EB virus?), encephalitis, hepatitis.

    Endocrine disorders—Cushing's disease (60% of patients; also from exogenous steroids), hypothyroidism (some experts recommend a careful thyroid evaluation in most (all?) depressed patients), apathetic hyperthyroidism, hyperparathyroidism (symptoms parallel levels of serum $Ca^{++}$), diabetes, Turner's syndrome.

    Blood—anemia (particularly Pernicious Anemia).

    Nutrition and electrolytes—pellagra, hyponatremia, hypokalemia, hypercalcemia, inappropriate ADH.

    Misc.—MS, Parkinson's disease, head trauma, stroke (post stroke depression; particularly L-frontal), early Huntington's disease, post-MI, PMS (?), menopause (relieved by estrogens).

**Mania**

Tumors—of brain.

Infections—encephalitis, influenza, syphilis (20% of patients with general paresis).

Misc.—MS, Wilson's disease, head trauma, psychomotor epilepsy, hyperthyroidism.

## SUBSTANCE-INDUCED MOOD DISORDER

Drugs of abuse, medications, and toxins all can produce mood disorders of various types (DSM-IV p 374). The likelihood of mood symptoms from use of a substance and the pattern of symptoms produced varies not only with the specific drug but also upon the dose, the duration of use, whether the issue is intoxication or withdrawal, and ill-specified and poorly understood individual factors in the patient. A modest list of likely agents include (see Chapter 13):

**Depression**

Drugs of Abuse—alcohol (often hard to tell "which is the chicken and which the egg"), sedative-hypnotics, opioids, PCP.

Medication—oral contraceptives, corticosteroids, reserpine (6% of patients), alpha-methyldopa, guanethidine, levodopa, indomethacin, benzodiazepines, opiates, cimetidine, propranolol, anticholinesterases, amphetamine withdrawal.

Misc.—heavy metal poisoning.

**Mania**

Drugs of Abuse—cocaine, amphetamines, hallucinogens, PCP.

Medication—steroids, L-dopa.

Misc.—organophosphates, petroleum distillates

## MOOD DISORDER NOS

BIPOLAR DISORDER NOS (DSM-IV p 366, 296.80) and DEPRESSIVE DISORDER NOS (DSM-IV p 350, 311) include the remaining (unusual) affective presentations.

## DIFFERENTIAL DIAGNOSIS

### Depression

Schizophrenic Disorders—particularly catatonics, but any type can look or be depressed during or after an episode. Poor premorbid adjustment, formal thought disorder with well-formed delusions and complex hallucinations, lack of cyclic history, and no family history for affective disorder all suggest schizophrenia.

Schizoaffective Disorder—a psychotic disorder that meets the criteria for schizophrenia, but with superimposed major mood symptoms for part of the time.

Generalized Anxiety Disorder—anxiety appears first and predominates. With the anxious patient, always consider depression.

Alcoholism and Drug Abuse—alcoholism and depression are both often present ("dual diagnosis" patients).

Obsessive Compulsive Disorder; Histrionic and Borderline Personality Disorders—are the full syndromes present?

Dementia—"pseudodepression" is common and differentiation is tricky, particularly in the elderly. Check for memory impairment and disorientation.

### Mania

Schizophrenic Disorders—often indistinguishable in acute cases. Check past personal and family history.

Schizoaffective Disorder

Borderline Personality Disorder

### PSYCHOBIOLOGICAL THEORIES

Psychoanalytic theory (Freud) postulates that a depressed patient has suffered a real or imagined loss of an ambivalently loved object, has reacted with unconscious rage which then has been turned against the self, and this has resulted in a lowered self-esteem and depression. Cognitive Theory postulates a "cognitive triad" of distorted perceptions in which (1) a person's negative interpretation of his own life experiences (2) causes a devaluation of himself which (3) causes depression.

Promising but unproven biological theories focus on brain norepinephrine (NE) and serotonin (5-HT) abnormalities. Biological and psychological theories need not be mutually exclusive. The catecholamine hypothesis suggests that low brain NE levels cause depression and elevated levels cause mania; however, urinary MHPG levels (a major metabolite of NE) are low in only some depressions. The indolamine hypothesis holds that low cerebral 5-HT (or the primary metabolite, 5-HIAA) causes depression and elevation causes mania, yet exceptions occur. The permissive hypothesis postulates that lowered NE produces depression and raised NE causes mania only if 5-HT levels are low. The known mechanisms of action of antidepressants support these theories—tricyclics block NE and 5-HT reuptake and MAOIs block oxidation of NE. In addition, recent research suggests that there may be frontal lobe/whole brain hypometabolism in depression or some fundamental abnormality of the circadian rhythms of depressed patients.

## TREATMENT OF DEPRESSION

Evaluate medically and psychiatrically to rule out secondary depression and to attempt to identify an affective syndrome. Always ask about vegetative features and evaluate suicidal potential (see Chapter 7). If the patient is (1) incapacitated by the disorder, (2) has a destructive home environment or limited environmental support, (3) is a suicide risk, or (4) has an associated medical illness requiring treatment—hospitalize. All depressed patients should receive psychotherapy—some must receive physical therapies in addition. The specific treatments used depend on the diagnosis, severity, patient's age, and past responses to therapy.

### Psychological Therapies

Supportive psychotherapy is always indicated. Be warm, empathic, understanding, and optimistic. Help the patient to identify and express concerns and to ventilate. Identify precipitating factors and help correct. Help solve external problems (eg, rent, job)—be directive, particularly during the acute episode and if the patient is immobilized. Train the patient to recognize signs of future decompensation. See the patient frequently (1–2 times/wk initially) and regularly, but not interminably—be available. Recognize that some depressed patients can provoke anger in you (via anger, hostility, unreasonable demands, etc.)—watch for it. Long-term insight-oriented psychotherapy may be of value in selected chronic minor depressions and some conflicted patients with a major depression in remission.

Behavior therapy may help mild to moderately severe depressives. Felt by some to be "learned helplessness," depressions are treated by giving patients skill training and providing success experiences. Cognitive therapy is clearly effective with some mild to moderately depressed patients. The patient is trained to recognize and eliminate negative expectations.

Partial sleep deprivation (awaken midway through the night and keep up until the next evening) helps lessen the symptoms of a major depression temporarily. Physical exercise (running, swimming) may produce improvement in depression, for poorly understood biological reasons.

### Physical Therapies (see Chapter 23)

All major and most chronic or unimproved minor depressions require a trial of antidepressants (70–80% of patients respond), even though an apparent precipitant of the depression is identified. Begin with an SSRI or tricyclic antidepressant but consider a trial with a different antidepressant, an MAOI (particularly in "atypical" depressions), or a drug combination if the first drug fails. Be alert to side effects and be aware that antidepressants "may" precipitate a manic episode in a few bipolar patients (10% with TCAs; possibly lower with SSRIs—but recognize that the whole "manic precipitation" concept is debated). Maintain for several months after remission, then taper, but some patients may require meds for long periods.

Lithium is moderately effective at maintaining remission in bipolar and some unipolar patients. Antidepressants and lithium may be started concurrently, and the lithium continued after remission. Lithium may be useful in treating acute bipolar depressions and a few unipolar depressions, but it can exacerbate symptoms in some patients. Psychotic, paranoid, or very agitated patients may require an antipsychotic, alone or with an antidepressant, lithium, or ECT—an antidepressant alone usually is not sufficient.

Electroconvulsive therapy (ECT) may be the treatment of choice (1) if medication fails after one or more 6-week trials, (2) if the patient's condition demands an immediate remission (eg, acutely suicidal), (3) in some psychotic depressions, or (4) in patients who can't tolerate medication (eg, some elderly cardiac patients). Up to 90% of patients respond.

## TREATMENT OF MANIA

Evaluate carefully but quickly. Is the patient medically ill or taking drugs? Has he been manic before? Is he taking lithium? What is the blood level?

If hypomanic, use outpatient treatment and work with the family, if possible. Consider short-term, low dose antipsychotics (eg, haloperidol 25 mg/day) but rely on treatment with lithium or carbamazepine longer term. If manic, hospitalize. Is the patient debilitated? Seriously sleep deprived?

1. Medicate acutely with antipsychotics (large doses may be required; eg, haloperidol 10-40 mg, during the first 24 hours). Consider adjunctive use of a benzodiazepine early on. Also, if drugs fail, ECT is an effective treatment for acute mania.
2. Be relaxed, reasonable, and controlled. Treat in quiet setting with minimal stimuli. Set firm limits.
3. Begin lithium carbonate; however, as many as 30% of manics stay partially symptomatic despite lithium. If lithium fails, consider carbamazepine. Other, (unproven) drugs that look promising for mania include clonazepam, lorazepam, clonidine, and sodium valproate. Even with treatment, long-term outcome is poor in a few patients.

### Suggested Readings

American Psychiatric Association Practice Guidelines: Practice guideline for major depressive disorder in adults. Am J Psychiatry 150(4, suppl):1–26, 1993.

Angst J: Course of unipolar, depressive, bipolar manic depressive, and schizoaffective disorders: Results of a progressive longitudinal study. Fortschr Neurol Psychiatr 48:30–39, 1980.

Beck AT, Hollon SD, Young JE, et al: Treatment of depression with cognitive therapy and amitriptyline. Arch Gen Psychiatry 42:142–148, 1985.

Chou JC: Recent advances in treatment of acute mania. J Clin Psychopharmacol 11:3–21, 1991.

Coryell W, Lavori P, Endicott J, et al: Outcome in schizoaffective, psychotic, and nonpsychotic depression. Arch Gen Psychiatry 41:787–791, 1984.

Coryell W, Endicott J, Keller M: Rapidly cycling affective disorder. Arch Gen Psychiatry 49:126–131, 1992.

Delgado PL, Charney DS, Price LH, et al: Serotonin function and the mechanism of antidepressant action. Arch Gen Psychiatry 47:411–418, 1990.

Egeland JA, Gerhard DS, Pauls DL, et al: Bipolar affective disorders linked to DNA markers on chromosome 11. Nature 325:783–787, 1987.

Ellicott A, Hammen C, Gitlin M, et al: Life events and the course of bipolar disorder. Am J Psychiatry 147:1194–1198, 1990.

Giles DE, Jarrett RB, Rush J, et al: Prospective assessment of electroencephalographic sleep in remitted major depression. Psychiatr Res 46:269–284, 1993.

Gold MS, Herridge P, Hapworth WE: Depression and "symptomless" autoimmune thyroiditis. Psychiatr Ann 17:750–757, 1987.

Goodnick PJ, Fieve RR, Schlegel A, et al: Predictors of interepisode symptoms and relapse in affective disorder patients treated with lithium carbonate. Am J Psychiatry 144:367–369, 1987.

Goodwin FK, Jamison KR: Manic-Depressive Illness. New York, Oxford University Press, 1990.

Harrow M, Goldberg JF, Grossman LS, et al: Outcome in manic disorders. Arch Gen Psychiatry 47:665–671, 1990.

Hellerstein DJ, Yanowitch P, Rosenthal J, et al: Long-term treatment of double depression. Prog Neuropsychopharmacol Biol Psychiatry 18:139–147, 1994.

Howland RH, Thase ME: A comprehensive review of cyclothymic disorder. J Nerv Ment Dis 181:485–493, 1993.

Joffe RT, Moul DE, Lam RW, et al: Light visor treatment for seasonal affective disorder. Psychiatr Res 46:29–39, 1993.

Karasu TB: Toward a clinical model of psychotherapy for depression. Am J Psychiatry 147:133–147, 1990.

Klein DF, Ross DC: Reanalysis of the National Institute of Mental Health treatment of depression collaborative research program general effectiveness report. Neuropsychopharmacology 8:241–251, 1993.

Martinot J, Hardy P, Feline A, et al: Left prefrontal glucose hypometabolism in the depressed state. Am J Psychiatry 147:1313–1317, 1990.

Mukherjee S, Sackeim HA, Schnur DB: Electroconvulsive therapy of acute manic episodes: A review of 50 years' experience. Am J Psychiatry 151:169–176, 1994.

Peet M: Induction of mania with selective serotonin reuptake inhibitors and tricyclic antidepressants. Br J Psychiatry 164:549–550, 1994.

Piccinelli M, Wilkinson G: Outcome of depression in psychiatric settings. Br J Psychiatry 164:297–304, 1994.

Pope HG, McElroy SL, Keck PE, et al: Valproate in the treatment of acute mania. Arch Gen Psychiatry 48:62–68, 1991.

Ribeiro SCM, Tandon R, Grunhaus L, et al: The DST as a predictor of outcome in depression: A metaanalysis. Am J Psychiatry 150:1618–1629, 1993.

Robinson RG: Depression and stroke. Psychiatr Ann 17:731–740, 1987.

Stasiek C, Zetin M: Organic manic disorders. Psychosomatics 26:394–402, 1985.

Task Force on Laboratory Tests in Psychiatry: The dexamethasone suppression test: An overview of its current status in psychiatry. An APA Task Force Report. Am J Psychiatry 144:1253–1262, 1987.

Tollefson GD, Holman SL, Saylor ME, et al: Fluoxetine, placebo, and tricyclic antidepressants in major depression with and without anxious features. J Clin Psychiatry 55:50–59, 1994.

# Chapter 5

# Delirium and Amnestic and Other Cognitive Disorders

The psychiatric conditions in this chapter are all caused by medical (organic) pathology. The most common is delirium, but several other specific presentations occur as well. In addition, organic processes contribute to dementia (see Chapter 6), intoxication and withdrawal (see Chapters 16 and 17), and many of the syndromes found in other chapters.

These syndromes are common, particularly among the elderly ($20\%^+$ of all acute medical inpatients develop some organic syndrome—usually delirium). Delirium is usually brief and reversible, and dementia is longer-lasting and more likely to be irreversible, yet none of these characterizations is completely true (eg, 15-20% of dementias are reversible). These conditions are clinically defined, and their course and characteristics are dependent on the nature, severity, course, and location of the causative organic pathology. First identify the syndrome, then determine the likely organic cause.

## DELIRIUM

This common condition may be caused by physical illness (D. DUE TO A GENERAL MEDICAL CONDITION; DSM-IV p 129, 293.0), drugs (SUBSTANCE INTOXICATION OR WITHDRAWAL D.; p 131), several causes simultaneously (D. DUE TO MULTIPLE ETIOLOGIES; p 132), or by unknown organic conditions. These patients may be confused, bizarre, or even "wild," and thus can be mistakenly thought to be suffering from other psychotic illnesses. Other delirious patients may appear somnolent or perfectly normal during the day but decompensate dramatically in the evening or night. Still other patients may have increasing difficulty functioning due to a mild delirium which is only revealed by specific mental status testing. Synonyms include acute brain syndrome, toxic psychosis, acute confusional state, and metabolic encephalopathy.

## Diagnosis

Delirium is a rapidly developing disorder of disturbed attention that fluctuates with time. Although the clinical presentation of delirium differs considerably from patient to patient, there are several characteristic features that help make the diagnosis.

Clouding of consciousness: The patient is not normally alert and may appear bewildered and confused. He may have noticeably decreased alertness (grading into stupor) or he may be hyperalert. Observe the patient.

Attention deficit: The patient usually is very distractible and unable to focus his attention sufficiently or for a long enough time to follow a train of thought or to understand what is occurring around him. Have the patient do serial 7's and/or a Random Letter Test.

Perceptual disturbances: These are common and include misinterpretations of environmental events, illusions (eg, the curtain blows and the patient believes someone is climbing in the window) and hallucinations (usually visual). The patient may or may not recognize these misperceptions as unreal.

Sleep-wake alteration: Insomnia is almost always present (all symptoms are usually worse at night and in the dark) while marked drowsiness may also occur.

Disorientation: Most frequently to time but also to place, situation, and (lastly) person. Ask for the date, time, and day of the week. "What place is this?" etc.

Memory impairment: The patient typically has a recent memory deficit and usually denies it (he may confabulate and may want to talk about the distant past). Ask about the recent past, eg, "Who brought you to the hospital? Did you have any tests yesterday? What did you have for breakfast?" etc. Name two objects and two words and ask the patient to repeat them in 5 minutes. Does he remember your name?

Incoherence: The patient may attempt to communicate but the speech may be confused or even unintelligible. Verbal perseveration may occur.

Altered psychomotor activity: Most delirious patients are restless and
agitated and may display perseveration of motion; some may be excessively somnolent; and some may fluctuate from one to the other
(usually restless at night and sleepy during the day).

Fluctuations: Most of the characteristics listed above vary in severity over
hours and days.

A delirium usually develops over days and may precede
signs of the organic condition causing it. Usually it lasts less
than a week (depending on the cause). Many of these patients
are significantly anxious or frightened by their experiences,
may become combative, and may develop some delusional ideas
based on their misperceptions. A few patients become dangerously suicidal—watch for it. Environmental conditions can significantly alter the presentation of a delirium. Change of setting
(eg, moving out of familiar surroundings), overstimulation, and
understimulation (eg, darkness, sensory deprivation) can all
worsen the symptoms, as can stress of any kind.

It is necessary to have a high index of suspicion and to ask
specific mental status questions if you are going to identify delirium early. Ask tactfully since many patients defensively resist
this probing. The early, prodromal symptoms that should alert
you to a developing delirium include:

Restlessness (particularly at night), anxiety
Daytime somnolence
Insomnia, vivid dreams and nightmares
Hypersensitivity to light and sound
Fleeting illusions and hallucinations
Distractibility; difficulty in thinking clearly

The EEG (although usually not necessary to make the diagnosis) has a characteristic pattern of diffuse slowing that is proportional to the severity of the delirium. It can help if there is
a question of the presence of a functional psychosis, drug use,
or a dissociative state. Delirium may also be accompanied by a
tremor, asterixis, diaphoresis, tachycardia, elevated BP, tachypnea, and flushing.

## ETIOLOGY AND DIFFERENTIAL DIAGNOSIS

The presence of a delirium usually means that the patient is
seriously medically ill. Delirium is a diagnosis that immediately

demands a search for causes. Most causes produce diffuse cerebral impairment and lie <u>outside</u> the CNS—usually due to some form of deranged metabolism (e.g., infection, fever, hypoxia, hypoglycemia, medication side effects, drug withdrawal states, hepatic encephalopathy, postoperative changes)—but also include CNS trauma and postictal states. The specific potential etiologies are too numerous to list (consult a more complete source), although usually the cause is evident. These patients all deserve a thorough physical and laboratory examination.

The major problem in differential diagnosis is in distinguishing a delirium from an acute functional psychosis. The delirious patient is usually more acute and confused, and the hallucinations are usually more disorganized and are more likely to be visual. Patients with functional psychoses usually don't have confusion, disorientation, and illusions, and they are more likely to have a formal thought disorder. <u>Always</u> check the personal and family history for serious psychiatric illness.

## TREATMENT

Provide adequate medical care for an identified cause of the delirium. Patients with delirium have an increased mortality rate. Provide for the patient's safety. Maintain around-the-clock observation (particularly at night). This may require someone in the room constantly—preferably someone with whom the patient is familiar. Use restraints only if absolutely necessary (they frequently increase agitation).

Keep the patient in a quiet, well-lighted room. Keep familiar objects around and use the same treatment personnel, if possible.

Frequently (and tactfully) reorient the patient. Introduce yourself again and describe what you are doing and why.

Anticipate the patient's anxiety and reassure him. Be calm and sympathetic.

Medication should be used cautiously. Use low doses. If psychotic features are prevalent, consider haloperidol or chlorpromazine. If sedation is called for (usually for marked agitation), consider the benzodiazepines (e.g., diazepam, clonazepam).

The following organic syndromes are considerably less common than delirium, dementia, and the substance abuse syndromes of intoxication and withdrawal. They are also more likely to be associated with focal organic pathology and with a few specific medical or neurological diseases.

### AMNESTIC SYNDROME
### (DUE TO A GENERAL MEDICAL CONDITION; DSM-IV p 160, 294.0)
### (SUBSTANCE-INDUCED; DSM-IV p 162)

These patients have severe memory deficits that usually appear suddenly after a CNS insult and that may be chronic. The deficits are both retrograde (old memories—ask about childhood, schooling, etc.) and anterograde (new memories—ask the patient to remember several facts for 5–10 minutes). The patients are often unaware that their memory is impaired. Unlike delirium, the sensorium is usually clear, although there may be disorientation. Unlike dementia, serious memory loss occurs without intellectual or other associated changes.

There are numerous potential causes that include CNS trauma, hypoxia, herpes simplex encephalitis, and some substance abuse (particularly alcohol and sedative-hypnotic abuse—see Chapters 16 and 17). Bilateral lesions of the medial temporal and/or diencephalic regions appear to be required. Treatment consists of correcting any medical/organic causes; and waiting.

### CATATONIC DISORDER DUE TO A GENERAL MEDICAL CONDITION
### (DSM-IV p 170, 393.89)

These patients display catatonia (immobility (stuporousness or the "waxy flexibility" of catalepsy) but sometimes extreme agitation; also mutism, slow and stereotyped movements, echolalia, and/or echopraxia) caused by a medical condition or a substance. The most common causes are neurological as well as metabolic (e.g., hypercalcemia or hepatic encephalopathy). Be sure to rule out catatonic schizophrenia (history of psychosis; no medical causes), but don't assume every catatonic patient is "just schizophrenic."

## PERSONALITY CHANGE DUE TO A GENERAL
## MEDICAL CONDITION
### (DSM-IV p 173, 310.1)

These patients display a personality change or a marked exacerbation of previous personality characteristics. Often this takes the form of a loss of control over impulses and emotions or the development of apathy, irritability, aggression, paranoia, or indifference. Impairment of social judgment is common. The usual cause is frontal lobe damage (the frontal lobe syndrome) due to stroke, tumor, CNS trauma, normal pressure hydrocephalus, general paresis, Huntington's chorea, or MS. Occasionally right-sided strokes may be responsible. Be careful not to mistake it for mild delirium or the early changes of dementia, schizophrenia, or major affective disorder.

### Suggested Readings

Dubin WR, Weiss KJ, Zeccardi JA: Organic brain syndrome: The psychiatric imposter. JAMA 249:60–62, 1983.

Francis J, Martin D, Kapoor WN: A prospective study of delirium in hospitalized elderly. JAMA 263:1097-1101, 1990.

Hill CD, Risby E, Morgan N: Cognitive deficits in delirium: Assessment over time. Psychopharmacol Bull 28:401-407, 1992.

Lipowski ZJ: Delirium (acute confusional state). In JAM Frederiks (ed.) Handbook of Clinical Neurology, Vol. 2, Neurobehavioural Disorders. New York, Elsevier Science Publishing Co., 1985.

Lipowski ZJ: Transient cognitive disorders (delirium, acute confusional states) in the elderly. Am J Psychiatry 140:1426–1436, 1983.

Lipowski ZJ: Delirium. New York, Oxford University Press, 1990.

Weddington WW: The mortality of delirium: An underappreciated problem? Psychosomatics 23:1232–1235, 1982.

Zisook S, Braff DL: Delirium: Recognition and management in the older patient. Geriatrics 41:67-78, 1986.

# Chapter 6

# Dementia

**DEMENTIA** (DSM-IV p 133) results from a broad loss of intellectual functions due to diffuse organic disease of the cerebral hemispheres (or subcortical structures as in Huntington's and Parkinson's diseases) of sufficient severity to impair social and/or occupational functioning. Dementia is a clinical presentation demanding a diagnosis—not a diagnosis itself. Causes are numerous, but clinical presentations are remarkably similar. Sixty percent of dementias are irreversible, but, since 25% are controllable and 15% are reversible, treatable causes must be identified.

## MAKING THE DIAGNOSIS

Dementia usually develops slowly and is easily overlooked. A rapid onset suggests a recent (and possibly treatable) insult although frequently a mild, unrecognized dementia is made worse and obvious by a medical illness (eg, pneumonia, CHF). Always interview the family—they frequently notice changes (in personality, memory, etc.) of which the patient is unaware. Unlike Delirium, clouding of consciousness is minimal (unless dementia and delirium are mixed)—make sure the patient is alert.

EARLY—**Effects include:** subtle changes in personality, impaired social skills, a decrease in the range of interests and enthusiasms, lability and shallowness of affect, agitation, numerous somatic complaints, vague psychiatric symptoms, and a gradual loss of intellectual skills and acuity. These are often first noticed in work settings where high performance is required. Patients may recognize a loss of abilities initially but vigorously deny it. Early dementia often precipitates a depression. Remember: early dementia may present primarily with emotional (usually depressive) rather than cognitive symptoms, but also emotional disorders may mimic early dementia—don't under or overdiagnose it.

### LATE—Parts of the full picture emerge:

Memory loss—Usually immediate and recent memory loss but gradually involves remote recall (medial temporal and diencephalic regions involved). Does patient forget appointments, the news, people he has just met, or places he has just been? Patient may confabulate, so check his information.

Ask patient to (1) repeat digits (normal—remember 6 forward, 4 backward) and (2) recall two words and three objects after 5 minutes. Does he know your name? the nurse? this place? the names of his visitors? last night's meal? Does he know his birth date? his hometown? the name of his high school?

Changes in mood and personality—Often exaggeration of previous personality (eg, more compulsive or more excitable). Depression, anxiety, and/or irritability early on—later, withdrawal and apathy. Has the patient become sloppy, belligerent, thoughtless of others, paranoid, socially inappropriate, fearful? Does he lack initiative or interest? Use vulgar language or jokes?

Loss of orientation—Particularly time (of day, day of week, date, season) but also place ("What place is this?") and, when severe, person. Has he been getting lost—in new places? in old neighborhood? at home? Does he know why he is here (situation)? He may not sleep well, wander around at night, and get lost.

Intellectual impairment—Patient is "less sharp" than he used to be. Does he have trouble doing things he could previously do easily? General information (last five Presidents, six large U.S. cities)? calculations (multiplication tables, serial 7's, make change)? similarities (How are a ball and an orange alike? a mouse and an elephant? a fly and a tree?).

Compromised judgment—Doesn't anticipate consequences. Does he act impulsively? "What should you do if you found a stamped, addressed envelope?" "If you noticed a fire in a theater?"

Psychotic symptoms—Hallucinations (usually simple), illusions, delusions, unshakable preoccupations, ideas of reference.

Language impairment—Often vague and imprecise; occasionally almost mute. Is there perseveration, blocking, or aphasia? (With early aphasia, suspect focal pathology.)

Ask about history of chronic medical or psychiatric disease, family psychiatric illness, drug or alcohol abuse, head injury, exposure to toxins.

## Physical Examination

Examine for the numerous medical causes of dementia, eg, endocrine, heart, kidney, lung, liver, infection (see below). Always perform a careful neurologic exam—identify any focal CNS causes of dementia. Always test for sense of smell (first cranial nerve)—may identify a large, unrecognized frontal lobe lesion. Always test hearing. Advanced diffuse disease displays ataxia, facial grimaces, agnosias, apraxias, motor impersistence, and/or perseveration, and pathological reflexes (grasp, snout, suck, glabella tap, tonic foot, etc.). Recognize that all types of physical illnesses occur more frequently in the demented (reasons for this are unclear). Survival time is reduced.

## Laboratory Examination

Select tests based on suspected etiology. Consider screening with: ESR, CBC, STS, SMA12, $T_3$ and $T_4$, vitamin $B_{12}$ and folate assays, UA, chest X-ray, and CT scan. Other tests based on likely causes include drug levels, EEG (20% of all elderly have an abnormal EEG), LP (rarely), arteriography, etc. The EEG is useful for identifying pathology in the usually silent CNS areas (frontal and temporal lobes)—investigate further if the dementia is mild but the EEG is grossly abnormal.

## Psychological Testing

These can (1) help identify a focal lesion, (2) provide a baseline, (3) help with the diagnosis, and (4) identify strengths to be used in planning treatment. Useful tests include: WAIS, Bender-Gestalt test, the Luria test, and the Halstead and Reitan Batteries (very time-consuming; don't use routinely). A brief but useful screening test is the Mini-Mental State Exam. Patients with even mild dementia often will show impaired constructional ability; thus, have them draw simple figures (eg, a diamond, a cross, and cube—can be done on initial interview).

## CAUSES

### Major Untreatable Dementias

**DEMENTIA OF THE ALZHEIMER TYPE** (DSM-IV p 142, 290.xx): Approx. 50%+ of all dementias (4% of people over 65), but—usually a diagnosis by exclusion. It is frequently over-diagnosed. Usually begins insidiously in the 50's (presenile dementia), 60's, or 70's and progresses to death in 6-10 years. Ceaseless pacing and a shuffling gait are common; social responses often remain intact until very late. Look for cortical atrophy and enlarged ventricles by CT scan. EEG is often normal for age early on—a good screening test since it is often abnormal with reversible causes of dementia (except for general paresis and NPH). Histologically there are senile plaques (degenerated nerve terminals surrounding a neurotoxic $\beta$-amyloid core), neurofibrillary tangles, and neuronal granulovacuolar degeneration. Recent evidence implicates primary degeneration of cholinergic neurons of the basal forebrain, particularly the nucleus basalis (although serotonergic and other neurons are increasingly being implicated—very heterogeneous). There is an increased incidence in women (1.5:1), post head injury patients, first-degree relatives (3-fold; particularly with presenile dementia), and Down's syndrome. (Moreover, a few presenile familial cases have been related to the amyloid precursor protein gene on the portion of chromosome 21 near the region associated with Down's syndrome; other cases have been associated with chromosome 14. Also, "normal" late onset Alzheimer's disease recently has been associated with the apolipoprotein E type 4 allele on chromosome 19—a possible breakthrough.)

**Huntington's Chorea:** A "subcortical dementia." Psychiatric symptoms, ranging from neurotic to psychotic (including dementia), may precede the chorea. Dementia always occurs terminally. Autosomal dominant (short arm of chromosome 4)—so check family history.

**Parkinson's Disease:** Lesion in the basal ganglia (subcortical). Depression (40%) and/or dementia in some patients. L-Dopa relieves temporarily only.

**Others:** Progressive Supranuclear Palsy, spinocerebellar degenerations, Pick's disease, Parkinsonism-Dementia Complex of Guam, SSPE, Creutzfeldt-Jakob disease, herpes simplex encephalitis, MS, HIV, head trauma.

### Treatable Forms of Dementia

**VASCULAR DEMENTIA** (DSM-IV p. 146, 290.4x): Ten percent of dementias. Differentiate from Alzheimer's Dementia by history of rapid onset and stepwise deterioration (can be difficult) in a patient in his 50's or early 60's and by presence of focal neurological impairment. EEG may show focal abnormalities. Caused by multiple thromboembolic episodes (numerous small cerebral infarcts pathologically) in a patient with atherosclerotic disease of the major vessels or valvular disease of the heart. Hypertension is usually present. Pseudobulbar phenomena are common: emotional lability, dysarthria, and dysphagia. Controlling BP may help.

**Normal Pressure Hydrocephalus (NPH):** A "classic triad" of gait ataxia, incontinence, and progressive dementia—either idiopathic or after cerebral trauma, hemorrhage, or infection. There is normal CSF pressure but dilated ventricles by CT scan and pneumoencephalography. Confirm with isotope cisternography. Treat with a lumboperitoneal or ventriculoatrial shunt—55% show improvement.

**SUBSTANCE-INDUCED PERSISTING DEMENTIA** (DSM-IV p. 154): A diagnosis by exclusion. Most commonly follows many years of heavy drinking and may be partly reversible with good nutrition and abstinence. Also 2° to chronic sedative-hypnotic abuse and toxins such as lead, mercury, solvents, and organophosphates.

**Drug Intoxication:** Common, particularly in the elderly (too many meds, misunderstood instructions, etc.). Watch for major and minor tranquilizers, analgesics (particularly digoxin, primidone, phenytoin, methyldopa). Reevaluate and stop, if possible.

**Brain Tumors:** Primarily metastatic tumors (from lung and breast) and meningiomas. Focal signs are usually present except in frontal lobe. Get CSF pressure and protein, EEG, and CT scan. EEG may be localizing.

**Brain Trauma:** Dementia is unusual except for subdural hematoma in the elderly—dementia, headache, and drowsiness developing over weeks or months with or without a history of trauma. Don't do LP. Get CT scan, then arteriography (diagnostic). May be reversible.

**Infection:** Any significant infection (eg, pneumonia, UTI) can produce delirium and worsen a dementia in the elderly patient. Dementia can be caused by brain abscess, CNS syphilis (general paresis—serological tests of blood and CSF usually positive), and tuberculosis and cryptococcal meningitis.

**Metabolic Disorders:** Most common are thyroid disorders—hypothyroidism (dementia even with near normal hormone levels; may be reversible; look for diffuse slowing on EEG) and also hyperthyroidism ("apathetic thyrotoxicosis" particularly in the elderly). Electrolyte imbalances are also common causes in the elderly, eg, hypo- and hypernatremia and hypercalcemia. Suspect Wilson's Disease if there are signs of liver failure, tremor, rigidity, and convulsions in a person younger than 40. Also consider Cushing's syndrome, hypoglycemia, and hyper- and hypoparathyroidism.

**Disorders of heart, lung, liver, kidney:** Particularly CHF, arrhythmias, SBE, chronic hypoxia and hypercapnia (eg, emphysema), hepatic encephalopathy, uremia, dialysis dementia.

**Other:** Malnutrition (particularly vitamin $B_{12}$ and folate deficiencies—check for pernicious anemia and combined system disease), remote effects of carcinoma, SLE, epilepsy.

## DIFFERENTIAL DIAGNOSIS

Normal aging may mimic mild dementia, particularly if the patient is stressed by environmental changes, social isolation, fatigue, or visual and hearing disorders (sensory deprivation). Many elderly will develop mild anxiety, depressive, or hypochondriacal disorders that mimic dementia, but with persistent questioning and encouragement, normal memory, orientation, etc. can be seen. Intellectual deterioration with schizophrenia is differentiated from dementia by a history of psychosis and social withdrawal and by the presence of a characteristic thought disorder. An Amytal interview may help distinguish dementia from catatonic schizophrenia. In delirium there is an altered and fluctuating level of consciousness. Delirium and dementia frequently coexist, but the delirium must clear before the diagnosis of dementia can be made.

A major depression is the most common cause of pseudodementia. Unlike the demented patient, these patients have a rapid, recent onset (family can usually date it), complain of a severe memory loss (usually mild when tested), have marked affective changes, emphasize their inabilities and failings, and frequently answer simple questions with "I don't know" (the demented patient usually attempts an answer). A temporary clearing during an interview and the lack of a deteriorating course helps identify these patients. Consider a DST and CT scan. These patients usually improve with antidepressants or ECT.

Don't mistake an aphasia due to a focal lesion for a dementia (although perhaps 10% of severely demented patients have a related aphasia).

## TREATMENT

### Supportive Treatment

— Provide good physical care, eg, good nutrition, eye glasses, hearing aids, protection (eg, stairs, stoves, medication), etc. Physical restraint is necessary at times.
— Keep in familiar settings, if possible. Surround with familiar objects; keep old friends engaged. Encourage the family's participation and understanding.
— Keep the patient involved—through personal contact, frequent orientation (remind him of the day, of the time). Discuss the news with him. Use calendars, radio, TV. Structure daily activities—make them predictable.
— Help maintain patient's self-esteem. Treat him like an adult. Plan toward his strengths. Be accepting, tolerant.
— Avoid dark, isolated settings; avoid overstimulation.

### Symptomatic Treatment

Psychiatric conditions may require <u>small</u> doses of appropriate medication.

— Acute anxiety, restlessness, aggression, agitation: eg, haloperidol 0.5 mg PO tid (or lower); thioridazine, 25 mg PO tid-qid. Stop after 4–6 weeks.
— Nonpsychotic anxiety, agitation: eg, diazepam 2 mg PO bid-tid; oxazepam 10 mg PO bid-tid. Stop after 4–6 weeks.
— Chronic agitation: SSRIs (eg, fluoxetine 10–20 mg/day) and/or buspirone (15 mg bid); also consider low-dose $\beta$-blockers.
— Depression: consider SSRIs first; with TCAs, begin slowly and work up to eg, desipramine 75-150 mg PO daily.
— Insomnia: use for short periods only, eg, temazepam 15 mg PO HS.

### Specific Treatment

— Identify and correct any treatable condition.
— No specific drug treatment for dementia has been found to be consistently useful, although many are being investigated, eg, cerebral

vasodilators, anticoagulants, cerebral metabolic stimulants, stimulants, hyperbaric oxygen. Increasing central cholinergic activity may relieve some symptoms in a few patients with Primary Degenerative Dementia temporarily. Acetylcholine precursors (choline, lecithin) are of little value, but anticholinesterases (eg, physostigmine—short-acting; and only with mild dementia) show promise.

Tacrine (Cognex; THA or tetrahydroaminoacridine) may produce modest cognitive improvement in moderate dementia. Begin at 40 mg and raise by 40 mg every 6 weeks until at 160 mg. Thirty percent have increased liver enzymes (ALT 3 × nl)—stop if ALT is 5 × nl. Nausea, vomiting, and diarrhea can also be problems.

## Suggested Readings

Bondareff W, Mountjoy CQ, Wischik CM, et al: Evidence of subtypes of Alzheimer's disease and implications for etiology. Arch Gen Psychiatry 50:350–356, 1993.

Caine ED, Shoulson I: Psychiatric syndromes in Huntington's disease. Am J Psychiatry 140:728–733, 1983.

David KL, Thal LJ, Gamzu ER, et al: A double-blind, placebo-controlled multicenter study of tacrine for Alzheimer's disease. N Engl J Med 327:1253–1259, 1992.

Eagger S, Morant N, Levy R, et al: Tacrine in Alzheimer's disease. Br J Psychiatry 160:36–40, 1992.

Farlow M, Gracon SI, Hershey LA, et al: A controlled trial of tacrine in Alzheimer's disease. JAMA 268:2523–2529, 1992.

Folstein MF, Folstein SE, McHugh PR: "Mini-mental state"—a practical method for grading the mental state of patients for the clinician. J Psychiatr Res 12:189–198, 1975.

Goate A, Chartier-Harllin M, Mullan M, et al: Segregation of a missense mutation in the amyloid precursor protein gene with familial Alzheimer's disease. Nature 349:704–706, 1991.

Jeste DV, Gierz M, Harris MJ: Pseudodementia: Myths and reality. Psychiatr Ann 20:71–79, 1990.

Kunik ME, Yudofsky SC, Silver JM, et al: Pharmacologic approach to management of agitation associated with dementia. J Clin Psychiatry 55(2, suppl):13–17, 1994.

Mace NL, Rabins PV: The 36-Hour Day. Baltimore, Johns Hopkins University Press, 1981.

Mayeux R, Stern Y, Williams JBW, et al: Clinical and biochemical features of depression in Parkinson's disease. Am J Psychiatry 143:756–759, 1986.

McDonald WM, Nemeroff CB: Neurotransmitters and neuropeptides in Alzheimer's disease. In, Davidson M (Ed), Alzheimer's Disease:

The Psychiatric Clinics of North America. Philadelphia, WB Saunders, 1991.

Molloy DW, Ahemayehu E, Roberts R: Reliability of a standardized minimental state exam compared to the traditional minimental state examination. Am J Psychiatry 148:102–105, 1991.

RaeGrant A, Blume W, Lau C, et al: The electroencephalogram in Alzheimer-type dementia. Arch Neurol 44:50–54, 1987.

Risse SC, Raskind MA, Nochlin D, et al: Neuropathological findings in patients with clinical diagnoses of probable Alzheimer's disease. Am J Psychiatry 147:168–172, 1990.

Schellenberg GD, Bird TD, Wijsman EM, et al: Genetic linkage evidence for a familial Alzheimer's disease locus on chromosome 14. Science 258:668–671, 1992.

Schneider LS, Sobin PB: Nonneuroleptic treatment of behavioral symptoms and agitation in Alzheimer's disease and other dementias. Psychopharmacol Bull 28:71–79, 1992.

Sloane PD, Mathew LJ, Scarborough M, et al: Physical and pharmacological restraint of nursing home patients with dementia. JAMA 265:1278–1282, 1991.

Stern RG, Mohs RC, Davidson M, et al: A longitudinal study of Alzheimer's disease. Am J Psychiatry 151:390–396, 1994.

Terry RD, Katzman R, Bick KL: Alzheimer Disease. New York, Raven Press, 1994.

Travis J: New piece in Alzheimer's puzzle. Science 261:828–829, 1993.

# Chapter 7

# Suicide and Assaultive Behaviors

## THE SUICIDAL PATIENT

### Epidemiology

— Reported suicides in the United States—30,000/yr (12/100,000).
— Suicide is underreported—often listed as accidental.
— Attempted suicide:successful suicide ratio is 20:1.
— Suicide increases with age; second leading cause of death in male adolescents and college students.
— Completers 3:1 (M:F); attempters 3:1 (F:M).
— Most common attempt is by drug ingestion; most likely to be fatal is by shooting.
— Most patients are <u>not</u> "psychotic or incompetent."

All clinicians will encounter suicidal patients. Many will not recognize them. Some of those patients will kill themselves.

### IDENTIFYING THE POTENTIALLY SUICIDAL PATIENT

One-fifth of suicides are unanticipated: accurate prediction is difficult, if not impossible, with present knowledge. Entertain the possibility when:

1. Suicide attempt: Patient seen in ER, medical ward, etc.
2. Overt or indirect suicide talk or threats: "You won't be bothered by me much longer" (most often made to family members).
3. Depressed or anxious mood due to a depression.
4. Significant recent loss: eg, spouse, job, self-esteem.
5. Unexpected change in behavior: making a will, intense talks with friends, giving away possessions.
6. Unexpected change in attitude: suddenly cheerful, angry, or withdrawn.

## ASSESSING SUICIDAL RISK

### Assessment Procedure

First, build rapport during a supportive, nonjudgmental interview. If not volunteered, investigate suicidal thoughts by asking questions of increasing specificity: eg, "Have you been feeling sad?"; "Have you thought of doing away with yourself?"; "How?"; etc. Asking about suicide does not precipitate it. After a serious attempt, wait until the patient is alert enough to cooperate.

The following must be learned about all suicidal patients:

1. The patient's intention—Why does he want to die?
2. Is a suicide plan made?—the more specific the plan, the more likely the act.
3. Method—the more lethal the technique, the more serious the plan.
4. Presence of psychiatric or organic factors, eg, psychotic depression, thought disorder, sedative self-medication, organicity.
5. Determine the role of impulsivity vs premeditation.
6. Is the precipitating crisis resolving?
7. Take an "inventory of loss."
8. Does the patient have plans for the future?
9. Does the patient have caring family or other supports?
10. Does the patient think he is going to commit suicide?

**Population Risk Factors:** Males, elderly, isolated, whites, American Indians, policemen.

### Individual Risk Factors:

— Sense of hopelessness, helplessness, loneliness, exhaustion, "unbearable" psychological pain.
— Psychiatric illness (in 90% of suicide patients), mainly:
  1. Major mood disorder (either 1° or 2°; 50% of all suicides), particularly with vegetative signs or constriction of thought; 15% lifetime suicide risk.
  2. Alcoholism (suicide rate 50 times norm—25% of all suicides) mostly chronic patients; mostly men; often after interpersonal loss; 34% lifetime risk. Much higher if also depressed and with poor social supports. Drug addiction (10% die by suicide).
  3. Schizophrenia, particularly when lonely, depressed, chronic, or with persecutory delusions or self-destructive command hallucinations; 10%$^+$ lifetime risk.
  4. Other: Psychoses due to organic conditions; personality disorders (borderline, antisocial).

— Failing health, particularly if previously independent (5% of all suicides).
— Intoxication; active use (abuse) of alcohol and drugs.
— Impaired impulse control for any reason; hostility.
— Past history of suicide attempts, particularly serious attempts.
— Nature of past or present suicide attempts: eg, shooting or jumping more lethal than most ingestions or wrist cutting. Warning given? Help available at the time?
— Family history of suicide; personal exposure to suicide; suicide itself may run in families genetically.
— Widowed, divorced, separated, single, unemployed, retired.
— Medical patients on renal dialysis.
— Family stresses or instability; few external supports.
— A change in status—up or down.
— Recent loss or rejection.
— Parental loss during childhood.

**Other Risk Factors:**
— Holidays, spring, anniversaries.
— Possible biochemical measures of suicide potential: decreased CSF 5-HIAA and HVA and increased MHPG; decreased urine NE/E ratio; increased adrenal weight; positive DST.

## INITIATING APPROPRIATE TREATMENT

The first question often is: "Should you hospitalize?" If the patient has pressing suicidal thoughts and/or decreased impulse control coupled with several risk factors, hospitalize, if only overnight. Be conservative. Don't write off patients as "just manipulative"—all statements of suicide intent initially should be taken seriously (particularly from adolescents). Manipulative suicide patients have "accidentally" killed themselves after being denied admission—60% of successful suicides have had previous suicide attempts. The most emotionally upset patient is not necessarily the most suicidal. The suicidal state is episodic; a patient may be "safe" just hours after a serious suicide attempt. Be very cautious of the patient who has trouble considering any alternative to suicide.

    The decision to hospitalize should be communicated to the patient decisively but optimistically. Hospitalization should be involuntary if necessary. Assure the patient's physical safety in the hospital through appropriate "suicide precautions," eg, close supervision, no isolation, no dangerous objects.

A patient of lesser risk may be followed as an outpatient if there is a reliable family to help monitor him—assess that support. If the patient is <u>not to</u> be hospitalized, specific plans for follow-up must be made with the patient. Be absolutely clear about this with him.

## Treatment Principles

1. Identify and treat psychiatric or medical conditions. Treat depression vigorously. Treat psychotic depressions with an antidepressant and antipsychotic drugs. If the patient is determinedly suicidal, use <u>ECT</u> rather than wait for a medication response. Phenothiazines and benzodiazepines may be briefly useful with the agitated patient.
2. Develop a therapeutic alliance with the patient. Be concerned and accepting. Attempt to understand why the patient wants to die. Allow him to express anger, "unacceptable" thoughts, and feelings of rejection and hopelessness. These patients often feel misunderstood and trapped but unable to ask for help. Reduce the psychological pain anyway you can.
3. Suicidal patients are usually <u>ambivalent about death</u> and may not know why they are trying to kill themselves. Point out that ambivalence to them—show them evidence of their desire to live. Be hopeful. Be definite. Make specific plans with and for the patient. Appeal to his mature rather than his regressive side.
4. The patients are often bewildered and have a narrowed focus of thought—deal with reality issues.
5. Don't minimize the seriousness of a suicide attempt to the patient.
6. Never agree to hold a suicide plan in confidence.
7. Help the patient to grieve over losses.
8. Do not explain away the patient's symptoms, eg, "I'd feel the same way myself."
9. Suicide potential can change rapidly. Reassess the patient's state of mind frequently.
10. Use community resources. Involve the family and significant others in treatment; use family therapy when appropriate. Actively try to reduce social isolation and withdrawal. Help make changes in the patient's environment where it is pathological.
11. Many suicides in depressives occur during the first 36 months after hospital discharge. <u>Don't lose contact</u> with the patient. Monitor closely during holidays.
12. Be active but insist that the patient ultimately take responsibility for his own life.
13. Tricyclics, MAO inhibitors, and many sedative-hypnotics have seri-

ous overdose potential. Some depressed outpatients store medication, so track drugs prescribed.

Theoretical explanations of suicide include the loss of a sense of identity with the social group (Durkheim), hostility turned against the self (Freud), a "cry for help," and a reflection of biologic, psychiatric conditions.

## THE VIOLENT PATIENT

Human aggression has complex and uncertain biological, psychosocial, and cultural roots. Implicated in violent behavior are lesions of the prefrontal cortex (Frontal Lobe Syndrome) and stimulation of the amygdala and limbic system. Also, elevated androgens and CSF norepinephrine or decreased CSF serotonin (similar to "violent" suicide) and GABA.

Prediction of violence is difficult. Anyone can become violent, yet some groups are at risk: young males 15-25; urban, black, violent cultural subgroups, alcoholics. Key individual predictors of violent behavior are:

1. A past history of violence.
2. Active use of alcohol.
3. Physical abuse as a child.
4. Some form of brain injury.

### Mental Disorders with Associated Violent Behavior

Although most mentally ill patients are not dangerous, some present an increased risk. (NOTE: Serious medical illness can first present with violent behavior.)

1. Organic brain syndromes—particularly with confusion or decreased impulse control; eg, the demented, drugs in the elderly, hypoglycemia, CNS infections, anoxia, metabolic acidosis.
2. Alcohol and drug abuse—particularly with intoxication, delirium, or delusional states of Etoh, amphetamines, cocaine, or PCP; also with intoxication from inhalants or "downers."
3. Schizophrenia, paranoid and catatonic types—particularly with command hallucinations or patients who drink.
4. Acute psychotic states of any origin.
5. Certain mentally retarded; XYY karyotype (possibly), and others.
6. Attention-deficit disorder with hyperactivity, in adults.

## Several Recognizable Patterns of Violence

1. Chronic, aggressive, self-aggrandizing life style—seen with ANTISO-CIAL PERSONALITY DISORDER and thus associated with drug and alcohol abuse, onset in youth, delinquency and adult crime, truancy and school failure. Patients fight frequently and are "constantly in trouble." Serious affective disorders are common in this population.
2. Episodic violence—explosive rages with little provocation, daily to several times/yr, brief, occasional amnesia for event and remorse about it. A mixed group of clinical presentations; CNS abnormalities in most.

If violence is directed: consider (1) INTERMITTENT EX-PLOSIVE DISORDER (DSM-IV p 612, 312.34)—usually males with history of violent outbursts, family history of violence, neurological soft signs, abnormal EEGs, normal between episodes; (2) PERSONALITY CHANGE DUE TO A GENERAL MEDICAL CONDITION, Disinhibited Type (DSM-IV p 173, 310.1)—neurologic origin (encephalitis, epilepsy, MS, tumor, poststroke, etc.), disturbed personality between episodes; or (3) rages in borderline or histrionic personality disorders; or with intoxication.

If violence poorly directed: consider temporal lobe epilepsy (get NP leads), alcohol idiosyncratic intoxication, or other neurologic syndromes.

### EVALUATING THREATS OF VIOLENCE

Take all ideas or threats of violence seriously. Assess risk factors. What is the patient's current mental state? Can he control his impulses and rage? Does he feel under great tension and fear losing control? Is there an intended victim? Is the victim covertly provoking the attack? Specific plans made? Sadistic fantasies present? Weapons available? Patient armed (always check)? Family support system present?

### MANAGEMENT OF THE VIOLENT PATIENT

1. First decide if patient is acutely out of control. If so, treat immediately with restraint and medication, not talk. See immediately—don't keep him waiting.

2. Approach an unfamiliar patient cautiously and from a position of strength (help available, open door). Be alert to warning signs: eg, restlessness, demandingness. If talking appears useful, try, but set clear limits during interview. Use physical controls if patient can't maintain but emphasize their temporary, helping nature. If patient arrives in restraints, don't remove until rapport established and some evaluation done—however, many patients do better without restraints. Restraints may increase agitation and cause hyperthermia. If force is needed to subdue, use overwhelming force—1 person to each limb. Don't take chances.

3. Medication—For the majority of acutely agitated patients: haloperidol 5 mg IM hourly × 3–4 ( + Ativan, 2–4 mg IM) or droperidol (5 mg IM, q45 min, × 2–3—Not FDA approved for that purpose, however). Has patient taken CNS depressants, is he delirious, or is a medical condition responsible for behavior? If so, hold meds and observe. ECT can control psychotic violence.

4. If patient is threatening and agitated but not wild, treat with respect—be civil, direct, confident, calm, reassuring. Don't challenge, provoke, or openly disagree with the patient. Eliminate red tape. Always explain what you are doing, and why. Violent patients are often frightened—find out why and of what.

5. Determine etiology of violence. Is a mental illness present? A brain injury? Drugs involved (get urine screen)? Are there identifiable environmental precipitants? Expect to intervene directly with the psychotic patient.

6. Most patients can be "talked down" with support, understanding (and medication)—however, hospitalize involuntarily if necessary. Is this really a criminal matter, and should the police be involved instead?

### ONGOING CARE

1. The chronically violent patient should receive medication trials. Treat psychosis with antipsychotics, seizures with anticonvulsants. For continued aggression, consider:

   SSRIs (eg, fluoxetine) and buspirone
   propranolol (160-600 mg/day, divided doses), may take 4-6 weeks for effect
   carbamazepine (600-1200 mg/day, divided doses)
   lithium (blood level 0.6-1.2 meq/l)
   stimulants in hyperactive adults

   Benzodiazepines can be useful during times of stress, but paradoxical rages occur in some patients.

2. Teach patient to recognize early signs of increasing anger and to develop ways to discharge tension. The severely brain damaged patient may need a structured environment and behavioral techniques.
3. Help patient to develop a support system and to learn to control environmental stresses. Maintain a channel of communication with the potentially violent patient—be available by phone. Also, you have some legal responsibility.

## Suggested Readings

Beck AT, Brown G, Berchick RJ, et al: Relationship between hopelessness and ultimate suicide: A replication with psychiatric outpatients. Am J Psychiatry 147:190–195, 1990.

Beck JC: The potentially violent patient: Legal duties, clinical practice, and risk management. Psychiatr Ann 17:695–699, 1987.

Clark DC, Young MA, et al: A field test of Motto's risk estimator for suicide. Am J Psychiatry 144:923–926, 1987.

Eichelman B: Toward a rational pharmacotherapy for aggressive and violent behavior. Hosp Commun Psychiatr 39:31–39, 1988.

Eichelman B: Neurochemical and psychopharmacologic aspects of aggressive behavior, in Meltzer H (ed): Psychopharmacology: The Third Generation of Progress. New York, Raven Press, 1988.

Goldstein RB, Black DW, Nasrallah A, et al: The prediction of suicide. Arch Gen Psychiatry 48:418–422, 1991.

Herrman H, McGorry P, Mills J, et al: Hidden severe psychiatric morbidity in sentenced prisoners. Am J Psychiatry 148:236–239, 1991.

Hodgins S: Mental disorder, intellectual deficiency, and crime. Arch Gen Psychiatry 49:476–483, 1992.

Motto JA, Heilbron DC, Juster RP: Development of a clinical instrument to estimate suicide risk. Am J Psychiatry 142:680–686, 1985.

Murphy GE, Wetzel RD, Robins E, et al: Multiple risk factors predict suicide in alcoholism. Arch Gen Psychiatry 49:459–463, 1992.

Ratey JJ, Gordon A: The psychopharmacology of aggression. Psychopharmacol Bull 29:65–73, 1993.

Robins E: The Final Months: A Study of the Lives of 134 Persons Who Committed Suicide. New York, Oxford University Press, 1981.

Roy A, Karoum F, Pollack S: Marked reduction in indexes of dopamine metabolism among patients with depression who attempt suicide. Arch Gen Psychiatry 49:447–450, 1992.

Tardiff K: Assessment and Management of Violent Patients. Washington, D.C., American Psychiatric Press, 1989.

Tonkonogy JM: Violence and temporal lobe lesion: Head CT and MRI data. J Neuropsychiatry 3:189–196, 1991.

# Chapter 8

# Anxiety Disorders

Anxiety is ubiquitous; anxiety disorders are not. Anxiety is an unpleasant and unjustified sense of apprehension often accompanied by physiological symptoms, while anxiety disorder connotes significant distress and dysfunction due to the anxiety. An anxiety disorder may be characterized by only anxiety, or it may display another symptom such as a phobia or an obsession and present anxiety when the primary symptom is resisted. Fear is also universal and can produce the symptom picture of acute anxiety states, yet, in contrast to anxiety, the cause is obvious and understandable. A feature common to all of the anxiety disorders is the unpleasant and unnatural quality of the symptoms (anxiety, phobia, obsession)—they are ego-alien or ego-dystonic. These tend to be chronic, relapsing conditions—be alert for suicide.

Anxiety is mediated through a complex system that involves (at least) the limbic system (amygdala, hippocampus), thalamus, and frontal cortex anatomically and norepinephrine (locus ceruleus), serotonin (dorsal raphe nucleus), and GABA (GABA$_A$ receptor coupled with the benzodiazepine receptor) neurochemically. We don't yet know how these parts work.

## CHRONIC, MILD ANXIETY

Tension, irritability, apprehension, and mild distractibility are common (particularly in medical and psychiatric patients), often related to environmental factors, and treated with supportive and reality-oriented therapy. Medications are of little value chronically although iatrogenic addiction is a serious problem. Environmentally induced, short-lived, mild anxiety (ADJUSTMENT DISORDER WITH ANXIETY, DSM-IV p 626, 309.24) usually resolves with the disappearance of the stress.

## CHRONIC, MODERATELY SEVERE ANXIETY

A diagnosis of GENERALIZED ANXIETY DISORDER (DSM-IV p 435, 300.02) is made with more severe, chronic anxiety (longer than 6 months; usually years, but waxing and waning) and including symptoms such as autonomic responses (palpitations, diarrhea, cold clammy extremities, sweating, urinary frequency), insomnia, poor concentration, fatigue, sighing, trembling, hypervigilance, and/or marked apprehension. It tends to run in families, has a moderate genetic component, and is associated with simple and social phobias and with major depression (40%+ of patients at some time). Usually no obvious etiologic stress is found, but look anyway.

Consider both medication and psychotherapy. Use benzodiazepines sparingly (diazepam, 5 mg, PO, tid-qid, or 10 mg HS) and for short periods (weeks several months); allow medication use to follow the fluctuating course of the illness. Consider buspirone for a first medication or for chronic use (20-30 mg/day; divided doses); a patient may not find it effective after the "instant relief" of a benzodiazepine. Tricyclic antidepressants, SSRIs, and MAOIs are useful in selected patients (particularly those who have depressive sxs), although some patients with autonomic symptoms improve with β-blockers (eg, propranolol 80-160 mg/day).

Encourage self-reliance, maintenance of productive activity, and reality-based cognitions. Train the patient in relaxation techniques; eg, biofeedback, meditation, self-hypnosis. More than 50% of patients become asymptomatic with time (months, years), but the rest retain a significant degree of impairment. Help the patient understand the chronic nature of the illness and the likelihood of having to live with some symptoms.

## ACUTE ANXIETY—PANIC ATTACKS

A PANIC DISORDER WITHOUT AGORAPHOBIA (DSM-IV p 402, 300.01) has dramatic, acute symptoms (peak within 10 minutes) lasting minutes to hours, is self-limited, and occurs in patients with or without chronic anxiety. Symptoms are perceived by the patient as medical and are characteristic of strong autonomic discharge—heart pounding, chest pains, trembling, choking, abdominal pain, sweating, dizziness, as well as disorganization, confusion, dread, and often a sense of impending doom or terror. Attacks may come "out of the blue" or may be initiated by crowds, stressful situations, or anticipation ("anticipatory anxiety"). They may be repeated several times daily, weekly, or monthly, and often disappear for months at a time (but may become chronic). A typical panic attack can be produced in 50-75% of patients with panic disorder, but not in normal patients, by the intravenous infusion of sodium lactate or the breathing of $CO_2$.

As with other anxiety conditions, it runs in families (15%[+] of 1° relatives; 30%[+] of monozygotic twins). (Genetic evidence suggests a single dominant gene with incomplete penetrance—perhaps on chromosome 16.) It is comorbid with major depression (50%), suicide, social and specific phobias, and alcoholism (however, family members are at risk only for panic disorder and social phobia). It occurs in women more frequently than in men (2:1), particularly those who have had a disturbed childhood and early difficulty separating from their parents (separation anxiety disorder). In its milder forms, panic disorder tends to grade into the Generalized Anxiety Disorder clinically, although it appears to be a distinct disorder. In addition, the majority of patients with panic also have agoraphobia (PANIC DISORDER WITH AGORAPHOBIA; DSM-IV p 402, 300.21; see below): combined, these conditions afflict about 3% of the population. Patients often receive the "million dollar workup" for angina, thyrotoxicosis, or abdominal complaints. Effective treatment exists.

1. Medication is essential for panic disorder. Several effective drugs are available, although response to any one is unpredictable. Some patients respond to initial doses of medication with dysphoria or marked jitteriness, so start slowly. Consider:
   A. SSRIs, but also other serotonergic drugs such as clomipramine.
   B. Tricyclic antidepressants (eg, imipramine or desipramine, 150–300 mg/day); expect 2–3 weeks for response.
   C. MAOIs (particularly phenelzine, 30–75[+] mg/day); effective with a broad spectrum of patients but may take 4–6 weeks for a response.
   D. Clonazepam (1–5 mg/day, bid); sedative but looks promising.
   E. Alprazolam (0.5–2 mg/day, tid-qid); patients respond rapidly, but depression, potential addiction, and need for frequent doses can be problems.

F. Other medication occasionally effective includes $\beta$-blockers (propranolol), carbamazepine (400–1200 mg/day), valproate (500–3000 mg/day), verapamil (240–480 mg/day).

Typical practice is to maintain meds for 6 months following improvement, then slowly discontinue. Unfortunately, the relapse rate is high: "half-dose" maintenance may work better.

2. Cognitive-behavioral therapy should be coupled with medication (see discussion under "agoraphobia"). Supportive psychotherapy is of use acutely but does not correct the condition or prevent relapses.

### ANXIETY WITH SPECIFIC FEARS—PHOBIC DISORDERS

Phobias are fears that are persistent and intense, are out of proportion to the stimulus, make little sense even to the sufferer, lead to avoidance of the feared object or situation, and when sufficiently distressful or disabling are termed a PHOBIC DISORDER. Common, mild, frequently transient fears (of the dark, heights, snakes) receive no diagnosis. Phobias may wax and wane over months or years and may disappear spontaneously, but serious cases may continue for decades and gradually take the form of a depressive disorder. The fears may generalize during their developing stages, eg, fear of a store generalizes to the street in front of the store and then to the entire shopping area.

More than 12% of the population may have a phobic disorder in some circumstances, yet in less than 1% is it significantly disabling. Many begin suddenly in women from stable families and of ages 15–30. Anxiety with ruminations may dominate the day-to-day picture, or anxiety may occur only when the phobic object is encountered directly. Relief occurs with escape, thus reinforcing the avoidance pattern—a vicious cycle. Phobics are at risk to abuse alcohol and drugs as self-medication. Three subtypes have been identified, all of which have a moderate genetic component:

**AGORAPHOBIA WITHOUT HISTORY OF PANIC DISORDER** (DSM-IV p 404, 300.22): Multiple phobias with chronic anxiety: specifically fears of open and/or closed spaces, crowded places, unfamiliar places, being alone, and, more generally, of a loss of a sense of security. Many other fears and hypochondriacal concerns may be present, as well as multiple other symptoms including fainting, obsessional thoughts, depersonalization (feel unreal, detached), and derealization (feel surroundings are unreal). Depression is common. This is the most disabling phobic disorder.

This may actually be a subset of panic disorder since most patients with agoraphobia also have panic attacks: PANIC DISORDER WITH AGORAPHOBIA. Typically, these combined patients develop their agoraphobia as an extension of a panic disorder, ie, unpredictable panic attacks cause them to avoid public places for fear of having an attack (anticipatory anxiety) which then reinforces the behavior (phobic avoidance). This is even more disabling than agoraphobia alone. It most commonly develops during the 20's — F:M = 2:1. Genetics are similar to panic disorder (10%+ of 1° relatives are similarly affected).

**SOCIAL PHOBIA** (DSM-IV p 416, 300.23): Fear of scrutiny from others during public speaking, using public lavatories, blushing, eating in public, etc. Typically begins during adolescence and is found in 2–4% of the population (F:M = 2:1). Some patients are troubled by specific and limited social activities while others suffer from generalized social exposure. Marked general anxiety is common in severe cases: patient controls by avoidance—can be socially crippling. Frequently associated with substance abuse and depression but don't mistake for the social withdrawal of primary depression, schizophrenia, or paranoid states; if symptoms have been present lifelong, consider Avoidant Personality Disorder.

**SPECIFIC PHOBIAS** (DSM-IV p 410, 300.29): Monophobias of animals, storms, heights, blood, needles, etc. Usually begin in childhood, are found in 10%+ of the population (more frequent among women), and have few associated symptoms or syndromes.

TREATMENT: 2-fold.

1. Cognitive-behavior therapy is essential in all three types of phobias. The key to treatment is exposure to the feared object or situation coupled with a reversing of the fearful expectations ("cognitions") about the upcoming encounter. Systematic desensitization (by reciprocal inhibition) utilizes a graded hierarchy of frightening stimuli allowing the patient to "work up" to facing the phobic object. In flooding, the patient faces the feared object or situation directly while with implosion the exposure is to the idea of the object or a

vivid account of the "terrible" consequences expected. Social skills training may also be required for those who are socially inept. Such treatment may require (and be enhanced by) support and/or anti-anxiety medication.

2. Medication. Minor tranquilizers are used temporarily to help the patient confront the phobia. In social phobias, $\beta$-blockers (eg, propranolol, atenolol) can be used to help control incapacitating autonomic symptoms (eg, before a speech) if the symptoms are specific, while MAOIs (eg, phenelzine) and SSRIs are effective with generalized social phobias.

In the agoraphobic, with or without panic attacks, use medication for panic disorder (TCAs, MAOIs, alprazolam). Once the panic attacks are controlled with meds, an agoraphobic usually needs supportive exposure to the feared situations (without experiencing panic) before the phobia resolves. "Half dose" maintenance meds may be necessary as well.

### POSTTRAUMATIC STRESS DISORDER (PTSD)
### (DSM-IV p427, 309.81)

If a patient suffers a severe loss or stress (eg, rape, serious car accident, harm to a child or spouse, natural disaster, combat, prison camp, etc.), he may develop the clinical syndrome of POSTTRAUMATIC STRESS DISORDER. A mixture of the following symptoms are present initially:

Marked anxiety
Personality change with irritability and poor concentration
An exaggerated startle response
Insomnia and nightmares
Intrusive thoughts of the event
Reliving the feelings experienced at the time
Avoidance of anything associated with the trauma
Emotional blunting which can impair interpersonal relationships and day-to-day functioning

Later, depression, emotional numbing, and preoccupation with the trauma may predominate. The more severe the stress, the more likely PTSD is (1) to develop and (2) to be long-lasting. It may resolve after months (lasts 1–3 months = acute) or, untreated, last for decades (>3 months = chronic). Occasional patients present primarily with physical symptoms or chronic pain. Comorbid psychiatric conditions include depression, anxiety and panic disorders, dissociative states, and substance abuse.

Patients with PTSD are more likely to have a personality disorder, a previous history of depression or substance abuse, a childhood history of physical abuse, or a family history of psychopathology, but presumably PTSD can occur in anyone who has experienced sufficient stress (found in 1–9% of the general population; higher in special populations). Psychophysiologic arousal at the time of the stress seems to be important in developing PTSD, while conditioned arousal keeps it going.

PTSD patients are notoriously noncompliant: 70–80%+ drop out of treatment, presumably because they can't tolerate reliving the event in therapy. Medication is useful in many cases: benzodiazepines briefly for anxiety but primarily tricyclic antidepressants (imipramine 150–300 mg/day), MAOIs (phenelzine 45–75 mg/day), or SSRIs in moderately high doses. Carbamazepine has been found useful in controlling flashbacks, nightmares, and intrusive recollections (400–600 mg/day; 5–10 mg/L) while propranolol (80–160 mg/day) may reduce sympathetic hyperarousal. Psychotherapy should accompany medication: primarily education, support, and cognitive-behavioral therapy. The patient should be engaged in treatment <u>as soon after the incident as possible.</u> (For example, the rape victim needs special and sensitive care often in the ER—after the assault, for psychiatric as well as legal reasons. Many of her interpersonal relationships may have been altered by that episode. Work with the family—the married victim often needs to establish a new equilibrium with her husband.)

### ACUTE STRESS DISORDER (DSM-IV p 431, 308.3)

Acute Stress Disorder is an expected reaction of anyone experiencing an adequately severe trauma, yet individuals require different amounts and types of stress to develop it. PTSD symptoms predominate: nightmares, reexperiencing the event, avoiding stimuli that remind one of the trauma, and symptoms of increased arousal such as irritability, hypervigilance, poor concentration, and marked startle response. In addition, patients may respond for several days with derealization, depersonalization, and as though they are in a daze.

Typically, acute stress disorder will disappear after 1–2

weeks (if that long), but if it lasts for longer than 1 month, the diagnosis needs to be changed to PTSD. The most useful therapy is to get the patient to come to terms with his acute stressor as soon as possible by having him "talk it through" and realize that life can return (and is returning) to normal. Sometimes it is necessary to use benzodiazepines briefly to facilitate this process. Failure to put his trauma into perspective and get on with his life all too often results in the development of PTSD.

## ANXIETY DISORDER DUE TO A GENERAL MEDICAL CONDITION (DSM-IV p 439, 293.89)

Medical conditions (most commonly cardiac disorders) can produce anxiety states, although often they generate no sense of apprehension or foreboding. If suggestive physical symptoms accompany anxiety, remember:

1. Abnormal EKGs and heart sounds help identify cardiac symptoms (chest pain, palpitations) due to angina pectoris, prolapse of the mitral valve, and cardiac arrhythmias (eg, PAT). Mitral valve prolapse syndrome (MVPS midsystolic click, late systolic murmur, and echocardiographic findings) occurs with increased frequency (15–40%$^+$) in patients with panic disorder; however, anxiety and panic disorders may not be increased in patients with MVPS. Thus, the relation between the two is not clear.

2. The apprehension and dyspnea associated with bronchial asthma or COLD ("pink puffers") usually has accompanying wheezing or characteristic spirometric and radiographic features.

3. Acute Intermittent Porphyria—anxiety with abdominal focus; look for fever, leukocytosis, pain in extremities, prior drug exposure, elevated urine porphobilinogen; Watson-Schwartz Test is positive.

4. Characteristic findings usually occur with duodenal ulcer (bleeding, relief of pain with food, persistent crater by X-ray, suggestive gastric analysis) and ulcerative colitis (bloody diarrhea, fever, weight loss, sigmoidoscopic findings) but without them, differentiation is sometimes difficult. Internal hemorrhage may be accompanied by pain and restlessness—the picture develops quickly.

5. The vertiginous, anxious patient with Ménière's Disease also has deafness, tinnitus, and nystagmus during the attack.

If there are no localizing features to the acute attack or if the anxiety is chronic, consider:

6. Hypoglycemia—at times indistinguishable from chronic or acute psychogenic anxiety; obtain blood glucose at the time of the episode; 5-hr GTT.

7. Hyperthyroidism—anxiety symptoms occur with rapid onset type; skin warm and moist rather than cold and clammy; look for exophthalmos; get $T_3$, $T_4$; check for goiter; consider TRH stimulation test.
8. Pheochromocytoma—anxiety attacks with hypertension; visual blurring, headache, perspiration, palpitations; get 24-hr urinary VMA or free catecholamines.

Other medical conditions can produce an anxiety syndrome: intracranial tumors, menstrual irregularities, hypothyroidism, hyper- and hypoparathyroidism, postconcussion syndrome, psychomotor epilepsy, Cushing's disease. Appropriate tests help differentiate.

### SUBSTANCE-INDUCED ANXIETY DISORDER (DSM-IV p 443)

Almost any drug of abuse can produce an anxiety syndrome on intoxication, while anxiety symptoms commonly predominate upon withdrawal from alcohol, hypnotic-sedatives, and cocaine. Similarly, a number of medications can produce anxiety with use: eg, antihypertensives and other cardiac drugs, thyroid, sympathomimetics and bronchodilators, anticholinergics, antiparkinsonian meds, lithium, and antipsychotics (see Chapter 13). Once the cause is identified and corrected, the anxiety usually promptly disappears.

### ANXIETY WITH OBSESSIONS AND COMPULSIONS
### OBSESSIVE COMPULSIVE DISORDER (DSM-IV p 422, 300.3)

Obsessions are repetitive ideas, images, and impulses that intrude upon a patient who feels powerless to stop them. They are unwanted, distressful, occasionally frightening or violent (eg, the impulse to leap before a car; the thought that he may attack his spouse), and often impair functioning. The patient can ruminate endlessly ("Did I lock the door?"); most develop rituals or compulsions (counting, touching, cleaning) to ward off unwanted happenings or to satisfy an obsession (eg, an obsession with dirt leading to handwashing rituals). Compulsions are thus obsessions made manifest and occur in 75%$^+$ of obsessives. The performance of the ritual relieves the anxiety from the obsession temporarily. Thinking is often magical ("My son won't have an accident if I stamp each foot 30 times.") and the patient is aware of this.

OCD afflicts 2% of the population, presents varying degrees of severity, and is chronic, with some spontaneous cures. OCD patients suffer depressive feelings (80%), major depression (30%), and Tourette's syndrome (5%); 8% of first-degree relatives have OCD. First symptoms occur by the 20's in 75%, may begin suddenly or slowly, and often have an episodic course. The clinical picture may be dominated by the rituals, which require direct treatment.

The cause of OCD is unknown, but CNS serotonin neurons are implicated in some cases. Moreover, CNS damage (eg, head trauma), the orbitofrontal cortex, caudate, neostriatum, globus pallidus, and thalamus play roles. There is an increase in anxiety disorders in family members (15%), but only slightly increased OCD.

### Differential

Obsessive-compulsive problems are common in serious psychiatric illnesses. 20% of serious depressions have obsessive symptoms—major symptoms and family history help separate—treatment may be identical. Schizophrenics have bizarre obsessions and are usually comfortable with them. (Be cautious: OCD can reach psychotic proportions, so don't over-diagnose schizophrenia.) Some organic conditions may present early with obsessions and compulsions.

### Treatment

Medication substantially reduces symptoms in 60%[+] and should be tried: clomipramine (Anafranil) is first choice (150–250 mg/day), then fluoxetine (40–80 mg/day); later possibly augmented with buspirone (5–20 mg tid) or clonazepam (0.5–2.5 mg bid-tid). Behavior therapy should be considered an essential complement to meds. For ritualizers, use a combination of exposure to the feared situation and response prevention (blocking the compulsive behaviors). For patients with just obsessions, use imaginal exposure (mentally experiencing what "could happen") and thought stopping (the therapist, and then later the patient, interrupts obsessional thought with the shouted word "Stop!").

From the combination of meds and psychotherapy, expect

moderate to significant improvement. Meds promote rapid change, but exposure sustains that change and may make meds unnecessary long-term. For the chronic, treatment-resistant, and disabled patient, consider very localized psychosurgery: either cingulotomy or bilateral anterior capsulotomy.

## Suggested Readings

Agras WS: Treatment of social phobias. J Clin Psychiatry 51(10, suppl):5–25, 1990.

Allgulander C, Lavori PW: Excess mortality among 3302 patients with 'pure' anxiety neurosis. Arch Gen Psychiatry 48:599–602, 1991.

Appleby L: Panic and suicidal behavior. Br J Psychiatry 164:719–721, 1994.

Aronson TA: A naturalistic study of imipramine in panic disorder and agoraphobia. Am J Psychiatry 144:1014–1019, 1987.

Barlow DH: Long-term outcome for patients with panic disorder treated with cognitive-behavioral therapy. J Clin Psychiatry 51(12, suppl A):17–23, 1990.

Beck A, Steer RA, Sanderson WC, et al: Panic disorder and suicidal ideation and behavior: Discrepant findings in psychiatric outpatients. Am J Psychiatry 148:1195–1199, 1991.

Brawman-Mintzer O, Lydiard RB, Emmanuel N, et al: Psychiatric comorbidity in patients with generalized anxiety disorder. Am J Psychiatry 150:1216–1218, 1993.

Buigues J, Vallejo J: Therapeutic response to phenelzine in patients with panic disorder and agoraphobia with panic attacks. J Clin Psychiatry 48:55–59, 1987.

Clark DM, Salkovskis PM, Hackman A, et al: A comparison of cognitive therapy, applied relaxation and imipramine in the treatment of panic disorder. Br J Psychiatry 164:759–768, 1994.

Cottraux J, Mollard E, Bouvard M, et al: Exposure therapy, fluvoximine, or combination treatment in obsessive-compulsive disorder. Psychiatric Res 49:63–75, 1993.

Durham RC, Allan T: Psychological treatment of generalized anxiety disorder. Br J Psychiatry 163:19–26, 1993.

Goldstein RB, Weissman MM, Adams PB, et al: Psychiatric disorders in relatives of probands with panic disorder and/or major depression. Arch Gen Psychiatry 51:383–394, 1994.

Hay P, Sochdev P, Cumming S, et al: Treatment of obsessive compulsive disorder by psychosurgery. Acta Psychiatr Scand 87:197–207, 1993.

Hewlett WA, Vinogradov S, Agras WS: Clonazepam treatment of obsessions and compulsions. J Clin Psychiatry 51:158–161, 1990.

Hoes MJAJM, Colla P, Van Doorn P, et al: Hyperventilation and panic attacks. J Clin Psychiatry 48:435–437, 1987.

Hollander E, Cohen LJ: The assessment and treatment of refractory anxiety. J Clin Psychiatry 55(2, suppl)]:27–31, 1994.

Jenike MA, Rauch SL: Managing the patient with treatment resistant obsessive compulsive disorder. J Clin Psychiatry 55(3, suppl):11–17, 1994.

Johnson J, Weissman MM, Klerman GL: Panic disorder, comorbidity, and suicide attempts. Arch Gen Psychiatry 47:805–808, 1990.

Katerndahl DA: Panic and prolapse. J Nerv Ment Dis 181:539–544, 1993.

Kendler DS, Neale MC, Kessler RC, et al: Generalized anxiety disorder in women. Arch Gen Psychiatry 49:267–272, 1992.

Kendler KS, Neale MC, Kessler RC, et al: The genetic epidemiology of phobias in women. Arch Gen Psychiatry 49:273–281, 1992.

Liebowitz MR, Schneier F, Campeas R, et al: Phenelzine vs atenolol in social phobia. Arch Gen Psychiatry 49:290–300, 1992.

Lydiard RB, Laraia MT, Ballenger JC, et al: Emergence of depressive symptoms in patients receiving alprazolam for panic disorder. Am J Psychiatry 144:664–665, 1987.

Mavissakalian M, Perel JM: Clinical experiments in maintenance and discontinuation of imipramine therapy in panic disorder with agoraphobia. Arch Gen Psychiatry 49:318–323, 1992.

McGuire PK, Bench CJ, Frith CD, et al: Functional anatomy of obsessive-compulsive phenomena. Br J Psychiatry 164:459–468, 1994.

Modigh K, Westberg P, Eriksson E: Superiority of clomipramine over imipramine in the treatment of panic disorder. J Clin Psychopharmacol 12:251–261, 1992.

Nutt D, Lawson C: Panic attacks: A neurochemical overview of models and mechanisms. Br J Psychiatry 160:165–178, 1992.

O'Sullivan G, Noshirvani H, Marks I, et al: Six-year follow-up after exposure and clomipramine therapy for obsessive compulsive disorder. J Clin Psychiatry 52:150–155, 1991.

Papp LA, Klein DF, Martinez J, et al: Diagnostic and substance specificity of carbondioxide-induced panic. Am J Psychiatry 150:250–257, 1993.

Rauch SL, Jenike MA, Alpert NM, et al: Regional cerebral blood flow measured during symptom provocation in obsessive-compulsive disorder using oxygen 15-labeled carbon dioxide and positron emission tomography. Arch Gen Psychiatry 51:62–70, 1994.

Rickels K, Downing R, Schweizer E, et al: Antidepressants for the treatment of generalized anxiety disorder. Arch Gen Psychiatry 50:884–895, 1993.

Schneier F, Liebowitz MR, Davies SO, et al: Fluoxetine in panic disorder. J Clin Psychopharmacol 10:119–121, 1990.

Schneier FR, Johnson J, Hornig CD, et al: Social phobia. Arch Gen Psychiatry 49:282–288, 1992.

Tesar GE, Rosenbaum JF, Pollack MH, et al: Clonazepam vs alprazolam in the treatment of panic disorder. J Clin Psychiatry 48(10, suppl):16–19, 1987.

Tomb D: The phenomenology of posttraumatic stress disorder. Psychiatr Clin North Am 17:237–250, 1994.

Zohar Y, Insel TR, Rasmussen SA: Psychobiology of Obsessive Compulsive Disorder. New York, Springer-Verlag Press, 1990.

# Chapter 9

# Dissociative Disorders

"Dissociation" is the splitting off of specific mental activities from the rest of normal consciousness, such as the splitting of thoughts or feelings from behavior (eg, to daydream through a boring lecture and yet end up with a complete set of notes without being aware of having taken them). Minor dissociation is a common human phenomenon. Dissociative disorders demonstrate severe dissociation which produces significant and diverse symptoms and impairs functioning. Such disorders are fairly common (10% lifetime risk), typically occur within the context of childhood physical and/or sexual abuse, and are frequently comorbid with major depression, PTSD, substance abuse, and borderline personality disorder.

### AMNESIA

Organic processes (usually involving the temporal lobes) account for the majority of cases of significant memory loss in adults. These processes include intoxication or withdrawal from drugs or alcohol, various dementias, acute or chronic metabolic conditions (eg, hypoglycemia, hepatic encephalopathy), brain trauma (ie, postconcussive amnesia), brain tumors (particularly in the temporal lobes), cerebrovascular accidents, epilepsy (particularly temporal lobe epilepsy), and various degenerative or infectious CNS diseases. Transient Global Amnesia (TGA) is a sudden, self-limited, massive loss of memory in middle-aged or elderly patients due to a temporary (presumably vascular) cause. Always look for an organic cause for amnesia first.

Loss of memory from psychological causes is DISSOCIATIVE AMNESIA (DSM-IV p 481, 300.12). Usually there is sudden anterograde loss of emotion-laden information after a severe physical or psychosocial stress. It occurs most frequently in women in their teens or 20s, or in men during the stress of war. The patient often appears confused and puzzled during the attack, but recovery is typically rapid, spontaneous, and complete. However, some people have amnesia, partial or complete, for past periods in their lives which may last for months or years.

If, usually after an acute stress, the patient suffers a severe memory loss, leaves home, and acts like a different person, he has DISSOCIATIVE FUGUE (DSM-IV p 484, 300.13). Although he presents himself well to strangers, on questioning he is usually unaware of his previous (real) identity and may seem somewhat perplexed about his current personal identity. However, occasional patients function for long periods of time in complex roles, undetected. The return of old memories and the old identity usually occurs abruptly within hours or days, but may not happen for months (or longer). Fugue is more common in alcohol abusers.

The differential diagnosis of both conditions includes:

1. Various organic conditions (see above).
2. Psychiatric conditions—Amnesia may often accompany severe depressive or anxiety states. Somnambulism may superficially resemble some fugues but has marked clouding of consciousness. PTSD, somatoform disorders, and other dissociative states often include amnesia as well.
3. Malingering and secondary gain in patients with antisocial personality disorder.

Evaluate these patients with a careful history and physical exam, liver enzymes, blood alcohol level, and drug screen. Further evaluation may include a CAT scan and a sleep-deprived EEG with NP leads. Are old skills preserved during the attack (uncommon in organic conditions)? Is there obvious secondary gain? Is there a personal or family history for mental illness or epilepsy? The Amytal interview is occasionally diagnostic—organic patients usually become more confused while patients with psychological amnesia may have a return of memory.

## DISSOCIATIVE IDENTITY DISORDER (DSM-IV p 487, 300.14)

Formerly known as multiple personality disorder (MPD), patients with this dramatic disorder (eg, *The Three Faces of Eve*) feel that they have at least two (and sometimes many) personalities within themselves. One of the personalities is usually dominant, yet any one of them may dominate from time to time. The patient's behavior is consistent with whatever personality is in "control" at that moment. Each personality may or may not be aware of the presence of the others.

This poorly understood (and hotly debated) psychiatric condition begins in childhood (possibly in response to abuse), is more common among females (3–9:1), tends to be chronic, and is replete with multiple symptoms such as anxiety, depression with suicidal impulses and acts, trances and amnesia, a multitude of somatic complaints, substance abuse and other "misbehavior," and psychotic-like symptoms. Once considered rare, it may be relatively common, particularly in milder forms and it is frequently mistaken for the more flamboyant personality disorders (particularly, borderline), somatization disorder, major depression, anxiety and panic disorders, and schizophrenia. In fact, DSM-IV criteria are often fulfilled for DID and several of these conditions as well.

Proper treatment may or may not center around a careful integration of the different personalities and personality fragments through 1–3 times/wk psychotherapy and hypnotherapy over years. This may be the best treatment or it may worsen the condition—treatment remains uncertain.

### DEPERSONALIZATION DISORDER
### (DSM-IV p 490, 300.6)

These patients experience periods during which they have a strong and unpleasant sense of their own unreality (depersonalization), often coupled with a sense that the environment is also unreal (derealization). The patient may feel mechanical and separated from his own thoughts, emotions, and self-identity. Although many people transiently experience this phenomenon in a mild form, the experience for those receiving a clinical diagnosis is much more intense and recurrent. An episode occurs suddenly (often during relaxation after stress), usually in persons in their teens or 20s, may last for minutes, hours, or days, and then gradually disappears. It may return many times over the years.

Psychotherapy has been of little value. Recently, however, anxiolytics and antidepressants (eg, fluoxetine) have seen some success. Rule out the symptom of depersonalization that may accompany psychiatric disorders (eg, schizophrenia, depression, anxiety disorders, and histrionic personality disorder) and organic conditions (eg, delirium, temporal lobe epilepsy, drug and alcohol use, brain tumor).

## Suggested Readings

Akhtar S, Brenner I: Differential diagnosis of fugue-like states. J Clin Psychiatry 40:381–385, 1979.

Allen JG, Smith WH: Diagnosing dissociative disorders. Bull Menninger Clin 57:328–343, 1993.

Bliss EL, Larson EM, Nakashima SR: Auditory hallucinations and schizophrenia. J Nerv Ment Dis 171:30–33, 1983.

Chu JA: The rational treatment of multiple personality disorder. Psychotherapy 31:94–100, 1994.

Frankel FH: Adult reconstruction of childhood events in multiple personality literature. Am J Psychiatry 150:954–958, 1993.

Hollander E, Liebowitz MR, DeCaria C, et al: Treatment of depersonalization with serotonin reuptake blockers. J Clin Psychopharmacol 10:200–203, 1990.

Khan AU: Clinical Disorders of Memory. New York, Plenum Medical Book Co., 1986.

Loewenstein RJ (Ed): Multiple Personality Disorder. The Psychiatric Clinics of North America, Vol 14, No 3, Philadelphia, WB Saunders, 1991.

Merskey H: The manufacture of personalities. Br J Psychiatry 160:327–340, 1992.

Mullen PE, Martin JL, Anderson JC, et al: Childhood sexual abuse and mental health in adult life. Br J Psychiatry 163:721–732, 1993.

Piper A: Multiple personality disorder. Br J Psychiatry 164:600–612, 1994.

Putnam FW: Diagnosis and Treatment of Multiple Personality Disorder. New York, Guilford Press, 1989.

Putnam FW, Loewenstein RJ: Treatment of multiple personality disorder: A survey of current practices. Am J Psychiatry 150:1048–1052, 1993.

Ross CA, Joshi S, Currie R: Dissociative experiences in the general population. Am J Psychiatry 147:1547–1552, 1990.

Ross CA: Epidemiology of multiple personality disorder and dissociation. Psychiatr Clin North Am 14:503–517, 1991.

Saxe GN, vanderKolk BA, Berkowitz R, et al: Dissociative disorders in psychiatric inpatients. Am J Psychiatry 150:1037–1042, 1993.

# Chapter 10

# Grief and the Dying Patient

Everyone endures personal losses; many suffer chronic illnesses. Everyone dies. Physicians attend at all of these events and need to recognize normal and abnormal human responses to loss (grief reaction and unresolved grief), illness, and death.

## GRIEF REACTION

### Normal Grief

**Symptoms:** BEREAVEMENT (DSM-IV p 684, V62.82) (grief, mourning) is a normal response to a significant loss (of spouse, parent, child—but also of health, limb, career, savings, status, etc). Expect to see it with major losses—be alert for future problems if the patient doesn't grieve (although 30% of widows mourn briefly and very little). If a loss is obviously approaching, mourning may begin before the loss actually occurs (anticipatory grief). Symptoms associated with divorce may also be coded as PARTNER RELATIONAL PROBLEM (DSM-IV p 681, V61.1).

Recognize grief by restlessness, distractibility, disorganization, preoccupation, "numbness," feelings of sadness, apathy, crying, anxious pining, a need to talk about the dead, and intense mental pain during the days, weeks, and months after a loss. Somatic distress is common and includes generalized weakness, a tightness in the throat, choking, shortness of breath, palpitations, headaches, and GI complaints. Do not be surprised if the patient displays marked but short-lived irritability, hostility, or anger toward you, others, or the dead (you didn't "do enough"; they don't "care enough"; he died; etc). This often alternates with listlessness, social withdrawal, depression, and feelings of guilt (about that which was left undone or could have been done differently). Patients become preoccupied with their loss. They constantly think about the dead and review past experiences, visit the grave, and may even briefly deny the death.

25–35% of patients have symptoms suggesting a major depression: anorexia, feelings of worthlessness, impaired memory, suicidal thoughts, and hopelessness. 10% have delusional thoughts and hallucinations. Be careful not to "overread" temporary bizarre behavior in the bereaved. Some patients develop psychophysiologic disorders, hypochondriasis, major anxiety symptoms, or phobias. A few begin to drink too much, some deteriorate physically, and major psychiatric illnesses (eg, acute schizophrenia) may be precipitated in those predisposed (eg, positive family history). Moreover, bereavement has been associated with increased ACTH and cortisol, decreased immune function and natural killer cell activity, and an increased rate of heart disease and malignancy. Death from suicide and illness is increased during the first year after the loss.

### Unresolved Grief

Loss not dealt with through a normal mourning process may produce chronic symptoms.

— Prolonged Grief: Grief develops into a chronic depression or a sub-syndromal depression that lasts for more than 1 year in as many as 30%. Lowered self-esteem and guilt tend to be prominent.

— Delayed Grief: The patient who doesn't grieve at the time of a loss is at risk for later depression, social withdrawal, anxiety disorders, panic attacks, overt or covert self-destructive behavior, alcoholism, and psychophysiological syndromes. Chronic anger and hostility, marked emotional inhibition, or distorted interpersonal relationships also may be displayed. Unresolved grief may be an unsuspected cause of psychiatric disability in many people—always inquire about a past history of significant losses.

— Distorted Grief: Exaggerated (bizarre, hysterical, euphoric, or psychosis-like) reactions occur in a few patients which have the effect of postponing the normal grieving process. Alternately, the patient may present with physical complaints (eg, pain or "chronic illness behavior") and may be mistaken for having a primary medical problem.

Persons at risk for developing an abnormal grief reaction include those who:

1. Received little support or understanding from others after their loss (eg, abortion, suicide, death of an illicit lover).
2. Are social isolates—either "psychological loners" or those without family or friends nearby. Multiple strong supports help truncate the mourning process.
3. Are inhibited, compulsive, or uncomfortable with any form of emotion.
4. Have experienced multiple recent losses or a sudden, severe, unexpected loss.
5. Have unresolved past losses.
6. Had ambivalent feelings about the deceased when alive and have reacted to the death with guilt.

## Treatment

Encouraging satisfactory mourning is an important activity for the physician.

— Encourage mourning. Say it is OK. Say it is important and necessary.
— Explain that the anguish he undoubtedly will experience during this process is essential and curative. However, do not force the patient—let him set the pace.
— Help the patient identify and experience his emotions—sadness, hopelessness, despair, anxiety, fear, anger. Assure him that these are normal, expected, and understandable. Do not be embarrassed by these emotions yourself.
— Help the patient review his loss. Be an active listener. Ask for a description of the deceased—ask for particulars, details, shared intimacies, etc. Become a support.
— See the patient frequently. Be interested. Be available, particularly over time. Recognize and tolerate relapses. Be alert to the presence of anniversaries.
— Do not use medication to attenuate normal grief—help the patient work through the grief instead. Sleeping medication may be useful. If anxiety or restlessness is excessive, consider a temporary use of minor tranquilizers (eg, diazepam 5 mg PO tid) as therapy is begun. Treat a major depression or psychosis with medication.
— Work with the family. Help develop a sympathetic support system. Mourners are social outcasts—help decrease the "social isolation of the bereaved." Self-help groups can be very valuable (eg, groups of parents who have lost a child, etc.).

— Keep the mourner "involved in life"—slowly at first, but insist on increasing independence.

## THE DYING PATIENT

Few patients stress physicians as much as those who are dying. This need not be. Even if little can be done to change a fatal outcome, careful handling by the physician and crucial others can help turn a patient's death (whether expected or untimely) into a time of genuine relief, satisfaction, and (even) growth. When time is so limited, new realities and priorities emerge that must be dealt with if life is to be concluded satisfactorily.

### Normal Responses in the Dying

The news that one is dying produces a special kind of grief reaction. A typical series of "stages" or psychological reactions to the threat of imminent death are seen frequently.

1st Stage—Shock and denial: Denial is the initial reaction of many patients to being told that they are dying—particularly severe in those "caught by surprise." They may refuse to believe the diagnosis, actively begin doctor shopping, or be dazed and appear oblivious to the significance of the diagnosis. This may be fleeting, but some patients may never pass beyond this stage.

2nd Stage—Anger: A frustrated, hopeless, angry, bitter "Why me?" response often accompanies the realization of impending death. The anger is directed at the physicians (or family, God, fate, etc.) for the "unfairness" of this turn of events.

3rd Stage—Bargaining: The patient attempts to bargain with physicians or God for more time—promising good behavior, good intentions, etc., in exchange for "a chance to see my boy be graduated from college," etc.

4th Stage—Depression: The patient despairs and begins to grieve. Be alert to suicide, particularly in the irritable, demanding, agitated depression.

5th Stage—Acceptance: The patient is quiet and resigned. He has little outside interests but seeks the presence of loved ones or a few close friends.

These stages are not necessarily stepwise and invariable. Just as often the person will shift back and forth between stages (eg, from denial to anger and then back to denial), exhibit varying degrees of denial throughout, but gradually become more detached. The younger the adult, the more likely the stages are to be turbulent and the problems severe.

Specific psychiatric problems occur often and should be identified and treated:

1. Depression is common but not "normal," and thus, if a depression is not relieved by support and time, a major depression may have developed. Consider treatment with antidepressants.
2. Organic brain syndromes (usually waxing and waning) develop frequently and can be frightening to patients. Help them see the disorders as separate from themselves—as just another thing to be experienced.
3. Acute anxiety is common but usually temporary, particularly if treated with medication.
4. Communication failures between the patient and loved ones are very common and troublesome—often taking the form of a "tyranny of silence" or a lack of understanding on either one's part of the distress of the other. These need to be dealt with directly.

## Treatment

### Telling the Patient

— Choose a quiet and private spot, be relaxed, sit down with the patient, and briefly reveal the diagnosis. Use the patient's response as an indicator of how much to tell.
— Patients need to know and need a chance to ask questions but, most of all, they need someone (usually the physician, but also spouse, pastor, etc.) available—someone to help them grieve.
— Be truthful (but allow them to deny if they insist on it) and realistically hopeful ("We will begin treatment. Sometimes remissions occur. etc."). Don't encourage false hopes, but don't dwell on the fatal outcome.
— Strong negative reactions do occur. Sedation can be helpful temporarily.

### Treating the Patient

— Be supportive, empathic, warm, a good listener, hopeful (eg, about goals to be achieved before death), and available. Get to know the patient as a person—attention to exclusively medical matters is "dehumanizing." Be tolerant of ups and downs. Recognize that the patient may become hostile toward you—be patient.
— Always take your lead from the patient. Some days some topics are too stressful. Other days they "have" to talk. Only force the issue if

their denial, anxiety, or anger is seriously obstructing good care. Occasionally confrontation may be required.

— Make them comfortable. Treat pain aggressively—narcotics are OK. Attend fastidiously to basic physical needs. Make their room pleasant and cheerful. Hallucinogens (eg, LSD) have been used experimentally with success.

— Certain fears are common and need to be looked for and dealt with: eg, fear of pain, of physical dependency, of being isolated, of losing control (emotional and physical), of being helpless, of the unknown, of leaving loved ones to flounder (financially or emotionally).

— It is essential to help the patient "work through" the process of dying. Help him set new priorities and goals (eg, get his affairs in order). Help him resolve old problems and feel good about current relationships. Help him be responsible. Encourage him to consider not only how he will die but also how he will live the rest of his life.

— Do not insist that patients march through the "stages of dying" in a set order and on schedule.

— Allow the patient "terminal dependency"—it is OK finally to regress.

## Treating the Family

— Family members show many of the signs of grief. Like the patient, they also may be angry, hostile, or denying. They may need treatment—help them mourn.

— It is important to keep the family (ie, loved ones) involved. Help the patient die "with their blessing."

— It can be enormously beneficial (to the patient, to the family) if the patient can be supportive to the family members in their grieving.

## Treating the Staff

— Recognize that the physician, nurses, aides, etc. are all affected by death. Anxiety, intellectualization, avoidance, and grieving frequently occur among staff—don't let them impair care. Staff conferences to ventilate and explore these issues may help.

## THE CHRONICALLY ILL PATIENT

Chronic illness is another form of stress that entails grieving. Like the dying patient, these patients may deny their illness, become angry and resentful, regress, or become depressed. Common to all these reactions is anxiety associated with a loss of health and attractiveness, a loss of self-esteem, and the threat of dependency or even death. Certain personality types are at risk, eg, the narcissistic or the very independent. Treatment principles useful with the grieving or dying patient apply here as well.

## Suggested Readings

Barry MJ: Therapeutic experience with patients referred for "prolonged grief reaction"—some second thoughts. Mayo Clin Proc 56:744–748, 1981.

Belitsky R, Jacobs S: Bereavement, attachment theory, and mental disorders. Psychiatr Ann 16:276, 1986.

Brown JH, Henteleff P, Barakat S, et al: Is it normal for terminally ill patients to desire death? Am J Psychiatry 143:208–211, 1986.

Clayton PJ: Mortality and morbidity in the first year of widowhood. Arch Gen Psychiatry 30:747–750, 1974.

Fredrick JF: The biochemistry of bereavement. Omega 13:295–303, 1982–1983.

Irwin M, Daniels M, Bloom ET, et al: Life events, depressive symptoms, and immune function. Am J Psychiatry 144:437–441, 1987.

Kubler-Ross E: On Death and Dying. London, Tavistock, 1970.

Marmar CR, Horowitz MJ, Weiss DS, et al: A controlled trial of brief psychotherapy and mutual-help group treatment of conjugal bereavement. Am J Psychiatry 145: 203–209, 1988.

Parkes CM: Bereavement: Studies of Grief in Adult Life. New York, International Universities Press, 1972.

Rynearson EK: Pathologic grief: The queen's croquet ground. Psychiatric Ann 20:295–303, 1990.

Spurrell MT, Creed FH: Lymphocyte response in depressed patients and subjects anticipating bereavement. Br J Psychiatry 162:60–64, 1993.

Zisook S, Shuchter SP: The first four years of widowhood. Psychiatr Ann 16:288–294, 1986.

Zisook S: Biopsychosocial Aspects of Bereavement. Washington, DC, American Psychiatric Press, 1987.

Zisook S, Shuchter SR, Sledge PA, et al: The spectrum of depressive phenomena after spousal bereavement. J Clin Psychiatry 55(4, suppl):29–36, 1994.

# Chapter 11

# Conditions that Mimic Physical Disease

It is essential to differentiate organic illness from psychogenic illness in patients complaining of physical symptoms. Patients with physical concerns in whom no medical illness can be found and/or who don't improve with treatment are common. These frustrating patients often exhaust one doctor after another and usually end up being labeled "hysterics" or "crocks." This occasionally angry response by the physician does a disservice to these patients since, although some may be consciously "faking it" (malingering), most patients have as yet undiagnosed organic conditions or have symptoms that are unconsciously and involuntarily produced.

There are several discrete involuntary psychiatric syndromes (somatoform disorders—see below) that mimic organic disease. These disorders have typical clinical presentations, family histories, recommended treatments, and likely prognoses.

Failure to identify an organic etiology for a physical symptom does not necessitate a diagnosis of a somatoform disorder or malingering—these are not diagnoses by exclusion but rather should be based on specific characteristics. Consider the following diagnoses in any patient with a poorly specified or uncertain medical condition.

### 1. Undetected Physical Illness

The possibility of an underlying, unrecognized illness must continue to be considered throughout the course of diagnosis and treatment, however long. Follow-up studies find 15–30% of conversion reaction diagnosis to represent misdiagnosed organic disease. Physical illness may produce symptoms that mimic a somatoform disorder or may predispose susceptible patients to develop concurrent psychiatric conditions (it's not "either, or"). Some patients with subtle CNS disease are at risk for conversion symptoms, so always carefully evaluate neurologically. The physical conditions commonly found (on follow-up) among these "false positive hysterics" include:

— CNS disease: Particularly epilepsy, MS, and postconcussion syndrome, but also CNS infections (eg, encephalitis), dementia, brain tumor, and cerebrovascular disease.
— Degenerative disorders: Of musculoskeletal and connective tissues; including SLE, polyarteritis nodosa, early rheumatoid arthritis, myasthenia gravis.
— Others: Syphilis, TB, hyper- and hypothyroidism, hyperparathyroidism, porphyria, hypoglycemia, duodenal and gallbladder disease, pancreatic disease, etc.

Be suspicious of any somatoform disorder that develops late in life. Psychological testing is of little help in differentiation— don't be misled by a "neurotic" picture on the MMPI into prematurely abandoning the search for a physical cause.

## SOMATOFORM DISORDERS

### 2. Conversion Disorder
### (DSM-IV p 457, 300.11)

A patient whose predominant problem is an obvious loss of function of some part of the nervous system which no identified organic pathology completely explains (conversion symptom), may have a conversion disorder. Conversion symptoms include:

Motor—paralysis, astasia-abasia, seizures, urinary retention, aphonia, globus hystericus ("lump in the throat" which prevents swallowing).
Sensory—paresthesia, anesthesia, anosmia, blindness, tunnel vision, deafness.
Other—unconsciousness, vomiting.

In addition, the particular symptom appears to serve one of two specific psychological purposes.

1. As primary gain, the symptom "buries" an unconscious mental conflict. An unacceptable, painful thought is repressed, and the emotional energy is converted to a physical symptom. Usually the specific

symptom "chosen" represents the conflict symbolically (eg, the negligent mother of a burned child develops anesthesia over the corresponding part of her body).

2. As secondary gain, the symptom gets the patient something he wants (eg, paralysis permits dependency on wife or justifies worker's compensation) or allows him to avoid something he doesn't want (eg, seizures prevent a court appearance).

As obvious as these relationships may be to the observer, the patient is unaware of them (unconscious), and the patient does not grasp their significance, even if they are explained (lacks insight).

### DIAGNOSIS

In the apparent absence of organic pathology, it is necessary to identify features in addition to a presumed conversion symptom before making the diagnosis. Realize also that as many as 25% of patients with conversion disorders have associated organic pathology (eg, epilepsy in a patient with pseudoseizures is common), so also investigate symptoms only partially explained by the physical abnormalities. Features associated with conversion disorders include:

— The symptom occurs abruptly and frequently follows an acute stress.
— There is often a past history of the same or a different conversion symptom.
— The disorder usually is seen first during adolescence or in the patient's 20s and in a person predisposed by a dependent, histrionic, antisocial, or passive-aggressive personality disorder.
— The patients often have associated moderate anxiety and depression.
— The patients are frequently immature, shallow, and demanding, although they tend to cooperate with examinations. They tend to have lower intelligence, limited insight, and lower socioeconomic status.
— Indifference to the symptom may be found (la belle indifference).

The individual neurological symptoms may have some characteristics that distinguish them from those of an organic etiology. In general, they tend to be variable, atypical, and inconsistent with anatomy.

**Conversion Seizures:** Seizures are often atypical and bizarre (patient may laugh or cry throughout seizure). Only infrequently is there incontinence, cyanosis, physical self-harm, tongue biting, or complete loss of consciousness during the seizure. Good muscle tone is preserved during the typically brief postictal stage (arm dropped onto face may land lightly or miss the face altogether). The onset is usually dramatic, and seizures rarely occur when the patient is alone. Sit patient quickly upright—seizures often stop.

**Conversion Unconsciousness:** The loss of consciousness is usually light and incomplete with the patient showing some awareness of environmental events, particularly when he feels unobserved. VS and reflexes are normal, and the patient usually responds to painful stimuli. The eyes are held tightly shut, and some movements may be purposive (eg, move to keep from falling from exam table).

**Conversion Paralysis:** The paralysis is often variable—even during one exam. Paralysis of one limb, part of a limb, or hemiparesis are most common but the specific involvement is often inconsistent with anatomy, and the related changes (eg, tone, etc.) are atypical. DTR changes are variable, and pathological reflexes (eg, Babinski) are not present. The paralyzed limbs often show little resistance to passive movement but resist the pull of gravity. If there is resistance to a forced movement, it tends to give way abruptly (vs gradually as in organic conditions). There may be movement when startled by a painful stimulus. Palpate the antagonists—they often contract to simulate agonist weakness. There are usually associated conversion sensory changes.

**Astasia-abasia:** This exaggerated and bizarre conversion ataxia varies from moment to moment. The patient falls toward walls and people, rarely falls to the floor, and rarely hurts himself despite a dramatic presentation.

**Conversion Sensory Changes:** These are often dramatic, sometimes vague, and usually inconsistent with anatomy (eg, "stocking and glove" anesthesia, loss of all senses on one side or below a certain level on a limb, loss of which stops exactly at midline. Careful testing differentiates most cases.

**Conversion Blindness:** Visual disturbances are usually blurring, double vision, or tunnel loss but may be total blindness. Response to a bright light (check with EEG) and avoidance of threatening objects are often inconsistent with the degree of presumed visual loss.

When the diagnosis is in doubt, a single dose of IV sodium amobarbital (Amytal) often temporarily removes the conversion symptom, thus clarifying the diagnosis. Slowly give a 10% solution intravenously (1 ml/min—maximum of 500 mg). When the patient's words begin to slur, stop administration and observe for disappearance of symptom.

### DIFFERENTIAL DIAGNOSIS

— Carefully rule out physical illness.
— Some patients with conversion symptoms require a primary diagnosis of major depression or schizophrenia.
— Two somatoform disorders (see below) have features in common with conversion disorders—somatization disorder and psychogenic pain disorder.
— Differentiation from malingering is difficult (see below).

### TREATMENT

Some patients have a short course and are "spontaneous cures"; a few may be chronic (eg, some paralyzed patients actually develop contractures), but most improve over weeks or months. A physical process is later identified in a significant minority (25%).

It is uncertain what treatment is best. Long-term psychoanalysis appears to effect real change in a few but is not for the majority of patients. Use minor tranquilizers if anxiety predominates. Behavior modification has had mixed success.

Crucial to any therapy is the formation of a supportive therapeutic alliance, but these patients are generally resistant to treatment. Direct confrontation about the "hysterical" nature of the symptom rarely works—the patient usually withdraws. Help the patient ventilate. Help the patient explore areas of stress in her life but relate that to symptoms only after an alliance has been formed. Gradually identify the symbolic nature of the symptoms, if present.

Work with the family. Help restructure the patient's environment to remove the secondary gain, if possible. Educate other involved medical personnel about the disorder—help them avoid countertherapeutic hostility.

### 3. Somatization Disorder
### (DSM-IV p 449, 300.81)

This syndrome, historically called hysteria or Briquet's syndrome, has been refined in the last few years and may or may not be coequal to the traditional diagnosis of hysteria. The patients have <u>numerous</u> vague and dramatic physical symptoms (usually presented in a dramatic way) which typically involve several organ systems.

— Conversion symptoms of all types, including <u>neurological</u>
— Vague and ill-defined <u>pains</u>
— Menstrual/<u>sexual</u> problems; inhibited orgasm
— GI, GU, and cardiopulmonary difficulties
— Poorly characterized altered states of consciousness

The symptoms wax and wane but usually are presented forcefully by the patient, who insists on examination and treatment. These patients often receive multiple operations and are at risk for iatrogenically induced drug addiction.

Analytically oriented researchers argue that symptoms are produced when forbidden impulses are repressed and the emotional energy associated with those drives is converted (conversion) into a physical symptom. Although definitive information remains incomplete, features currently associated with Briquet's syndrome include:

— A chronic condition beginning in adolescence or during the 20s.
— Primarily in women; as much as 1% of all women.
— Anxiety, irritability, and depression common; frequent suicide attempts (but few successful).
— Patients usually of lower intelligence and lower socioeconomic groups.
— Frequent interpersonal and marital problems.
— Patients often have a previous or concurrent history of antisocial behavior and a poor school history.
— Patients may have histrionic, dependent, or antisocial personality disorder.

— First-degree female relatives have a 20% incidence of somatization disorder. First-degree male relatives have increased prevalence of alcoholism and antisocial personality disorder.

Somatization disorder is difficult to distinguish from malingering, and occasionally there are elements of both present. It is essential to rule out inconstant and confusing medical syndromes (eg, SLE, acute intermittent porphyria, temporal lobe epilepsy, MS, hyperparathyroidism), although most can be differentiated from the full Briquet's syndrome (reliable diagnostic screening tests are available). Follow-up studies find few cases of undiagnosed organic illness (unlike conversion disorder). Rule out somatization in schizophrenia and depression.

**TREATMENT**

Treatment success is limited. Focus usually should be placed on management rather than cure. Develop a therapeutic alliance by being sympathetic and interested in the patient and her health but don't make that your exclusive focus. Gradually encourage an examination of the patient's general life problems and coping styles. Help the patient develop mature social, occupational, and intimate interpersonal skills. Treat depression and anxiety with medication, if indicated, but recognize the risk for addiction.

## 4. Pain Disorder
## (DSM-IV p 461, 307.8x)

These patients (often women) experience pain for which no cause can be found. It appears suddenly, usually after a stress, and may disappear in days or last years. It is frequently accompanied by organic illness that, however, doesn't adequately explain the severity of the pain. This condition is very similar to conversion disorder, and the patients may differ only by experiencing pain rather than neurological deficit as the predominant symptom. Treatments are also similar.

## 5. Hypochondriasis
## (DSM-IV p 465, 300.7)

Although many people may mentally expand a minor symptom into a major physical illness (particularly during times of stress), they rarely become preoccupied with it and can easily be dissuaded when examination and laboratory tests are normal. The hypochondriac, on the other hand, is convinced he is ill, angrily rejects evidence to the contrary, insists on further tests and treatments, and feverishly doctor shops. The patient appears pleased only if assured he is sick, and he eagerly seeks additional medical attention. This common chronic condition begins in adolescence or middle age, is common among the elderly, and is resistant to therapy. The patient rarely sees a psychiatrist but rather drifts from internist to surgeon to neurologist, etc.

The patient is hyperalert to symptoms and presents them in great detail during the history. He usually has some specific idea of "what the trouble is" and merely may want the physician to concur. Physicians frequently become angry and rejecting toward the patient, which leads to further "shopping around." In severe cases, the patient becomes an invalid.

Many of these patients display anxiety or depression. Hypochondriacal features occur frequently in serious psychiatric conditions like schizophrenia, major depression, dysthymic disorder, and organic brain syndromes. Rule out other somatoform disorders, chronic factitious disorder, and malingering.

Treatment is unpromising. Symptoms may disappear if an associated depression or psychosis is successfully treated. Don't expect a "cure" but rather work with the patient to help control his symptoms. Assure the patient that the problem is persistent but not debilitating or fatal. See the patient frequently for short periods of time. Assure him that you will be available if needed but schedule regular appointments (to be kept whether or not he is feeling ill). Consider giving a mild medication (eg, antihistamine, vitamin) which can be a focus of attention during appointments and will be evidence that he is taken seriously. This form of palliation can restore the patient to functional health more readily than any definitive medical treatment.

### 6. Body Dysmorphic Disorder (DSM-IV p 468, 300.7):

This disorder of young adults can be minor or incapacitating: patients can become preoccupied with an imagined physical defect, which they feel negatively affects their appearance, and seek surgical correction or become socially withdrawn or even housebound. Although in its minor forms it is surprisingly common, little is known of its etiology, family patterns, biology, or treatment. It occasionally reaches psychotic proportions. SSRI antidepressants may help some.

### 7. Undifferentiated Somatoform Disorder
### (DSM-IV p 451, 300.81):

This residual category contains patients complaining of nonspecific weakness, fatigue, and vague but incapacitating medical symptoms (GI, GU, etc.). They share elements of the other somatoform disorders but without adequate focus. Thoroughly evaluated and completely unexplained "chronic fatigue syndrome" patients would go here. These patients are not uncommon; treat similarly to hypochondriasis.

### SIMULATION OF PHYSICAL SYMPTOMS

Two categories of patients voluntarily mimic physical symptoms:

### 8. Malingering
### (DSM-IV p 683, V65.2)

These people knowingly fake symptoms for some obvious gain. They may be trying to get drugs, avoid the law, get a bed for the night, etc. Despite their physical complaints, they tend to be evasive and uncooperative during evaluation and therapy, and they avoid medical procedures. When exposed, they may angrily give up their symptoms and sign out AMA. Antisocial personality disorder and drug abuse are common associated conditions.

### 9. Factitious Disorder with Predominantly
### Physical Signs and Symptoms
### (DSM-IV p 474, 300.19):

These patients also knowingly fake symptoms but do so for psychological reasons: they usually prefer the sick role and may move from hospital to hospital in order to receive care. They are usually loners with an early childhood background of trauma and deprivation. They are unable to establish close interpersonal relationships and generally have severe personality disorders. Unlike many malingerers, they follow through with medical procedures and are at risk for drug addiction and for the complications of multiple operations.

Both groups of patients can be difficult to distinguish from the somatoform disorders and from organic illness, yet careful and repeated examinations will usually uncover their deceptions. The most common presentations include:

— Abdominal pain: May have an abdomen "like a railroad yard."
— Heart: Complains of pain. May induce arrhythmias with digitalis or produce tachycardia with amphetamines or thyroid.
— Bleeding: Patient may take anticoagulants or add blood from a scratch to lab samples.
— Neurological: Weakness, seizures, unconsciousness—difficult to differentiate from conversion symptoms.
— Fever: Produced by manipulating the thermometer (eg, hot coffee in the mouth).
— Skin: Look for lesions in a linear pattern in areas the patient can reach.

Although both groups produce symptoms consciously, they should be dealt with differently. The malingerer should be handled formally (and often legally). The patient with a factitious disorder should be treated sympathetically and every effort made to convince him to enter psychotherapy (difficult). Unlike the malingerer, these patients are unable to control their self-destructive behavior, and that should be tactfully pointed out to them.

### Suggested Readings

Barsky AJ, Wyshak G, Klerman GL: Hypochondriasis. Arch Gen Psychiatry 43:493–500, 1986.

Bass C, Benjamin S: The management of chronic somatisation. Br J Psychiatry 162:472–480, 1993.

Creed F, Guthrie E: Techniques for interviewing the somatising patient. Br J Psychiatry 162:467–471, 1993.

Fishbain DA, Goldberg M: The misdiagnosis of conversion disorder in a psychiatric emergency service. Gen Hosp Psychiatry 13:177–181, 1991.

Ford CV: The somatizing disorders. Psychosomatics 27:327–337,1986.

Ford CV, Folks DG: Conversion disorders: An overview. Psychosomatics 26:371–383, 1985.

Golding JM, Smith GR, Kashner RM: Does somatization disorder occur in men? Arch Gen Psychiatry 48:231–235, 1991.

Gould R, Muller BL, Goldberg MA, et al: The validity of hysterical signs and symptoms. J Nerv Ment Dis 74:593–598, 1986.

Henderson LM, Bell BA, Miller JD: A neurosurgical Munchausen tale. J Neurol Neurosurg Psychiatry 46:437–439, 1983.

Katon W, Lin E, Von Korff M, et al: Somatization: A spectrum of severity. Am J Psychiatry 148:34–40, 1991.

Kellner R: Prognosis of treated hypochondriasis. Acta Psychiatr Scand 67:69–79, 1983.

Kellner R: Psychotherapeutic strategies in hypochondriasis: A clinical study. Am J Psychother 36:146–157, 1982.

Lee G, Loring DW, Martin RC: Rey's 15-item visual memory test for the detection of malingering. Psychol Assess 4:43–46, 1992.

McElroy SL, Phillips KA, Keck PE, et al: Body dysmorphic disorder: Does it have a psychotic subtype? J Clin Psychiatry 54:389–395, 1993.

Noyes R, Kathol RG, Fisher MM, et al: The validity of DSM-IIIR hypochondriasis. Arch Gen Psychiatry 50:961–970, 1993.

Phillips KA: Body dysmorphic disorder: The distress of imagined ugliness. Am J Psychiatry 148:1138–1149, 1991.

Phillips KA, McElroy SL, Keck PE, et al: Body dysmorphic disorder: 30 cases of imagined ugliness. Am J Psychiatry 150:302–308, 1993.

Powell R, Boast N: The million dollar man. Br J Psychiatry 162:253–256, 1993.

Sigvardsson S, von Knorring A, Bohman M, Cloninger R: An adoptions study of somatoform disorders. Arch Gen Psychiatry 41:853–859, 1984.

Spivak H, Rodin G, Sutherland A: The psychology of factitious disorders. Psychosomatics 35:25–34, 1994.

Starcevic V: Reassurance and treatment of hypochondriasis. Gen Hosp Psychiatry 13:122–127, 1991.

Stern J, Murphy M, Bass C: Personality disorders in patients with somatization disorder. Br J Psychiatry 163:785–789, 1993.

Swartz MS, McCracken J: Emergency room management of conversion disorders. Hosp Commun Psychiatry 37:828–832, 1986.

Theodore WH: Pseudoseizures: Differential diagnosis. J Neuropsychiatry 1:67–69, 1989.

*Chapter 12*

# Psychosomatic Disorders

There are two overlapping classifications here. A PSYCHOSO-MATIC DISORDER (not in DSM-IV) is a physical disease partially caused or exacerbated by psychological factors while the new DSM-IV category, PSYCHOLOGICAL FACTORS AFFECTING MEDICAL CONDITION (DSM-IV p 678, 316), broadly identifies those psychological and social factors that influence the development and maintenance of medical disease. Both classifications apply only to those conditions in which psychological and/or behavioral influence is of major significance (but be aware that any physical disease may be modified by psychological stress). Neither the term "psychosomatic" nor the DSM-IV category refers to (1) a physical symptom or clinical presentation caused by psychological factors for which there is no organic basis (eg, conversion disorder, pain disorder, somatization disorder) or (2) a patient with knowingly spurious physical complaints (eg, factitious disorder, malingering), but the DSM-IV condition does allow for physical complaints due to habit disorders (eg, dyspnea due to excessive smoking, problems from obesity).

### Mechanisms of Disease Production

There are many specific diseases that are influenced greatly by the "psyche" (see below) but, although much studied, the mechanisms by which the brain produces such organic pathology are unclear.

**Psychological Mechanisms**

"Stress," either internal or external, is required but is much more likely to cause disease if:

1. The stress is severe (eg, death of a loved one, divorce or separation, major illness or injury, financial crisis, incarceration). Holmes and Rahe developed a ranked scale of stressful life events (rated by life change units LCU) and found a close correlation between an event's stress (in LCUs) and the patient's likelihood of developing a physical illness.
2. The stress is chronic.
3. The patient perceives the stress as stressful.
4. The patient has an increased level of general instability, eg, difficult job, troubled marriage, urban dweller, socially disrupted environment, etc.

It was once thought (F. Dunbar) that specific superficial personality traits produced specific organic diseases (eg, that there is a "coronary personality," an "ulcer personality," etc.). It was also held (F. Alexander) that specific deep and unconscious, unresolved neurotic conflicts caused specific physical disorders. Currently, the specificity that is generally accepted associates the "Type A" personality (ie, sense of time urgency, impatience, aggressiveness, upward striving, competitiveness, tendency to anger when frustrated, and particularly a "cynical hostility") with coronary artery disease. More generally accepted are nonspecific hypotheses that link a wide variety of stresses to the development of disease in an individual placed at risk by one or more of the following:

1. A genetic susceptibility.
2. A degree of chronic debilitation, a current illness, or "an organ vulnerability."
3. A tendency to react to stress with anger, resentment, frustration, anxiety, or depression.
4. A "psychological susceptibility" (eg, patient is pessimistic and "expects the worst" vs being optimistic and actively working to overcome stress).
5. An "alexithymic" personality eg, a person who is in poor contact with his emotions and has an impoverished fantasy life.

**Physiological mechanisms**

These mechanisms are poorly understood, and only the broad outline can be sketched. Stress is perceived cognitively (by the cerebral cortex) but, once recognized, is mediated primarily by the limbic system which, under chronic stress, chronically stimulates the hypothalamus and the vegetative centers in the brain stem. This stimulation produces a direct effect on the various organs by:

1. Activation of the autonomic nervous system (sympathetic and adrenal medulla; parasympathetic).
2. Involvement of the neuroendocrine system, ie, releasing hormones from the hypothalamus travel through the pituitary portal system to the anterior pituitary where they cause the release of the trophic hormones (eg, ACTH, TSH, GH, FSH) which either act directly or release other hormones from the endocrine glands (eg, cortisol, thyroxin, epinephrine, NE, sex hormones). These produce a variety of changes in structures throughout the body. Hans Selye (1976) emphasized the central role of cortisol as a primary mediator of the body's stress response (general adaptation syndrome, GAS)—if cortisol is released too chronically, various organs are damaged, producing psychosomatic diseases.

The details have yet to be worked out—there remain more questions than answers. The recently identified hormones, endorphins, may play a major role in stress response regulation. Central to all of these physiological systems is the concept of homeostasis—psychosomatic diseases occur when the body's "natural balance" is upset, particularly if it is chronically upset.

Although psychosomatic medicine has been concerned primarily with those diseases believed to be "psychosomatic," recently the concept has been broadened to include (or overlap with) the new field of Behavioral Medicine. The essence of behavioral medicine is the application of behavior modification techniques derived from learning theory to various medical problems, eg, chronic pain, hypertension and other psychosomatic diseases, habit disorders, etc. Techniques used include behavioral self-management methods, biofeedback, hypnosis, and various relaxation procedures.

## Specific Psychosomatic Disorders

Although (1) stress can increase the susceptibility to any disease and (2) most diseases are currently viewed as multifactorially determined, those that most clearly have a major psychosomatic contribution include the following disorders.

### CARDIOVASCULAR

**Coronary artery disease:** More common in "Type A" personalities. These patients have increased serum cholesterol, low-density lipoproteins, and triglycerides; also increased urinary 17-ketosteroids, 17-hydroxycorticosteroids, and NE. Sudden death by MI is increased in patients experiencing a severe recent loss (first 6 months).

**Hypertension:** Chronic psychosocial stress probably plays a role in its development in genetically predisposed patients. Mechanism is uncertain but may not be related to the brief hypertension that occurs during periods of acute stress. May occur more frequently in Type A people and in compulsive people who "store resentment" and who handle angry feelings poorly. Treat first with antihypertensives. Relaxation therapy (eg, progressive relaxation, meditation, hypnosis) is an effective adjunct to drugs—biofeedback may also help.

**Arrhythmias:** Palpitation, sinus tachycardia, and worsening of preexisting arrhythmias may all be produced by stress—probably via a sympathetic-parasympathetic imbalance.

**Hypotension** (fainting): Produced by fear—probably due to peripheral vasodilation and a decreased ventricular filling.

**Congestive heart failure:** Frequently develops after periods of stress. Anxiety tends to exacerbate the condition.

**Raynaud's disease:** Can often be treated effectively with progressive relaxation or biofeedback.

**Migraine:** Attacks are often precipitated by stress. Treatment should include medication and biofeedback. Consider relaxation and psychotherapy also.

### RESPIRATORY

**Bronchial asthma:** Occurs in people with a genetic predisposition—made worse by acute and chronic stress. These patients are at risk for developing neurotic emotional reactions secondary to the respiratory disorder. There is good evidence that a wide variety of problem-solving and stress-reducing techniques (eg, psychotherapy, family therapy, systematic desensitization, hypnosis, etc.) are effective at preventing attacks in many asthmatics and should be used in conjunction with medication.

**Hay fever:** Patients have an increased sensitivity to their allergens when stressed but may also develop characteristic symptoms when no allergens can be identified.

**Tuberculosis:** Chronic stress often precedes development of the disease.

**Hyperventilation syndrome:** A common ER presentation (see Chapter 8). Differentiate from panic disorder.

GASTROINTESTINAL

**Peptic ulcer:** Stress contributes to ulcer development, probably through its influence on the hypothalamic-pituitary-adrenal axis. The chronically frustrated and angry patient with increased gastric HCL (hypersecretor) is at risk. Help the patient develop more stress-free life patterns. Relaxation therapy may be of value.

**Ulcerative colitis:** Stressful emotional factors often precede disease development and can induce a relapse but the mechanism is unclear. Nonconfrontive, supportive psychotherapy is indicated to help the patient adapt better to stress and to his illness and to help him deal with the frequently associated anxiety and depression, but psychiatric care alone will not prevent relapses. Other intestinal conditions that are markedly influenced by psychosocial stress include regional enteritis (Crohn's disease) and irritable bowel syndrome. "Functional gastrointestinal disorders" may be associated with a history of physical and sexual abuse in women.

**Obesity:** Genetic and psychological factors interact. Improper conditioning around food habits, an overvaluation of food, and a negative body image (eg, "fatso") are central. "Binge eaters" are particularly susceptible to stress. Supportive psychotherapy may be of some value but behavior modification is most useful. Long-term success is limited—initial weight loss is frequent but relapses are very common. A change in lifestyle appears essential.

**ANOREXIA NERVOSA** (DSM-IV p 544, 307.1): This disorder of profound weight loss without loss of appetite usually develops in adolescence (F:M = 10:1), continues through the early 20s, and may end in death by starvation (5–10%). It is increasingly common in upper middle class females.

These patients have a disturbed body image (feel fat despite dramatic visual evidence to the contrary) and are preoccupied with losing weight. They diet, exercise, and dangerously abuse diuretics and laxatives, even while family members and professionals attempt to stop them. Many anorexics (50% at some time during their course) also binge eat.

A related condition, BULIMIA NERVOSA (DSM-IV p 549, 307.51), is a chronic disorder characterized primarily by episodic eating binges in adolescent or early adult females (F:M = 10–20:1) of normal weight who follow the gorging by self-induced vomiting (purging) or by inducing diarrhea with laxatives. These individuals are weight conscious and markedly depressed by their uncontrolled eating. Self-deprecation and suicidal ruminations are common, as is substance abuse (25%). Endocrinological, family history, and treatment findings are similar to those of anorexia, and many patients slip back and forth between the two conditions over time.

Anorexics often have hormone imbalances (eg, amenorrhea), numerous signs of starvation (eg, edema, bradycardia, and hypothermia), and associated features like ritual behavior (eg, handwashing). The etiology is uncertain. In a few patients, anorexia is comorbid with avoidant and bulimia comorbid with borderline personality disorders. The families frequently have disturbed interpersonal patterns and an increased incidence of eating and affective disorders. Be certain to rule out a primary affective or schizophrenic disorder.

Treatment of anorexia should be comprehensive: hospitalization for severe cases, individual and family therapy, behavior modification, and possibly antidepressants. In its early stages this condition is frequently overlooked yet treatment can be lifesaving. Develop a high index of suspicion in thin, young females. Bulimics benefit most from the combination of cognitive therapy and antidepressants (eg, fluoxetine, 20–60 mg/day) (but with frequent relapses), while a few require antipsychotics. Long-term ($10^+$ years) outcome of bulimics finds $50\%^+$ symptom free and most of the rest with reduced symptoms. Anorexics, if they survive, tend to be chronically thin women.

## MUSCULOSKELETAL

**Rheumatoid arthritis:** Symptoms frequently worsen after emotional stress. Stress may be acting as an immunosuppressant. Depression is common in these patients. Psychotherapy is of little value in altering the course of the disease.

**Tension headaches:** Caused by chronic muscular tension. Treat with mild analgesics and EMG feedback from the frontalis muscles or with relaxation techniques (often coupled with vigorous activity).

**Spasmodic torticollis:** Exacerbated by stress. EMG biofeedback may be useful.

**Low back pain:** Treat multimodally.

## ENDOCRINE

Conditions that are exacerbated by stress include hyperthyroidism and diabetes mellitus. Acute and chronic stress may precipitate a thyroid crisis in genetically predisposed patients. Ketosis may be produced and maintained by stress in diabetics. Patients with either condition should receive psychotherapy if they have adopted self-destructive life habits and if they experience frequent relapses.

## GENITOURINARY

Most gynecological disorders reflect primarily an endocrine imbalance, but many of these conditions also can be influenced significantly by psychosocial stress. Psychosomatic influences are most evident for: menstrual disorders (premenstrual tension, amenorrhea, oligomenorrhea), dyspareunia, frigidity pseudocyesis, premature ejaculation, and impotence. Spontaneous abortion can be produced by major stress.

## CHRONIC PAIN

Chronic pain patients are common. The sources of their pain may or may not be identifiable. They often have been thoroughly evaluated medically, have experienced several unsuccessful surgical or medical procedures, and may or may not be currently iatrogenically addicted to analgesics (be wary of requests for Demerol, Percodan, Codeine, Darvon, Talwin, Valium, etc.). Nothing has helped, and the patients show evidence of depression, hopelessness, chronic anxiety, insomnia, chronic anger, interpersonal withdrawal, and/or somatic preoccupation. Their lives may be totally dominated by the pain.

Be certain that you are not dealing with conditions that mimic or complicate chronic pain (see chapter 11):

1. Unrecognized, treatable organic pathology.
2. Primary depression, anxiety disorder, or psychosis.
3. Unrecognized, early delirium or dementia.
4. Drug addiction.
5. Conversion disorder.
6. Somatization disorder.
7. Pain disorder.
8. Hypochondriasis.
9. Histrionic personality disorder.
10. Malingering.
11. Compensation factors.

Always treat the chronic pain patient globally. Do not become overly concerned about whether the pain is "real" or "psychological"—it invariably will have elements of both, and treatments will be similar. Use whatever medical and surgical means are of value but do not stop there. Always explore and apply the multiplicity of psychological treatments that are available.

First, detoxify the patient, if necessary.

Take the patient and his pain seriously. Be interested, sympathetic, and hopeful. Be a continuing presence—see the patient regularly and do not abandon him.

Help the patient identify and accept reasonable expectations. Encourage him to continue functioning—avoid hospitalization.

Recognize that chronic administration of analgesics has limited usefulness and great risks yet can be done therapeutically. Attempt to use no drugs or nonaddicting drugs (eg, antidepressants (particularly useful; use low to normal doses), major tranquilizers, antihistamines). Codeine is the preferable narcotic.

Have the patient keep a pain diary. Work with the patient over time to help him determine what variables improve or worsen the pain.

Consider the variety of psychological techniques available, eg, hypnosis, biofeedback, relaxation therapy, etc. Encourage the patient to discover that he is "in control of his own pain." Use these methods within the context of a good therapeutic alliance. Consider family and group therapy. Help others in the patient's environment become more appropriately responsive to his pain.

Consider some physical procedures, eg, nerve block, dorsal column stimulators, acupuncture, rhizotomy, etc. Avoid surgery if possible.

Recognize that not all patients will improve markedly.

**OTHER**

**Skin:** A wide variety of psychosocial stressors can exacerbate certain skin conditions, including psoriasis, chronic urticaria, pruritus, and neurodermatitis (eczema). Research suggests that (1) warts (a contagious disease) responds to hypnosis and (2) TRICHOTILLOMANIA (hair pulling, $1\%^+$ of population (maybe); DSM-IV p 621, 312.39) may respond to fluoxetine or clomipramine (related to OCD?).

**Malignant disease:** Psychological stressors appear to influence the development (but perhaps not the course) of a malignancy. This may be related to the effect of stress on the immune system. Much work remains to be done, yet there is some suggestion that psychological treatments (eg, hypnosis) may play a future role in cancer treatment.

**Hematological:** Stress may aid clotting among hemophiliacs. Changes in levels of various blood elements may occur in normal patients under acute stress.

**Accident proneness:** Some people are chronically at risk for accidental trauma due to psychological characteristics (eg, impulsive, anxious, hostile).

**Seizures:** Emotional stress can trigger seizures (both neurogenic and conversion). Psychotherapy and stress management is effective in helping to control seizure disorders, particularly in patients with partial seizures.

## Suggested Readings

Agras WS, Rossiter EM, Arnow B, et al: One-year follow-up of psychosocial and pharmacologic treatments for bulimia nervosa. J Clin Psychiatry 55:179–183, 1994.

Axelrod J, Reisine TD: Stress hormones: Their interaction and regulation. Science 224:452–459, 1984.

Brandt J, Celentano D, Stewart W, et al: Personality and disorder in a community sample of migraine headache sufferers. Am J Psychiatry 147:30–38, 1990.

Cassileth BR, Lusk EJ, Miller DS, et al: Psychosocial correlates of survival in advanced malignant disease? N Engl J Med 312:1551–1555, 1985.

Christodoulou GN, Alevizos BH, Konstantakakis E: Peptic ulcer in adults. Psychother Psychosomat 39:55–64, 1983.

Collings S, King M: Ten-year follow-up of 50 patients with bulimia nervosa. Br J Psychiatry 164:80–87, 1994.

Drossman DA, Leserman J, Hachman G, et al: Sexual and physical abuse in women with functional or organic gastrointestinal disorders. Ann Internal Med 113:828–833, 1990.

Fairburn CG, Jones R, Peveler RC, et al: Three psychological treatments for bulimia nervosa. Arch Gen Psychiatry 48:463–469, 1991.

Fluoxetine Bulimia Nervosa Collaborative Study Group: Fluoxetine in the treatment of bulimia nervosa. Arch Gen Psychiatry 49:139–147, 1992.

Friedman M, Rosenman RH: Type A behavior pattern: Its association with coronary heart disease. Ann Clin Res 3:300–312, 1971.

Herzog DB, Sacks NR: Bulimia nervosa: Comparison of treatment responders vs nonresponders. Psychopharmacol Bull 29:121–125, 1993.

Holderness CC, BrooksGunn J, Warren MP: Comorbidity of eating disorders and substance abuse: Review of the literature. Int J Eat Disord 16:1–34, 1994.

Holmes TH, Rahe RH: The social readjustment rating scale. J Psychosomat Res 11:213–318, 1967.

Katon W, Egan K, Miller D: Chronic Pain: Lifetime psychiatric diagnoses and family history. Am J Psychiatry 142:1156–1160, 1985.

Kemmer FW, Bisping R, Steingruber HJ, et al: Psychological stress and metabolic control in patients with type 1 diabetes mellitus. N Engl J Med 314:1078–1084, 1986.

Latimer PR: Irritable bowel syndrome. Psychosomatics 24:205–218, 1983.

Lesser IM: Alexithymia. N Engl J Med 312:690–692, 1985.

Magni G: The use of antidepressants in the treatment of chronic pain: A review of current evidence. Drugs 42:730–748, 1991.

Selye H: The Stress of Life, 2nd ed. New York, McGraw-Hill Book Co, 1976.

Sharp CW, Freeman CPL: The medical complications of anorexia nervosa. Br J Psychiatry 162:452–462, 1993.

Skodol AD, Oldham JM, Hyler SE, et al: Comorbidity of DSM-IIIR eating disorders and personality disorders. Int J Eat Disord 14:403–416, 1993.

Stunkard AJ: The current status of treatment for obesity in adults. Res Publ Assoc Res Nerv Ment Dis 62:157–173, 1984.

Surman OS, Gottlieb SK, Hackett TP, Silverberg, EL: Hypnosis in the treatment of warts. Arch Gen Psychiatry 28:439–341, 1973.

Vollhardt BR, Ackerman SH, Grayzel AI, Barland P: Psychologically distinguishable groups of rheumatoid arthritis patients. Psychosomat Med 44:353–362, 1982.

Walsh BT, Hadigan CM, Devlin MJ, et al: Long-term outcome of antidepressant treatment for bulimia nervosa. Am J Psychiatry 148:1206–1212, 1991.

Winchel RM, Jones JS, Stanley B, et al: Clinical characteristics of trichotillomania and its response to fluoxetine. J Clin Psychiatry 53:304–308, 1992.

Wolman BB: Psychosomatic Disorders. New York, Plenum, 1988.

*Chapter 13*

# Psychiatric Symptoms of Nonpsychiatric Medication

Many medical patients develop psychiatric symptoms due to treatment with medical drugs—(1) as a common side effect, (2) as an idiosyncratic response, (3) from administration of toxic amounts, or (4) as the result of an untoward combination of drugs. Unrecognized, the responsible medications might be continued. Likely offenders include:

### Anticonvulsants

Phenytoin, phenacemide: Irritability, emotional lability, confusion, and occasionally hallucinations and psychotic thinking—at times with normal blood levels. Symptoms occur more frequently in patients who also demonstrate tremor and ataxia.

Phenobarbital: Normal blood levels occasionally may produce irritability and/or confusion in the elderly while excessive dosage will produce oversedation. Symptoms of withdrawal may occur if phenobarbital is stopped abruptly.

### Antiinflammatory Agents

Phenylbutazone (Butazolidin): Anxiety, nervousness, emotional lability.

Indomethacin (Indocin): Dizziness, disorientation, and confusion; also occasionally depression, hallucinations, and psychosis.

Salicylates: In high doses, can produce elation and euphoria grading into depression and confusion.

### Hormones

Exogenous thyroid: Excess can result in symptoms varying from restlessness and anxiety to a psychosis mimicking mania or acute schizophre-

**128**

nia. Inadequately treated patients may display symptoms of hypothyroidism; eg, fatigue, depression, psychosis (myxedema madness).

Adrenal corticosteroids (eg, cortisone, dexamethasone, prednisone): In addition to physical complications, excessive or chronic use can produce widely varying affective syndromes (eg, euphoria and hypomania, fatigue and depression) and/or degrees of a toxic psychosis. Steroid withdrawal can produce complaints of weakness and fatigue—suspect pseudotumor cerebri if coupled with headache, vomiting, and confusion.

Estrogens: Restlessness, a sense of well-being, euphoria.

Progesterones: May produce fatigue, irritability, tearfulness, and depression when given either alone or in combination as oral contraceptives (2-30% of patients).

Androgens: Restlessness, agitation, aggressiveness, euphoria.

## Anticholinergics

An anticholinergic psychosis (see Chapter 23) can be caused by a variety of medical drugs; they also can produce milder peripheral (dry mouth, hypotension) and central (lability, distractibility, restlessness) side effects.

Antihistamines: eg, Benadryl, Phenergan, Teldrin, Ornade, Dramamine.

Antispasmodics: eg, Banthine.

Ophthalmic drops: eg, atropine, homatropine, cyclopentolate.

Antiparkinsonian drugs: eg, Cogentin, Artane, Tremin, Kemadrin, Akineton.

Others: Compoz, Excedrin PM, Sleep-Eze, Sominex; anything containing scopolamine.

Treat psychosis with physostigmine 1–2 mg, IM or slowly IV; repeat in 20 minutes if needed.

## Antihypertensives and Cardiac Drugs

Rauwolfia alkaloids (reserpine): Can cause nightmares, confusion, and profound depression in susceptible patients taking normal doses.

Diuretics (thiazides, furosemide, ethacrynic acid): Fatigue and mild depression.

Methyldopa (Aldomet): Persistent lassitude; verbal memory impairment; depression with obtundation and confusion (on normal dosage).

Guanethidine (Ismelin): mild depression.

Clonidine: sedation, depression; antagonized by tricyclic antidepressants; hypomania on withdrawal sometimes.

Propranolol (Inderal) and other β-blockers: fatigue, insomnia, nightmares, verbal memory impairment, and depression; hyperactivity, paranoia, rarely confusion and a toxic psychosis.

Digitalis and the cardiac glycosides: Fatigue, apathy, depression, and/or toxic delirium particularly in the elderly.

Antiarrhythmics (quinidine, procainamide, lidocaine): mild confusion; mild-to-major delirium; occasionally depression.

## Sympathomimetics

Both catecholamine and noncatecholamine stimulants may produce restlessness, anxiety, fear and panic, weakness, dizziness, irritability, and insomnia in recommended dosages.

## Bromide

Acute intoxication is rare—bromide is too irritating to allow ingestion of large doses. Symptoms of chronic intoxication (weeks, months) (bromism) range from mild disorientation to full toxic psychosis. Look for "classic" acneiform rash of face and hair roots (30% of patients) in persons using some older over-the-counter sedatives (eg, Bromo-Seltzer).

## L-Dopa

The depression and apathy of Parkinson's disease may be relieved, but anxiety and agitation are produced frequently. Fifteen percent of patients develop more serious psychiatric problems including an acute organic brain syndrome with confusion or frank delirium, hypomania, acute psychosis, or major depression. Often hard to differentiate from the progression of the disease.

## Hypoglycemics (insulin, tolbutamide)

Symptoms of hypoglycemia—restlessness, anxiety, disorientation.

## Antibiotics and Related Drugs

Tetracyclines: Can produce emotional lability, depression, and confusion from vitamin deficiencies secondary to alteration of colonic bacteria.

Nalidixic acid and nitrofurantoin: Lethargy; rarely confusion.

Isoniazid (INH): Euphoria, transient memory loss, agitation, psychotic reaction, paranoia, catatonic-like syndrome.

Cycloserine: Lethargy and confusion, agitation, severe depression, psychosis, paranoid reactions.

## Antineoplastics

Acute organic brain syndromes and depression can be produced by a variety of these agents—either by a direct CNS effect or due to involvement of other systems (eg, anemia).

### Suggested Readings

Avorn J, Everitt DE, Weiss S: Increased antidepressant use in patients prescribed betablockers. JAMA 255:357–360, 1986.

Benson D, Peterson LG, Bartay J: Neuropsychiatric manifestations of antihypertensive medications. Psychiatr Med 1:205–214, 1983.

Bernstein JG: Drug interactions, in Cassem NH: Handbook of General Hospital Psychiatry. St Louis, CV Mosby Co, 1991.

Carpenter WT, Gruen PH: Cortisol's effects on human mental functioning. J Clin Psychopharmacol 2:91–101, 1982.

David K: Psychological effects of nonpsychiatric drugs, in Barchas J: Psychopharmacology: From Theory to Practice. New York, Oxford University Press, 1977.

Drugs That Cause Psychiatric Symptoms. Med Lett 28:81–86, August 29, 1986.

Glassman R, Salzman C: Interactions between psychotropic and other drugs: An update. Hosp Commun Psychiatry 38:236–242, 1987.

Lewis DA, Smith RE: Steroid-induced psychiatric syndromes. J Affect Disord 5:319–332, 1983.

Shader RI: Psychiatric Complication of Medical Drugs. New York, Raven Press, 1972.

Solomon S, Hotchkiss E, Saravay SM, et al: Impairment of memory function by antihypertensive medication. Arch Gen Psychiatry 40:1109–1112, 1983.

# Chapter 14

# Psychiatric Presentations of Medical Disease

Physical and psychiatric illnesses are closely interwoven. Both medical and psychiatric physicians should appreciate this inter-relationship.

— 60% of patients needing mental health care are being treated by medical physicians.

— 50-80% of the patients treated in medical clinics have a diagnosable psychiatric illness, and 10-20% of medical patients suffer primarily from an emotional disorder.

— 50% of patients in psychiatric clinic populations have undiagnosed medical conditions.

— 10% of self-referred psychiatric patients have symptoms that are due solely to a medical illness.

Always evaluate psychiatric patients medically. Be particularly alert to patients presenting with depression, confusion, memory loss, anxiety, personality changes, psychosis of rapid onset, visual hallucinations, and illusions. Always be suspicious of symptoms of sudden onset in a patient, particularly one over 35 years old, who previously has been problem-free. Recognize that patients (or their physicians) often can identify a "precipitating event" for even the most organic of psychiatric conditions—don't be fooled.

Always consider psychiatric possibilities for physical symptoms in medical patients. Take a good history including past emotional problems. Why is the patient coming for help now?

## PSYCHIATRIC SYMPTOMS

There are only a few typical psychiatric presentations and many different medical illnesses that can cause them. Some of the most common associations are listed below, although almost any physical condition can contribute to symptom production (Table 14.1).

## MEDICAL DISEASES

No medical illness produces pathognomonic psychiatric symptoms, yet each has a typical range of presentations. Some of the most characteristic are listed below, but more comprehensive sources are available. In many of these diseases, the patient develops psychiatric pathology before any medical signs or symptoms are noticed.

### Endocrine

Hyperthyroidism—anxiety, restlessness, emotional lability, weight loss, sweating, fine tremor, atypical depression with confusion in older patients.

Hypothyroidism—depression, fatigue, apathy, occasionally anxiety and psychosis ("myxedema madness"), dry skin, EEG slowing, cold intolerance.

Hyperparathyroidism—anxiety and irritability; depression, apathy, and fatigue; confusion and delirium; abdominal and bone pain, kidney stones, duodenal ulcer. Symptoms progress to psychosis and coma as the serum calcium levels rise.

Hypoparathyroidism—similar to hyper- but with anxiety and emotional lability more common; seizures, tetany.

Hypoadrenalism (Addison's disease)—fatigue, apathy, depression, weakness, occasional confusion.

Pheochromocytoma—anxiety, restlessness, apprehension and panic, flushing, headaches; all during attacks.

Hypoglycemia—symptoms vary with blood sugar; episodic anxiety, tremor, sweating, personality changes, bizarre behavior.

Diabetes mellitus—depression, apathy, confusion, intellectual dullness.

Premenstrual syndrome (PMS)—as many as 25% of women develop significant physical/psychological discomfort during the 4–5 days prior to menses, ending shortly after flow begins. Common symptoms include irritability, tension, tearfulness, moderate depression, a sense of bloating, swelling of the extremities, and headaches, but may in-

**Table 14.1**
**Common Associations for Psychiatric Symptoms**

| Presentation | Disease |
|---|---|
| Anxiety | hyperthyroidism |
| | hypoglycemia |
| | pneumonia |
| | acute intermittent porphyria |
| | pheochromocytoma |
| | mitral valve prolapse |
| | angina pectoris |
| | cardiac arrhythmias |
| | hyper- and hypoparathyroidism |
| | hypothyroidism |
| | Cushing's disease |
| | menstrual irregularities |
| Depression | hypothyroidism |
| | debilitating disease |
| | pneumonia, other infections |
| | Cushing's disease |
| | Addison's disease |
| | pancreatic carcinoma |
| | intracranial tumors |
| | Pernicious anemia |
| | hyper- and hypoparathyroidism |
| Confusion, memory loss | Numerous medical conditions (see Chapters 5 and 6) |
| Mixed psychotic-hysterical symptoms | MS |
| | Wilson's disease |
| | SLE |
| | intracranial tumors |
| | hyperthyroidism |
| | psychomotor epilepsy |
| | general paresis |
| | Huntingtons's chorea |
| | metachromatic leukodystrophy |
| | porphyria |

clude more severe symptoms such as profound depression, aggressiveness, and even psychosis. The etiology is unknown but may be related to hormonal imbalance: possibly prolactin, estrogen, or prostaglandins. Women with a preexisting mood disorder may be at risk for problems. No treatment is certain, but progestogenic oral contraceptives, bromocriptine, Li, and/or psychotherapy may help.

## Infections

Depression, anxiety, OBS, and acute psychosis all can occur due to a variety of infectious processes, depending upon the patient's sensitivity, age, and physical condition, the site of the infection, and the agent. Particularly common are symptoms with pneumonia (particularly delirium with bacterial and depression with viral), infectious mononucleosis (anxiety and psychosis may be the first symptoms of mono; depression is commonly late), viral hepatitis (the posthepatitic syndrome—weakness, irritability, lethargy, depression), syphilis (general paresis), and TB.

## Other

Acute intermittent porphyria—15% of cases present first with psychiatric symptoms: anxiety, irritability, emotional outbursts, depression, acute psychosis; abdominal pain, peripheral neuropathies and bulbar palsies, vomiting and constipation.

Hepatolenticular degeneration (Wilson's disease)—May present with a labile mood, explosive outbursts, and psychotic behavior in a young man before the development of cirrhosis, portal hypertension, rigidity, Kayser-Fleischer rings, and dementia.

Pellagra—dementia, diarrhea, and dermatitis; also depression, personality changes, and a confusional psychosis.

Systematic lupus erythematosus (SLE)—Patient may present with confusion, an affective state, and psychotic behavior before physical signs appear.

Pernicious anemia—depression and fatigue but also an organic psychosis. Look at blood for characteristic megaloblastic anemia.

Pancreatic carcinoma—severe depression in 40%+ of patients. Also depression with CA of lung and brain.

Prolapse of the mitral valve—associated with generalized anxiety disorder, panic disorder, and agoraphobia with panic attacks, but the significance of the association is not known.

COPD—anxiety, depression, and mild-moderate organicity are common.

Irritable bowel syndrome—GI pain, distention, and gas; also psychiatric sxs of autonomic arousal such as anxiety, panic, weakness, fatigue, headaches, tremor, insomnia, etc. Is this fundamentally a psychiatric illness?

## Suggested Readings

Borer MS, Bhanot VK: Hyperparathyroidism: Neuropsychiatric manifestations. Psychosomatics 26:597–601, 1985.

Bornstein RA, McLean DR, Ho K: Neuropsychological and electrophysiological examination of a patient with Wilson's disease. Int J Neuroscience 26:239–247, 1985.

Cassem NH: Handbook of General Hospital Psychiatry. St Louis, CV Mosby, 1991.

Cummings JL: Organic psychosis. Psychosomatics 29:16–26, 1988.

DeJong R, Rubinow DR, RoyByrne P, et al: Premenstrual mood disorder and psychiatric illness. Am J Psychiatry 142:1359–1361, 1985.

Dvdoredsky AE, Cooley HW: Comparative severity of illness in patients with combined medical and psychiatric diagnoses. Psychosomatics 27:625–630, 1986.

Garza-Trevino ES: Medical Psychiatry. Singapore, World Scientific, 1989.

Grant I, Prigatano GP, Heaton RK, et al: Progressive neuropsychologic impairment and hypoxemia. Arch Gen Psychiatry 44:999–1006, 1987.

Hall RCW: Psychiatric effects of thyroid hormone disturbance. Psychosomatics 24:7–11, 1983.

Hayes JR, Butler NE, Martin CR: Misunderstood somatopsychic concomitants of medical disorders. Psychosomatics 27:128–133, 1986.

Keye WR: Medical treatment of premenstrual syndrome. Can J Psychiatry 30:483–488, 1985.

Krystal A, Krisknan KRR, Raitiere M, et al: Differential diagnosis and pathophysiology of Cushing's syndrome and primary affective disorder. J Neuropsychiatry Clin Neuroscience 2:34–43, 1990.

Lishman WA: Organic Psychiatry. Oxford, Blackwell Publishers, 1987.

Price WA, DiMarzio L: Premenstrual tension syndrome in rapid cycling bipolar affective disorder. J Clin Psychiatry 47:415–417, 1986.

Raj A, Sheehan DV: Medical evaluation of panic attacks. J Clin Psychiatry 48:309–313, 1987.

Rubinow DR, Roy-Byrne P: Premenstrual syndromes. Am J Psychiatry 141:163–172, 1984.

Silberfarb, PM, Greer S: Psychological concomitants of cancer. Am J Psychother 36:470–478, 1982.

Stoudemire A, Fogel BS: Principles of Medical Psychiatry. New York, Grune & Stratton, 1987.

Stoudemire A, Fogel BS: Medical Psychiatric Practice, Vol I. Washington, D.C., American Psychiatric Press, 1991.

Tishler PV, Woodward B, O'Connor J, et al: High prevalence of intermittent acute porphyria in a psychiatric patient population. Am J Psychiatry 142:1430–1436, 1985.

Walker EA, Roy-Byrne PP, Katon WJ: Irritable bowel syndrome and psychiatric illness. Am J Psychiatry 147:565–572, 1990.

# Chapter 15

# Psychiatric Presentations of Neurological Disease

Many of the psychiatric symptoms caused by various neurological diseases (eg, CNS tumor, trauma, seizure, infection) can be correlated directly to the CNS site involved.

**Frontal lobes**

Prefrontal damage—the frontal lobe syndrome occurs with unilateral or bilateral damage (personality changes, irritability, euphoria, apathy, pseudodepression, impulsivity, social inappropriateness). Do not mistake for depression or mania. Intelligence is usually unimpaired in unilateral damage. Symptoms are milder if only one side is involved. If the premotor area is involved (on left), there may also be apraxia of the left hand and Broca's (expressive) aphasia. Don't confuse with psychosis.

**Temporal lobes**

Stimulation or lesions may produce visual and olfactory hallucinations, noncomplex auditory hallucinations, and aggressive psychotic behavior.

Dominant lobe lesion may produce agnosia for sounds, intonations, and music.

Bilateral lesions may produce the amnestic disorder of Korsakoff and the Kluver-Bucy syndrome (placidity and hypersexuality).

**139**

**Parietal lobes**

Dominant lobe lesions may produce language difficulties (eg, inability to express or understand spoken words, perform simple tasks, read, and/or write), tactile agnosia, apraxia, and intellectual deterioration.

Nondominant lobe lesions may produce anosognosia.

**Occipital lobes**

Some lesions produce crude, flashing visual illusions and hallucinations.

**Limbic system**

Effects are diverse but usually involve primitive and emotional behavior, eg, emotional lability, fear, rage, impulsivity, depression, memory loss. Also amnestic syndrome when mamillary bodies involved (Korsakoff's syndrome).

## Neurological Diseases

Neurological disorders can produce a variety of psychiatric symptoms consult a comprehensive source for detailed descriptions of specific conditions. Some major diseases are presented below.

Parkinson's disease—frequently accompanied by apathy and depression (40%$^+$), dementia (40%), and anxiety (40%).

Huntington's chorea—may present first with psychiatric symptoms (eg, emotional lability, impulsiveness, depression, hallucinations, delusions). Don't mistake for schizophrenia, major depression, or mania. Look for family history, movement disorder, and dementia.

Multiple sclerosis (MS)—early psychiatric symptoms are common, particularly emotional lability, euphoria, transient psychotic episodes, depression, and an "hysterical" presentation.

Intracranial tumors—50% of patients develop psychiatric symptoms, and occasionally they may be the presenting symptoms. Pattern is site-related, although there is usually a degree of generalized organicity. Early personality changes are often subtle—"He's not the same person any more." Aphasias due to tumor (or any other cause) may mimic psychotic language disorders—there are qualitative differences between these two types of speech.

Head trauma—a postconcussion syndrome: includes irritability, emotional lability, and personality changes. Depression and mania may occur.

CNS infection—typically presents with OBS (usually irritability and restlessness initially). General paresis (CNS syphilis) usually presents as a gradually developing dementia but can produce a variety of confusing symptoms eg, may mimic schizophrenia, mania, depression, somatization disorder.

Stroke—poststroke depression is common ($50\%^+$ of pts) but the type of mood disorder tends to vary with the anatomical location of the damage: major depression (L-frontal; R-parietal); dysthymia (L- and R-posterior); unnatural cheerfulness, anxiety, and anhedonia (R-frontal); and mania (R-basotemporal). Major depression lasts for 9–12 months and responds to antidepressants or ECT. This localization work is poorly refined as yet.

AIDS—Some combination of apathy and depression, anxiety and agitation, and denial occur in many AIDS patients and requires therapy. Minor memory, language, and concentration abnormalities develop early in many; $50\%^+$ develop serious neurological complications later that often grade into delirium and dementia.

**TOURETTE'S DISORDER** (DSM-IV p 103, 307.23): This neuropsychiatric syndrome of uncertain etiology usually develops in latency or early adolescence with the onset of one or more poorly controlled symptoms, including head or extremity tics, eyeblinks, and the spasmodic production of coughs or grunts which occasionally can include verbal obscenities (coprolalia). It is often severe and lifelong, occurs (along with other tic phenomena) with increased incidence in families, may (or may not) have a major genetic component, and is associated (genetically?) with obsessive-compulsive disorder and with hyperactivity (ADHD) and learning disorders in family members. All symptoms are worsened by stress and may be improved by psychotherapy, but primary treatment is pharmacological: haloperidol (the mainstay; 80–90% of patients improve; 2–12 mg/day), but consider clonidine (0.1–0.5 mg/day), pimozide (2–12 mg/day), clonazepam, or fluphenazine. Stimulant medication can precipitate or worsen Tourette symptoms but can also help, so use cautiously, if at all.

## Suggested Readings

Comings DE, Comings BG: A controlled family history study of Tourette's syndrome, I: Attention-deficit hyperactivity disorder and learning disorders. J Clin Psychiatry 51:275–280, 1990.

Erenberg G, Cruse RP, Rothner AD: Gilles de la Tourette syndrome: Effects of stimulant drugs. Neurology 35:1346–1348, 1985.

Handelsman L, Song S, Losonczy M, et al: Magnetic resonance abnormalities in HIV infection. Psychiatric Res 47:175–186, 1993.

Leckman JF, Hardin MT, Riddle MA, et al: Clonidine treatment of Gilles de la Tourette's syndrome. Arch Gen Psychiatry 48:324–328, 1991.

Lunn S, Skydsbjerg M, Schulsinger H, et al: A preliminary report on the neuropsychologic sequelae of human immunodeficiency virus. Arch Gen Psychiatry 48:139–142, 1991.

Maj M, Satz P, Jonssen R, et al: WHO neuropsychiatric AIDS study: Neuropsychological and neurological findings. Arch Gen Psychiatry 51:51–61, 1994.

Mendel S, Sataloff RT, Schapiro SR: Minor Head Trauma. New York, Springer-Verlag, 1993.

Robertson MM, Channon S, Baker J, et al: The psychopathology of Gilles de la Tourette's syndrome. Br J Psychiatry 162:114–117, 1993.

Robinson RG, Boston JD, Starkstein SE, Price TR: Comparison of mania and depression after brain injury: Causal factors. Am J Psychiatry 145:172–178, 1988.

Robinson RG, Starkstein SE: Current research in affective disorders following stroke. J Neuropsychiatry Clin Neurosci 2:1–14, 1990.

Rundell JR, Wise MG: Neurosyphilis: A psychiatric perspective. Psychosomatics 26:287–295, 1985.

Sandor P, Musisi S, Moldofsky H, et al: Tourette syndrome: A followup study. J Clin Psychopharmacol 10:197–199, 1990.

Sano M, Stern Y, Cote L, et al: Depression in Parkinson's disease: A biochemical model. J Neuropsychiatry 2:88–92, 1990.

Schubert DSP, Foliart RH: Increased depression in multiple sclerosis patients. Psychosomatics 34:124–130, 1993.

Simon RP: Neurosyphilis. Arch Neurol 42:606–613, 1985.

Stern RA, Bachman DL: Depressive symptoms following stroke. Am J Psychiatry 148:351–356, 1991.

Stern Y, Marder K, Bell K, et al: Multidisciplinary baseline assessment of homosexual men with and without human immunodeficiency virus infection. Arch Gen Psychiatry 48:131–138, 1991.

# Chapter 16

# Psychiatry of Alcohol

Alcohol is the major substance of abuse. Sixty-eight percent of Americans drink, 12% are heavy drinkers (men 2:1), 10 million have alcohol abuse problems, the life-time risk for alcoholism is 13%, and 50% of homicides and auto deaths are alcohol-related. Certain populations are at risk: eg, urban blacks, some Indian tribes, bartenders, musicians. Mixed abuse of alcohol and other drugs, however, is extremely common.

### CLASSIFICATION

Normal (recreational) drinking grades into pathological use. ALCOHOL ABUSE (DSM-IV p 196, 305.00) is diagnosed if there is clearly recurrent (but not continuous) impaired social and occupational functioning due to alcohol use over a 1-year period. Individual patterns can vary from continuous consumption for a time to periodic binges, but all demonstrate the inability to abstain from drinking or to stop drinking once started. Such drinking usually results in depression and anxiety. Beginning often as evening and weekend drinking, the pattern usually becomes established by the late 20s in males (later in females) with gradual deterioration in some during their 30s and 40s. Spontaneous remissions can occur. Blackouts (anterograde amnesia for events that occurred during acute intoxication but while conscious and quite functional) often follow more severe drinking.

If the patient also demonstrates tolerance (increased amounts needed to achieve effect), withdrawal, and/or compulsive and continuous use, he has ALCOHOL DEPENDENCE (ALCOHOLISM) (DSM-IV p 195, 303.90). Broader definitions of alcoholism are used by some; eg, "patients with significant

**143**

impairment due to persistent and excessive alcohol use, possibly involving physiological, psychological, or social dysfunction" (AMA Manual of Alcoholism).

The etiology of alcoholism is unknown. Evidence for genetic, biological characteristics grows but is not without controversy. Adoption studies indicate a genetic factor in some families: increased frequency of alcohol abuse and sociopathy among male, and possible increased somatization among female, relatives of alcoholics. Recent research identifies two groups of alcoholics:

Type 1—adult onset; steady, gradually escalating consumption; guilty, worried, rigid, perfectionistic, dependent, introverted; modest family history; both males and females; some recover completely; 75% of alcoholics.

Type 2—alcohol-seeking from adolescence and early adulthood; impulsive; distractible; risk-taking; antisocial characteristics with recklessness and aggression; strong family history; primarily males; very treatment resistant; 25% of all alcoholics.

Moreover, certain biological features seem to be inherited by 1° relatives (particularly males) of alcoholics: eg, a resistance to intoxication, a subnormal cortisol rise after drinking, and a subnormal epinephrine release after stress. At the least, heritable subtypes seem to exist.

Cultural groups are differently affected (eg, low among Jews and Orientals). All social strata are affected—fewer than 5% are "skid row" types. There is no "typical alcoholic personality." Patients with chronic anxiety, mood disorders (particularly females), schizophrenia, dementia, and antisocial personality disorder are at risk to "self-medicate" with alcohol. Always rule out these primary psychiatric disorders.

## RECOGNIZING THE ALCOHOLIC

The majority of alcohol abusers go unrecognized by physicians until their social and occupational life and their physical health have been significantly harmed. Early recognition is important. These patients frequently conceal alcohol use—keep a high index of suspicion. Be suspicious if the predominant complaints include:

1. Chronic anxiety and tension
2. Insomnia
3. Chronic depression
4. Headaches, blackouts
5. Nausea and vomiting, vague GI problems
6. Tachycardia, palpitations
7. Frequent falls or minor injuries

Ask about absenteeism, job loss, financial difficulties, family trouble. Ask, "Do you drink?" Be encouraging and nonjudgmental. Get drinking specifics (number of beers/day, oz/glass, drink alone?, etc). Interview relatives and friends, if possible.

Use a brief screening questionnaire. Two are quick and reliable: the MAST (Michigan Alcoholism Screening Test—24 "yes or no" questions; can be administered by an office worker) and the CAGE (consists of 4 questions; 2 or more positive answers are suggestive of alcoholism)

1. "Have you ever felt you should cut down on your drinking?"
2. "Have people annoyed you by criticizing your drinking?"
3. "Have you ever felt bad or guilty about your drinking?"
4. "Have you ever had a drink first thing in the morning to steady your nerves or get rid of a hangover (Eye-Opener)?"

Chronic drinking frequently elevates serum γ-glutamyltransferase (GGT) and RBC MCV. These measures, coupled with evidence of more acute alcoholic insult (protein, Alk Phos, LDH, SGOT, SGPT, etc.) constitute a fairly reliable laboratory screen for alcoholism. (Recent work suggests that inhibition of platelet MAO by ethanol and stimulation of platelet adenylate cyclase by other chemicals may be a specific test for alcoholism. Time will tell.)

## CLINICAL PRESENTATIONS

When presenting acutely, always determine the patient's recent drinking history:

1. Is he currently intoxicated?
2. Time since last drink?

## Intoxication Syndromes

ALCOHOL INTOXICATION (DSM-IV p 196, 303.00): Alcohol is a CNS depressant that initially disinhibits, then depresses. Early intoxication includes liveliness, a sense of well-being, and a smell of alcohol on the breath (blood alcohol levels up to 100 mg/100 ml); grading into irritability, emotional lability, and incoordination (100–150 mg/100 ml); which grades into apathy, slurred speech, and ataxia (150–250 mg/100 ml); which can become alcoholic coma (above 250–400 mg/100 ml; an emergency—get blood alcohol level and check for presence of other drugs; treat with intubation, CPR, etc., if necessary). Blood alcohol levels vary with drinking experience and thus are only approximate.

Acute intoxication can mimic schizophrenia, mania, depression, hysteria, etc., so delay detailed interview and final diagnosis until patient is sober. Evaluate carefully for medical problems (see below)—differential includes hypoglycemia, CNS infection, and toxic psychosis of other etiology. Intoxicated patients may be uncooperative, assaultive, and dangerous—be civil, nonthreatening, accepting, respectful, patient, but prepared with force. Attempt nonpharmacological management (quiet room, support, coffee), but sedation may be necessary: eg, diazepam 5–20 mg or IM (erratically absorbed), but be cautious of oversedation. Decide if the patient just needs to "sleep it off," is at risk for withdrawal, or is becoming comatose. Should he go home with family, be observed overnight, be hospitalized, or go to jail? Be familiar with community resources.

Alcohol idiosyncratic intoxication or Pathological Intoxication is an unusual and controversial condition (not currently in DSM-IV) of marked aggressiveness and emotional lability, occasionally of psychotic proportions, which follows ingestion of small quantities of alcohol in an otherwise normal person. Etiology is unknown. Some patients retain this pattern for life. Episodes appear suddenly and may last for hours or a day or more, often with amnesia for the episode afterward. Sedate (benzodiazepines, Haldol) and control until sober. Rule out temporal lobe epilepsy. Alcoholic paranoia has a similar presentation but with strong paranoid delusions. It usually occurs in chronic alcoholics who are actively drinking.

## Alcohol Withdrawal Syndromes

These may occur in heavy drinkers or alcoholics who stop drinking or who just reduce their consumption. Don't overlook them in the "closet" alcoholic eg, the businessman or housewife who temporarily abstains while in the hospital for other reasons. If the patient is withdrawing, delay final diagnostic conclusions.

ALCOHOL WITHDRAWAL (DSM-IV p 197, 291.8)—tremulousness, hyperreflexia, weakness, nausea, and vomiting, "dry heaves," anxiety, insomnia and bad dreams, mild illusions and hallucinations, hypervigilance, paresthesias, numbness, tinnitus, and/or blurred vision beginning with the first 12-18 hours of reduced drinking, leading to a vicious cycle. There is no EEG slowing—instead, the waves are normal or fast. Debilitated, medically ill patients are at risk. Alcoholic convulsions (generalized, self-limited, single or in small groups) occur in some, usually in the first 2 days of withdrawal, but sometimes later. If the seizure is focal—suspect CNS pathology (eg, subdural).

ALCOHOL WITHDRAWAL DELIRIUM (Delirium Tremens, DTs) (DSM-IV p 131, 291.0) is a life-threatening delirium with disorientation, agitation, memory disturbances, hallucinations (usually visual, but also tactile, auditory, vestibular, etc.), delusions, powerful autonomic discharge (hypertension, tachycardia, sweating), tremor, ataxia, and fever beginning 28 days after reduced drinking. Tremulousness and seizures can precede, and often are mistaken for, the much less common DTs. Malnourishment and medical illness increases the risk of delirium. Mortality rate is 10-15% for the complete syndrome (often from secondary infection or acute heart failure). Fewer than 5% of alcoholics ever experience DTs.

ALCOHOL-INDUCED PSYCHOTIC DISORDER, WITH HALLUCINATIONS (DSM-IV p 314, 291.3) displays striking auditory hallucinations (voices, sounds) and mixed other withdrawal symptoms (mild tremor, anger, apprehension) but the patient typically has a clear sensorium and is oriented. It usually occurs in the first 3 days after cessation of drinking in patients who have had years of heavy drinking. Patients may be dangerous or self-destructive while hallucinating. Usually self-limited (within 1 week), occasional cases last for months or become chronic. Differential includes alcoholic paranoia and toxic psychosis (amphetamine, cocaine). Differentiation from paranoid schizophrenia is difficult in chronic cases (look for other signs of schizophrenia).

## COMPLICATIONS OF CHRONIC ALCOHOLISM

Chronic alcoholics have numerous complicating diseases.

**Medical:** gastritis, gastric ulcer, diarrhea, anemia, hypertension, pancreatitis, cirrhosis (in less than 10% of alcoholics—alcohol plus poor diet), persistent impotence, insomnia. (NOTE: The majority of alcoholics die 15 years early, but not of these diseases—rather, they die of heart disease and cancer.)

### Neurological:

1. Peripheral neuropathy (vitamin B deficiencies)
2. Alcoholic cerebellar degeneration
3. Central pontine myelinolysis
4. Marchiafava-Bignami disease
5. Cerebral atrophy
6. Alcoholic myopathy and cardiomyopathy
7. Wernicke's encephalopathy (vertical and horizontal nystagmus, sixth nerve palsies, ataxia, and confusion)—due to thiamine deficiency (give 50 mg IV and 50 mg IM, then 50 mg IM daily until patient is eating). An emergency—if treated early, it usually quickly clears.

### Psychiatric:

1. ALCOHOL-INDUCED PERSISTING AMNESTIC DISORDER (Korsakoff's disease) (DSM-IV p 162, 291.1) is a profound recent short-term memory loss (retrograde and anterograde) with confabulation, which follows untreated Wernicke's encephalopathy or develops insidiously. Typically, events are remembered for several minutes (ie, immediate memory is OK) and then are forgotten. Due to thiamine deficiency—lesions in the mamillary bodies and thalamus. Treat as in Wernicke's disease. Impairment is often life-long, yet 75% improve with time.
2. ALCOHOL-INDUCED PERSISTING DEMENTIA (DSM-IV p 154, 291.2) refers to a dementia (ie, all intellectual functions affected), ranging from mild to severe, after many years of alcohol abuse and with no other obvious etiology. Few alcoholics are affected and the predisposition is unknown.
3. Suicide.

4. Drug abuse.
5. Accidents.

**Other:**

1. Fetal Alcohol Syndrome describes small, hyperactive, retarded children with variable anatomical abnormalities including ptosis, epicanthal folds, hypoplastic maxilla, cleft lip and palate, microcephaly, and hypospadias. Although not definite, it is thought to be due to a teratogenic effect on the fetus caused by alcohol consumed by the mother while pregnant. It is one of the most common causes of retardation.

## TREATMENT OF WITHDRAWAL

Treatment varies with the severity of the symptoms. When in doubt, hospitalize temporarily; however, many patients manifesting mild withdrawal symptoms can be treated in a supportive environment, with good nutrition, and without medication.

1. Be clear and unambiguous. Identify yourself. Explain procedures. Place patient in a lighted room. Include family and familiar people. Use restraints if needed. Keep under constant observation.
2. Carefully evaluate (PE, chest X-ray, chemistry, electrolytes including calcium and magnesium, CBC, CT, occult blood in stool, occasionally an LP). Incidence of complicating disorders is high, eg, pneumonia, TB, UTIs, hypoglycemia, diabetic ketoacidosis, anemia, shock, gastritis with hematemesis, acute hemorrhagic pancreatitis, cirrhosis and hepatic failure, meningitis. Be particularly careful to exclude (1) a subdural hematoma due to a fall and (2) withdrawal from other substances. Treat these conditions if present.
3. Use medication—to assure sleep, prevent exhaustion, reduce agitation. Sedate until calm (but avoid oversedation) then taper over 4–8 days (ie, decrease by approximately 20% of total first day's dose each day). The delirium often resolves within 1 day. Benzodiazepines currently are preferred—barbiturates, chloral hydrate, and carbamazepine may also be useful. Phenothiazines lower seizure threshold, but may be useful with chronic psychotics and alcoholic hallucinosis.
   Tremulousness: eg, chlordiazepoxide 25-50 mg PO (or diazepam, 10–20 mg), q4–6 hr until comfortable. Lorazepam (6-12 mg/day) may be a better choice in patients with liver disease or confusion.
   Delirium: eg, chlordiazepoxide 50-100 mg, PO or IM every hour until calm (able to stay in bed), then q4 hours. IM doses are often poorly absorbed—can lead to early undersedation, then cumulative oversedation. If patient is severe, give IV slowly.

Clonidine, a sympathetic inhibitor, may relieve sweating, tremor, and tachycardia, but doesn't prevent DTs. $\beta$-blockers (eg, atenolol, 50–100 mg/day) used with benzodiazepines may shorten the course.

4. If withdrawal seizures persist, consider 5–10 mg of diazepam slowly by IV or 100–150 mg of phenobarbital IM. If a primary seizure disorder exists, begin diphenylhydantoin.

5. Give thiamine 100 mg IM, then 50 mg PO tid × 4 days. Also provide a high carbohydrate diet and multivitamins daily (and for weeks/months).

6. Correct fluid and electrolyte imbalances—particularly hypokalemia (replace carefully over 24 hours or longer via IV) and significant hypomagnesemia (may exacerbate seizures—give magnesium sulfate 2–4 ml of 50% solution IM q6 hours x 2 days).

7. Record pulse, BP, and temp every half-hour initially. Treat shock with fluids, whole blood, and vasopressors.

8. Check for and treat: hypoglycemia, prolonged PT (give vitamin K 10 mg IM), fever (aspirin, sponge baths—rule out superimposed infection).

9. Anxiety, irritability, depression, and insomnia may persist for weeks after the acute episode—a vulnerable period for the alcoholic. Even serious depression may spontaneously resolve after several weeks of sobriety—don't over (or under) treat. Antianxiety agents may be of use for 1–2 weeks.

## TREATMENT OF ALCOHOLISM

Successful treatment of alcoholism is difficult but not hopeless. However, there is no definitive treatment: the majority of alcoholics who become abstinent do it in addition to treatment, not because of treatment (see George Vaillant's 50-year follow-up study of male alcoholics).

1. Identify its presence. Get your facts straight (family drinking history, recent intake).

2. Develop a personal rapport with the patient—be warm and supportive but firm. Be open and matter of fact about the drinking but insist on abstinence. Encourage patient to maintain employment and social involvement.

3. Treat all medical complications of drinking.

4. Treat any complicating primary psychiatric illness (eg, schizophrenia, affective disorder, anxiety disorder). If the patient is likely to drink, recognize that tricyclics potentiate the CNS depressant effect of alcohol and that alcohol can promote lithium toxicity.

5. Enlist family members in treatment. Evaluate family's contribution to the problem. Consider family therapy; marital therapy.

6. Lithium may help a few patients stay sober (unpredictable); there are more promising drugs on the way.

7. Consider disulfiram (Antabuse) use in cooperative but backsliding patients. It inhibits aldehyde dehydrogenase leading to toxic acetaldehyde buildup 15-30 minutes after alcohol consumption, which leads to anxiety and apprehension, sweating, nausea and vomiting, tachycardia, headache, and hypotension. Give 500 mg PO qd x 1 wk, then maintain on 250 mg daily (range 125-500 mg). Carefully inform patient of the possible reactions. Effects last up to 2 weeks after last dose; however, not every patient shows an Antabuse reaction. Occasional adverse effects include sedation, a metallic taste, mild GI disturbances, mild ataxia, and a peripheral neuropathy. Question its use in thoroughly irresponsible patients—hepatotoxicity and toxic psychoses can occur and severe reactions (to a large alcohol challenge) can lead to shock and coma. Contraindicated in patients with unstable medical conditions or histories of psychosis, OBS, MI, or heart failure. Biggest problem with disulfiram—patients stop taking it so they can drink.

8. Group therapy appears to be the most effective technique. In most cases, work with or refer patient to a specialized multidisciplinary treatment team. Make referral personally, with the patient present. AA (Alcoholics Anonymous) can help some (although it has a very high initial dropout rate)—encourage patient to give it a try. Also useful: Alanon (spouses of alcoholics). Hospitalize in an alcohol unit (milieu therapy) if even temporary sobriety cannot be achieved.

9. Be patient. Keep trying.

## Suggested Readings

Chick J, Gough K, Falkowski W, et al: Disulfiram treatment of alcoholism. Br J Psychiatry 161:84–89, 1992.

Cloninger CR: Neurogenetic adaptive mechanisms in alcoholism. Science 236:410–416, 1987.

Comings DE, Comings BG, Muhleman D, et al: The Dopamine $D_2$ receptor locus as a modifying gene in neuropsychiatric disorders. JAMA 266:1793–1800, 1991.

Ewing JA: Detecting alcoholism: The CAGE questionnaire. JAMA 252:1905–1907, 1984.

Gelernter J, O'Malley S, Risch N, et al: No association between an allele at the $D_2$ dopamine receptor gene (DRD2) and alcoholism. JAMA 266:1801–1807, 1991.

Holden C: Is alcoholism treatment effective? Science 236:20–22, 1987.

Holden C: Probing the complex genetics of alcoholism. Science 251:163–164, 1991.

Irwin M, Schuckit M, Smith TL: Clinical importance of age at onset in

Type 1 and Type 2 primary alcoholics. Arch Gen Psychiatry 47:320–324, 1990.

Kaufman E: The family of the alcoholic patient. Psychosomatics 27:347–360, 1986.

Kraus ML, et al: Randomized clinical trial of atenolol in patients with alcohol withdrawal. N Engl J Med 313:905,1985.

Litten RZ, Allen JP: Pharmacotherapies for alcoholism: Promising agents and clinical issues. Alcohol Clin Exp Res 15:620–633, 1991.

Malcolm R, Ballenger JC, Sturgis ET, et al: Double-blind controlled trial comparing carbamazepine to oxazepam treatment of alcohol withdrawal. Am J Psychiatry 146:617–621, 1989.

Mathew RJ, Wilson WH, Blazer DG, et al: Psychiatric disorders in adult children of alcoholics. Am J Psychiatry 150:793–800, 1993.

Pickens RW, Svikis DS, McGue M, et al: Heterogeneity in the inheritance of alcoholism. Arch Gen Psychiatry 48:19–28, 1991.

Powers JS, Spickard A: Michigan Alcoholism Screening Test to diagnose early alcoholism in a general practice. South Med J 77:852–856, 1984.

Reuler JB, Girard DE, Cooney TG: Wernicke's encephalopathy. N Engl J Med 312:1035–1040, 1985.

Rubino FA: Neurological complications of alcoholism. Psychiatr Clin North Am 15:359–372, 1992.

Schuckit MA, Gold E, Risch C: Plasma cortisol levels following ethanol in sons of alcoholics and controls. Arch Gen Psychiatry 44:942–945, 1987.

Schuckit MA, Smith TL, Anthenelli R, et al: Clinical course of alcoholism in 636 male inpatients. Am J Psychiatry 150:786–792, 1993.

Sellers E, Naranjo C: New strategies for the treatment of alcohol withdrawal. Psychopharmacol Bull 22:88–92, 1986.

Streissguth AP, Aase JM, Clarren SK, et al: Fetal alcohol syndrome in adolescents and adults. JAMA 265:1961–1967, 1991.

Swartz CM, Drews V, Cadoret R: Decreased epinephrine in familial alcoholism. Arch Gen Psychiatry 44:938–941, 1987.

Tabakoff B, Hoffman PL, Lee JM, et al: Differences in platelet enzyme activity between alcoholics and nonalcoholics. N Engl J Med 318:134–139, 1988.

Whitfield C, et al: Detoxification of 1,024 alcoholic patients without psychoactive drugs. JAMA 239:1049–1053, 1978.

Wilson A, Blanchard R, Davidson W, McRae L, Maini K: Disulfiram implantation: a dose response trial. J Clin Psychiatry 45:242–247, 1984.

# Chapter 17

# Psychiatry of Drug Abuse

Drug abusers are common (6% lifetime prevalence in the US), often unrecognized, and poorly understood. There is great variability in the degree of drug use from patient to patient; multiple drug use is common. Abuse occurs if the patient (1) uses drugs in a dangerous, self-defeating, self-destructive way, (2) has difficulty controlling his use even though the use is sporadic, and (3) has impaired social and/or occupational functioning because of that use, all within a 1-year period. Drug dependence requires the presence of tolerance, withdrawal, and/or continuous, compulsive use over a 1-year period. Patients may be classified by the type of drug abused (see below) or by the pattern and reason for abuse. Some recognized patterns of use (abuse) include:

— Recreational use—Patient takes drugs for "fun" and is not physically or psychologically dependent upon them. He may also take them "just to be part of the group" or because it is a countercultural requirement. This often fades into compulsive use, with time.

— Iatrogenic addiction—Patient addicted "by mistake." Patient (and physician) may or may not recognize the addiction. Many of these patients are convinced that they must have the drug to function (eg, to sleep, to interact with others) and may go to great lengths to talk their physicians into prescribing medication.

— The chronic drug addict—These patients usually abuse "street" drugs. Many have underlying depressions. Many have antisocial personalities. Some take drugs in an effort to self-medicate a chronic psychiatric disorder (eg, major depression, schizophrenia).

Abusers are not "all alike," but they do have many common features, including the frequent presence of marked depression and anxiety, increased dependency needs (often hidden), low self-esteem, a familial association (genetic?) with antisocial personality disorder and alcoholism, a disrupted family life, and a chronic course resistant to treatment. Drug use to "self-medicate" in specific psychiatric illnesses (anxiety, depression, panic disorder, schizophrenia) accounts for some abuse.

Treatment of chronic drug abusers is difficult—frequently an inpatient setting is required. Whether inpatients or outpatients, drug abusers should be treated firmly but with support and understanding. Set clear limits and stick to them. Insist on dealing with the patient only when he is not intoxicated. Be reasonably confrontative. You will be tested and manipulated by many patients—don't respond with retribution. Follow many of the principles used in dealing with the alcoholic patient (see Chapter 16).

The most common drugs of abuse, their clinical presentations, and treatment follow. Abusers of multiple drugs are common.

## OPIOIDS

### Drugs Involved

opium
morphine
diacetylmorphine (Heroin, horse, smack)
methadone
codeine
oxycodone (eg, Percodan, in mixture)
hydromorphone (Dilaudid)
levorphanol (Levo-Dromoran)
pentazocine (Talwin)
meperidine (Demerol)
propoxyphene (Darvon)

Some of these compounds are naturally occurring (opium and its constituents morphine and codeine) while the others are semi-synthetic or wholly synthetic. Some of these drugs have legitimate uses (eg, morphine, meperidine) while others are solely substances of abuse (eg, heroin). Most are obtained illegally "on the street" and are used primarily by a young, lower socioeconomic population while others are abused more widely (eg, Demerol, Dilaudid, and Percodan are common drugs of abuse among professionals). Common routes of administration are IV (heroin, morphine, methadone—"mainlining"), SC (heroin, meperidine—"skin popping"), nasally (heroin, cocaine—"snorting"), orally (methadone, Percodan), and smoked (opium). It is frequently very difficult to determine the daily dose used because (1) the abuser often overestimates the dose and (2) the amount of active drug in a "bag" bought on the street is uncertain. Frequently a bag of heroin is 95% adulterants (eg, quinine, mannitol, lactose).

Abuse (OPIOID ABUSE, DSM-IV p 249, 305.50) and dependency (OPIOID DEPENDENCE, DSM-IV p 248, 304.00) are common in some populations, and the search for drugs or money for drugs accounts for the majority of the crime in some communities. Some people (less than 50%) are able to abuse opioids without becoming dependent (ie, without tolerance and/or withdrawal), and they often use them recreationally without addiction. Those persons who become dependent represent a high risk group.

— 1%[+] of all heroin addicts in the US die each year. The most common cause is an inadvertently fatal OD, eg, an addict using "bags" of 5% heroin accidentally buys a supply containing 15% heroin. Also common is death during violent crime or, increasingly, due to AIDS.
— 25%[+] of addicts have a personality disorder—usually antisocial type. They also have a high incidence of depression and anxiety. Suicide rate is elevated.
— Heroin addicts are at a markedly increased risk (due to dirty needles, poor nutrition, etc.) for developing certain medical illnesses.

AIDS, but also

Hepatitis, serum and infectious
Subacute bacterial endocarditis
Tetanus
Pneumonia; pulmonary edema, embolus, abscess; TB
Cellulitis, thrombophlebitis, septicemia
UTIs, glomerulonephritis, nephrosis
Osteomyelitis
Transverse myelitis
Polyneuropathy (Guillain Barre = P type)
VD

Nasal septum perforation (due to "snorting")
Needle "tracts" on the arms (and legs)

Always carefully evaluate hospitalized addicts medically. Recognize that the analgesic properties of the opioids may obscure acute medical problems. The majority of addicts "grow out of" their habit over the years (or die), thus there are relatively few older abusers.

Treatment of the opioid addict usually means treatment of the acute episodes (eg, intoxication and withdrawal—see below). "Cure" of the addiction does occur in some well-motivated patients, yet most addicts continue their abuse over at least several years. The two major forms of long-term treatment (both with equivocal results) are:

1. Methadone Maintenance—Patients are maintained as outpatients on daily doses of methadone of 40–120 mg. This level controls the craving for (and eliminates the euphoria from) heroin. The patient can then develop some skills, hold a job, go to school, etc.: psychotherapy can help some, but treatment demands careful limit setting. Moderately motivated patients may succeed by this route. LAAM, a chemical congener of methadone (levomethadyl acetate), has recently found use as a long-acting replacement for methadone (patient takes it $3\times$/wk). Unfortunately, many of these patients continue to abuse other drugs while taking methadone (cocaine and "crack" are common).

2. Residential, drug-free, self-help programs—Patients (usually highly motivated) stay 1-2 years (or more) in a close "therapeutic community" which insists on the drug-free state and on personal responsibility. Confrontation and behavior modification are frequently used. Poor "candidates" usually drop out.

The two major features of illicit opioid use which bring patients to medical attention are intoxication (and overdosage) and withdrawal.

**OPIOID INTOXICATION** (DSM-IV p 249, 292.89): It develops rapidly after an IV dose (1-5 min). The time course varies with the drug used (see Table 17.1).

The abstinence syndrome begins after this period of time in the dependent patient. It is because of these kinetics that many heroin addicts "shoot up" 3–4 $\times$/day, or more.

Symptoms are similar for most of the narcotics.

Psychological symptoms—a "rush" immediately follows IV administration (described as a "whole body orgasm" with the

**Table 17.1**
**Time Course for Opioid Intoxication**

| Drug | Duration of action (hr) |
| --- | --- |
| heroin | 4–6 |
| methadone | 12–24 |
| meperidine | 2–4 |

focus in the abdomen). This is accompanied by euphoria and a sense of well-being or dysphoria (usually anxiety and fear), a drowsiness and "nodding off," apathy, psychomotor retardation, and difficulty concentrating.

Physical symptoms—miosis (pupillary constriction), slurred speech, respiratory depression, hypotension, hypothermia, bradycardia, constipation, and nausea and vomiting. Skin ulcers are common with meperidine injection. Seizures may occur in the patient tolerant to meperidine.

An overdose (either accidental or intentional) is a medical emergency—these patients may die of respiratory depression and pulmonary edema. Look for needle tracts and pinpoint pupils in the unconscious patient but recognize that if the patient already has experienced significant CNS anoxia, the pupils may be dilated. Seizures occasionally occur (particularly with meperidine).

Treat the OD with intensive medical care (ICU) and the narcotic antagonist naloxone (Narcan). Give 0.4 mg IV and repeat 5 times at 3-min intervals. Expect a rapid response (ie, clearing in 1-2 min), and if this doesn't occur after four doses, suspect another etiology for the coma. If the patient improves, continue monitoring—patient may need additional doses of naloxone since it has a much shorter half-life than either heroin or methadone. Excessive naloxone may throw a dependent patient directly from coma into withdrawal—don't be confused. Multiple drugs may have been taken—be alert to the possibility of a more slowly developing coma from a second agent.

**OPIOID WITHDRAWAL** (DSM-IV 251, 392.0): Despite its reputation as a dramatic and traumatic withdrawal syndrome, opioid withdrawal is uncomfortable but usually not life threatening in healthy young adults and is not nearly as dangerous or difficult to manage as the withdrawal from sedative hypnotic drugs.

Symptoms are similar for each of the narcotics, but the time course varies (dependent partly on the "size of the habit") (see Table 17.2).

Psychological symptoms—Early there is often intense drug craving followed by severe anxiety, restlessness, irritability, insomnia, and decreased appetite. In this state, the hospitalized patient is frequently extremely demanding and manipulative.

Physical symptoms—Yawning, diaphoresis, tearing, rhinorrhea, pupillary dilation, piloerection (hard to "fake" so look for it), muscle twitching, and hot flashes. Later·there is nausea and vomiting, fever, hypertension, tachycardia, tachypnea, diarrhea, and abdominal cramps. Seizures occur with meperidine withdrawal.

Babies born to addicted mothers, including those on methadone maintenance, often experience an abstinence syndrome, including a high-pitched cry, irritability, tremor, fever, decreased food intake, vomiting, yawning, and hyperbilirubinemia.

Withdraw these patients gradually by using oral methadone to lessen the symptom severity. After a complete history and physical (including urine screen for opioids and other drugs), wait for signs of withdrawal and then give methadone 10 mg PO. Establish the stabilization dose over the first 12 days by adding 5-10 mg of methadone on a qid schedule as the patient continues to show signs of abstinence (recognize that some patients will vigorously demand more drugs even while they are sedated by their current dose). Once stabilized, give the methadone on a qd or bid schedule and reduce the total daily

**Table 17.2**
**Time Course for Opioid Withdrawal**

| Drug | Time after last dose that symptoms begin | Symptoms peak | Symptoms disappear |
|------|------------------------------------------|---------------|--------------------|
| heroin | 4–8 hr | 1–3 days | 7–10 days |
| methadone | 12–48 hr | 4–6 days | 10–21 days |
| meperidine | 2–4 hr | 8–12 hr | 4–5 days |

amount by 5 mg/day (or 10–20% of the stabilization dose). Most withdrawals from heroin addiction take 7–10 days—methadone addiction withdrawals should be done more slowly (eg, 2–3 weeks). Alternate methods of opiate withdrawal using clonidine (Catapres) or LAAM have recently been developed which show evidence of being safer and more effective than methadone withdrawal. Withdraw patients from Talwin using decreasing doses of the drug.

If a patient is withdrawing from both opioids and sedative hypnotics (not uncommon), concentrate on a safe sedative-hypnotic withdrawal by maintaining the patient on 10–30 mg of methadone until the first withdrawal has been completed.

## SEDATIVE HYPNOTICS

The minimum dependency-producing dose listed in Table 17.3 should be considered only approximate (for some patients the addictive dose is much lower)—there are individual differences as well as a required period of continuous administration (usually at least 1–3 months) before withdrawal symptoms occur. Oral use is the rule. Street synonyms for some of the sedative-

**Table 17.3
Dependency-Producing Dose for
Sedative-Hypnotics**

| Drug | Dose (mg/day) |
| --- | --- |
| meprobamate (Equanil, Miltown) | 1600 |
| methaqualone (Quaalude, Sopor) | 600 |
| glutethimide (Doriden) | 250 |
| ethchlorvynol (Placidyl) | 1000 |
| chloral hydrate (Noctec) | 600 |
| secobarbital (Seconal) | 600 |
| pentobarbital (Nembutal) | 600 |
| amobarbital (Amytal) | 300 |
| chlordiazepoxide (Librium) | 200 |
| diazepam (Valium) | 40 |
| | |
| oxazepam (Serax) | |
| flurazepam (Dalmane) | |
| methyprylon (Noludar) | |
| phenobarbital (luminal) | |

hypnotics include downers, reds, blues, blue velvet, yellows, yellow jackets, sopers, ludes.

## Clinical Syndromes

The same variety of syndromes occurs with sedative-hypnotic use as occurs with alcohol. There is cross-tolerance between alcohol and the sedative-hypnotics as well as among the various drugs themselves. The clinical picture varies little from drug to drug although withdrawal phenomena are more severe with the shorter acting drugs and more prolonged with those that have a longer half-life.

**SEDATIVE, HYPNOTIC, OR ANXIOLYTIC INTOXICATION** (DSM-IV p 263, 292.89): Symptoms of intoxication are dose related. Mild intoxication includes a sense of well-being, talkativeness, irritability, and emotional disinhibition. Increased doses produce apathy, confusion, stupor, and coma. Physical signs of intoxication include slurred speech, ataxic gait, incoordination, reduced DTRs, lateral nystagmus, and constricted pupils. Look for fast activity on the EEG. Fatalities are frequent with sedative-hypnotic ODs, usually due to respiratory depression (uncommon with the benzodiazepines).

Always evaluate sedative-hypnotic-abusing patients who present with intoxication for an overt or covert OD. If they are becoming increasingly lethargic, treat as a medical emergency with hospitalization and intensive medical care. Obtain blood and/or urine levels.

**SEDATIVE, HYPNOTIC, OR ANXIOLYTIC ABUSE** (DSM-IV p 263, 305.40): This condition results from the pathological use of one or more of this class of drugs for more than 1 month. These patients frequently can't abstain from use, once started—a psychological addiction. Abuse of sedative-hypnotics is common and, unlike other substances of abuse, there are two distinct populations and patterns of abuse.

1. Males and females in their teens or 20s who obtain these drugs illegally and use them (as well as many other kinds) for "fun" and to get "high" or to block things out and "get away from the hassle."
2. Middle-aged females who are frequently chronically anxious or depressed and who obtain legal prescriptions from (one or more) physicians for complaints of anxiety and insomnia, gradually increase

the dosage themselves in an effort to cope, and often become physiologically addicted. Although these patients are common, they are disproportionately frequently seen by physicians because they ultimately have to "doctor shop" to obtain drugs. Recognize them. Recognize also that these patients frequently vigorously deny their illness both to their physicians and, sometimes, to themselves.

Without exception, if the patient takes enough drug long enough, he will develop tolerance to it and/or signs of physiological withdrawal when it is stopped; ie, SEDATIVE, HYPNOTIC, OR ANXIOLYTIC DEPENDENCE (DSM-IV p 262, 304.10). Some evidence suggests that there is a familial pattern to the abuse of these substances (eg, family members also abuse sedative-hypnotics and alcohol).

SEDATIVE, HYPNOTIC, OR ANXIOLYTIC WITHDRAWAL (DSM-IV p 264, 292.0): This is the most dangerous of the drug withdrawal syndromes and can occur both in the dependent person who abstains and also in the person who merely reduces his dose. Its severity depends upon the particular drug abused, the duration of use, and daily dose used (degree of tolerance). Keep a high index of suspicion. Recognize it (1) by a history of significant drug use (often denied by the patient), (2) by characteristic abstinence symptoms (see below), and (3) by a tolerance test.

**Withdrawal Symptoms**

Psychological: A subjective sense of severe anxiety, restlessness, apprehension, irritability, insomnia, and anorexia which has developed gradually over the past 24 hours (1–3 days with the longer acting sedative-hypnotics) and is worsening hour by hour. Delirium may occur (SEDATIVE, HYPNOTIC, OR ANXIOLYTIC WITHDRAWAL DELIRIUM, DSM-IV p 131, 292.81) with visual hallucinations and formication (sense of insects crawling on the skin).

Physical: Tremulousness (coarse tremor—primarily the upper extremities), weakness, nausea and vomiting, orthostatic hypotension, tachycardia, hyperreflexia, diaphoresis. After several days this may progress to delirium, hyperpyrexia, and coma. Seizures may occur (typically after 2–5 days)—usually generalized and single or a short series, but occasionally status epilepticus.

**Tolerance Test**

There are several methods of determining the degree of dependence (and thus the probable severity and length of withdrawal). One method is given below. It can be used regardless of the particular sedative-hypnotic drug of abuse (ie, they are all cross-tolerant).

1. Hospitalize the patient for the test if possible.
2. Administer test to a patient who is comfortable or only mildly anxious (not to a patient who is intoxicated or presently withdrawing—test would be invalid).
3. Give 200 mg of pentobarbital orally.
4. At 1 hour, evaluate the patient. If he is:
   a. asleep but arousable—patient has no tolerance.
   b. grossly ataxic, coarse tremor, and nystagmus—daily tolerance is 400–500 mg of pentobarbital.
   c. mildly ataxic, mild nystagmus—daily tolerance is 600 mg.
   d. comfortable, slight lateral nystagmus—daily tolerance is 800 mg.
   e. asymptomatic or has continuing signs of mild withdrawal—daily tolerance is 1000 mg, or more. Wait 3–4 hours, then give an oral dose of 300 mg of pentobarbital. Failure to become symptomatic at this larger dose suggests a daily tolerance of more than 1600 mg.

Treat withdrawal vigorously and carefully. Usually hospitalize unless the addiction is mild and the patient reliable. Evaluate for medical illness. Withdrawal can be accomplished safely using several different sedative-hypnotics although the most commonly used are pentobarbital, diazepam, and phenobarbital.

To withdraw with pentobarbital, give the estimated daily tolerance dose (obtained either by reliable history of all cross tolerant drugs and alcohol used or by a tolerance test) equally divided on a Q6 hr schedule for the first and second days and then reduce 10% of the initial dose each day. Expect the patient to be somewhat uncomfortable but, if signs of serious withdrawal (or intoxication) appear, slow (or quicken) the decrease slightly. If the patient is showing serious withdrawal symptoms before treatment, give enough pentobarbital over several hours to make him comfortable, then begin the withdrawal procedure.

**SEDATIVE, HYPNOTIC, OR ANXIOLYTIC-INDUCED PERSISTING AMNESTIC DISORDER** (DSM-IV p 162, 292.83): This profound, short-term, anterograde and retrograde memory loss after extensive sedative-hypnotic use is usually reversible unlike Korsakoff's syndrome from alcohol-induced thiamine deficiency.

## HALLUCINOGENS

### Drugs Involved

lysergic acid diethylamide (LSD-25, acid)
dimethyltryptamine (DMT)
trimethoxyamphetamine (TMA)
psilocybin
mescaline (peyote, tops, cactus)
phencyclidine (PCP, angel dust, hog)
thiocyclidine (TCP)
ketamine (Ketalar)
cannabis (marijuana, hashish, pot, weed, grass, reefer)
delta-9-tetrahydrocannabinol (THC)

### LSD, Mescaline, and Others

Patients take these drugs orally, develop symptoms in 10–45 minutes, and are back to normal in several hours (eg, LSD) to 12 days. New synthetic drugs, with different characteristics, are created and "hit the streets" regularly, in both this class and among the stimulants: the world of designer drugs. The typical consequence of ingestion (HALLUCINOGEN INTOXICATION; DSM-IV p 232, 292.89) is:

Psychological symptoms—Marked perceptual distortions (changing object shapes, changing body image), illusions and hallucinations (mostly visual geometric designs, but also auditory and tactile), depersonalization, derealization, and synesthesias (stimuli in one modality produce sensations in another, eg, sounds become colors)—all occurring in a clear sensorium. The patient is usually aware that what he is experiencing is due to drugs (ie, has insight—unlike the patient with amphetamine psychosis). Occasionally the patient experiences strong depressive or anxious feelings (eg, panic—a "bad trip"), but more typically the mood is euphoric and the patient feels he is receiving profound, staggering insights.

Physical symptoms—Tachycardia, palpitations, diaphoresis, pupillary dilation (responsive to light), blurred vision, tremor, incoordination, hyperreflexia, hyperthermia, piloerection.

The psychological symptoms are particularly sensitive to the "set" or expectations of the patient prior to drug usage. Occasionally the patient will experience brief hallucinations weeks, months, or even years after the period of drug use: HALLUCINOGEN PERSISTING PERCEPTION DISORDER; DSM-IV p 234, 292.89 (flashbacks). Flashback experiences may be continued for years, even in the absence of additional LSD usage, if marijuana is used regularly. Although primarily used as recreational drugs, a few patients disrupt their lives with drug use (HALLUCINOGEN ABUSE, DSM-IV p 231, 305.30). There are no withdrawal symptoms, although slight tolerance does develop.

Two clinical syndromes that may (infrequently) follow the use of these drugs by one or more days are:

**HALLUCINOGEN-INDUCED PSYCHOTIC DISORDER, WITH DELUSIONS** (DSM-IV p 314, 292.11) Delusions that occur with drug use may persist for a variable length of time after the drug is out of the body.

**HALLUCINOGEN-INDUCED MOOD DISORDER** (DSM-IV p 375, 292.84) A persistence of a dysphoric mood (usually depression or anxiety) for days, weeks, or longer after taking the drug. The presentation may be identical to or gradually develop into a major mood disorder.

Treatment for "bad trips" usually consists of support ("talking down"): patient usually clears within hours. Benzodiazepines and phenothiazines may be used (eg, diazepam 10–15 mg; haloperidol 4–5 mg).

### Phencyclidine (PCP)

PCP abuse (PHENCYCLIDINE ABUSE, DSM-IV p 257, 305.90; PCP DEPENDENCE, 304.90) is most common among youth. It is eaten, smoked, or taken IV. Symptoms begin in 2–60 minutes, depending on the route of administration.

Psychological symptoms—Low doses produce euphoria, grandiosity, a feeling of "numbness," and emotional lability. Higher doses cause symptoms that range from perceptual distortions, anxiety, excitation, confusion, and synesthesias to a paranoid psychosis, rigidity, and a catatonic-like state to convulsions, coma, and death. Violent (and self-destructive) behavior is common when intoxicated.

Physical symptoms—Tachycardia, hypertension, vertical and horizontal nystagmus, ataxia, dysarthria, myoclonus, decreased pain sensitivity, diaphoresis, seizures.

The patient usually clears in 3–6 hr. The symptom picture can be quite variable and can include a delirium usually lasting several days but which may last weeks or longer (PHENCYCLIDINE INTOXICATION DELIRIUM, DSM-IV p 131, 292.81), delusions (PCP-INDUCED PSYCHOTIC DISORDER, WITH DELUSIONS, 292.11), or a varying organic mood disorder (PCP-INDUCED MOOD DISORDER, 292.84). Long-term organic symptoms may occur (memory loss, word-finding difficulty). Diagnosis is based on the clinical picture, a history of PCP use, the presence of PCP in urine, and (possibly) hair analysis. Chronic, unadmitted PCP use can easily be misdiagnosed as "atypical psychosis," so be wary.

Treatment is controversial. ODs can be fatal. Hospitalize and use gastric suction, urine acidification, and symptomatic medical maintenance. If agitation must be controlled, use haloperidol (perhaps combined with ascorbic acid). Decrease external stimulation.

### Cannabis

The active ingredient of cannabis is delta-9-tetrahydrocannabinol (THC). The various forms (eg, marijuana, hashish) are all either smoked or eaten, and the differences in the effects they produce depend primarily on their concentrations of THC. Cannabis is used widely and usually produces mild physical and psychological alterations (CANNABIS INTOXICATION, DSM-IV p 218, 292.89) which occur shortly after intake and last 2–4 hr.

Psychological symptoms—The primary effect is a sense of well-being, mild euphoria, and relaxation. Mild alterations and intensifications of perceptions occur (greater with the more concentrated forms), as does a sense of indifference and slowed time. A few persons find the use of cannabis dysphoric and develop depression, anxiety, panic, or even a delusional syndrome (usually paranoid, often with depersonalization) (CANNABIS-INDUCED PSYCHOTIC DISORDER, WITH DELUSIONS (p 314, 292.11)). Impaired psychomotor performance and recent memory during and shortly after use are common (expected).

Physical symptoms—Tachycardia, conjunctival injection, dry mouth, increased appetite.

Toxic psychoses have been reported with high dose use. Some persons are socially and occupationally handicapped by chronic drug use (look for morning hangover) (CANNABIS ABUSE, DSM-IV p 217, 305.20). These patients are frequently apathetic and "amotivational," but this may be more a reflection of their personality structure than an effect of cannabis. If there is also a significant degree of tolerance, the patient has CANNABIS DEPENDENCE (DSM-IV p 216, 304.30).

Treat "bad trips" with support. Surreptitious use of marijuana can be detected by a urine screen for delta-9-THC-11-oic acid (THCA) up to several weeks after use.

## STIMULANTS

### Drugs Involved

amphetamine (Benzedrine)
dextroamphetamine (Dexedrine)
methamphetamine (Methedrine, "speed," "ice")
2,5-dimethoxy-4-methylamphetamine (DOM, STP)
3,4-methylenedioxymethamphetamine (MDMA, ecstasy, Adam)
phenmetrazine (Preludin)
cocaine (including "crack")

These are effective orally (except cocaine) and nasally (cocaine), but produce a more rapid and intense effect by smoking (cocaine ("crack"); crystal methamphetamine ("ice")) and IV (an orgasm-like "rush"). Street terms for amphetamines include speed, bennies, uppers, diet pills, crystal, double crosses, and ice; for cocaine include coke, snow, and crack (rock); and "speedball" for amphetamine or cocaine with an opioid. Crack, the alkaloidal, freebase form of cocaine HCl, is inexpensive, widely available, and extremely addicting. Use of a new, smokable form of methamphetamine (ice) which produces a crack-like effect is spreading.

## Clinical Syndromes

The effects of AMPHETAMINE INTOXICATION (DSM-IV p 207, 292.89) and COCAINE INTOXICATION (DSM-IV p 224, 292.89) occur within minutes (depending on route) and consist of:

Psychological symptoms—Hyperalertness, restlessness, psychomotor agitation, pacing, talkativeness and pressure of speech, sense of well-being, elation. Frequently aggressiveness, violent behavior, and poor judgment occur as well.

Physical symptoms—Tachycardia, hypertension, pupillary dilation, chills and diaphoresis, anorexia, nausea and vomiting, insomnia. Occasionally there are stereotyped repetitive movements (eg, endlessly taking something apart and then reassembling it).

With brief use, symptoms usually disappear within hours of stopping the drug. All these symptoms may disappear as tolerance develops.

If drug use becomes a consuming pattern that lasts for at least 1 month and that interferes with social and occupational functioning, the patient has AMPHETAMINE ABUSE (DSM-IV p 206, 305.70) or COCAINE ABUSE (DSM-IV p 223, 305.60). Abuse usually develops over months and may include a pattern of "runs" of frequent, large-dose IV administration over days or weeks. After a run, the person frequently sleeps for 12–18 hr, then may begin another run. High dose use places the patient at risk for developing:

**AMPHETAMINE DEPENDENCE** (DSM-IV p 206, 304.40) —ie, tolerance and/or withdrawal present.

**AMPHETAMINE INTOXICATION DELIRIUM** (DSM-IV p 131, 292.81)—A characteristic organic delirium (see Chapter 5) develops shortly after taking the drug and disappears as the blood level drops. Violence is common during these episodes.

**AMPHETAMINE-INDUCED PSYCHOTIC DISORDER, WITH DELUSIONS** (DSM-IV p 314, 292.11) Patient becomes markedly paranoid and develops persecutory delusions within a setting of clear consciousness, often accompanied by hostility, anxiety, ideas of reference, and psychomotor agitation. This condition may last for one week or longer than 1 year. It easily can be mistaken for paranoid schizophrenia, which it closely resembles.

**AMPHETAMINE WITHDRAWAL** (DSM-IV p 208, 292.0)— Cessation of drug in heavy user may be followed by mild to severe depression (watch for suicide), profound fatigue, irritability, anxiety, fearfulness, nightmares, and insomnia or hypersomnia. Severe symptoms seldom last more than 1 week but may be followed by chronic low-level depression and/or anxiety. Abnormal EEG patterns may last for weeks.

Cocaine produces similar syndromes. Serious medical complications occur with cocaine (and particularly crack): MI ($2°$ to coronary artery constriction) and anoxia $2°$ to seizures can be fatal. Depression, paranoia and paranoid psychosis, marked anxiety, malnutrition, and pneumonia may follow use. Crack, when smoked, typically produces a high within seconds, followed by a dysphoric crash several minutes later—leading to rapidly repeated administrations and addiction. It is a very bad drug. "Ice" is smoked similarly but produces a high lasting for hours—will it become the new crack?

Make the diagnosis by the clinical picture and history of drug use. Most sympathomimetics and cocaine can be identified by a urine drug screen (cocaine is difficult—check with your lab).

## Treatment

Stop the drug. If the patient is mildly or moderately excited, try to "talk him down" and use benzodiazepines (eg, diazepam 10–20 mg PO). The patient may be agitated and violent—take appropriate precautions (eg, restraints). Treat severe intoxication, delirium, and delusional symptoms with an antipsychotic (eg, haloperidol 10 mg PO or 5–10 mg IM). Acidify the urine with ascorbic acid or ammonium chloride (maintain pH at 4–5). Be alert to potential suicide and to medical complications (eg, MI, stroke, intracranial hemorrhage). Severe withdrawal depressions may respond to antidepressants.

Cure is difficult. Consider hospitalization if symptoms or habit are severe or if life is severely disrupted. Group therapy (in or outpatient) should be tried at some point. Desipramine (200–250 mg/day), bupropion, or amantadine (Symmetrel 200–300 mg/day) may (?) decrease cocaine withdrawal cravings in a few, particularly depressed patients, yet neither meds nor

formal psychotherapy has demonstrated prolonged effective
ness.

## INHALANTS

The types of glues, solvents, and cleaners "sniffed" for their psychic effects are numerous and include gasoline, kerosene, plas-
tic and rubber cements, airplane and household glues, paints,
lacquers, enamels, paint thinners, solvents, aerosols, furniture
polishes, fingernail polish removers, nitrous oxide, cleaning
fluids, etc. Several active constituents are probably involved in
most substances. This is a major abuse problem, particularly
among late latency and early to middle adolescent children,
and particularly among lower socioeconomic groups. This is often a group activity.

The effects from this variety of substance are usually quite
similar—typically mild euphoria, confusion, disorientation, impulsivity, and ataxia—all of which may progress to a toxic psychosis, seizures, and coma (INHALANT INTOXICATION;
DSM-IV p 239, 292.89). Repeated and chronic abuse is common
(INHALANT ABUSE; DSM-IV p 238, 305.90), but withdrawal
symptoms have not been noticed. Death has occurred from as-
phyxiation, aspiration, cardiac arrhythmias, and kidney, liver,
and bone marrow damage. An acute brain syndrome (delirium)
typically occurs but only in the unusual or very severe case does
the patient appear to develop a degree of chronic CNS damage.

Physical restraint and medical support may be needed in
the acute situation, but the patient usually clears over hours or
days. Evaluate carefully for liver, kidney, and pulmonary damage. Encourage these children (and a few adults) and their families to enter therapy.

## ANABOLIC STEROIDS

Not a problem in the "normal" doses used by patients with conditions like hypogonadism, anabolic steroids (most commonly
testosterone and nandrolone) used in massive doses by athletes
produce euphoria, irritability, and aggressiveness on use and
depression on withdrawal. Approximately 25% of persons using
supraphysiologic doses develop a major mood disorder at some
point; a few become dangerously aggressive.

## Suggested Readings

Carroll KM, Rounsaville BJ, Gordon LT, et al: Psychotherapy and pharmacotherapy for ambulatory cocaine abusers. Arch Gen Psychiatry 51:177–187, 1994.

Chait LD, Zacny JP: Reinforcing and subjective effects of oral delta-9-THC and smoked marijuana in humans. Psychopharmacology 107:255–262, 1992.

Charney DS, Heninger GR, Kleber HD: The combined use of clonidine and naltrexone as a rapid, safe, and effective treatment of abrupt withdrawal from methadone. Am J Psychiatry 143:831–837, 1986.

Cregler LL, Mark H: Medical complications of cocaine abuse. N Engl J Med 315:1495–1500, 1986.

Dinwiddie SH, Zorumski CF, Rubin EH: Psychiatric correlates of chronic solvent abuse. J Clin Psychiatry 48:334–337, 1987.

Evans AC, Raistrick D: Phenomenology of intoxication with toluene-based adhesives and butane gas. Br J Psychiatry 150:769–773, 1987.

Evans AC, Raistrick D: Patterns of use and related harm with toluene-based adhesives and butane gas. Br J Psychiatry 150:773–776, 1987.

Gawin FH: Cocaine addiction: Psychology and neurophysiology. Science 251:1580–1586, 1991.

Giannini AJ, Loiselle RH, DiMarzio LR, Giannini MC: Augmentation of haloperidol by ascorbic acid in phencyclidine intoxication. Am J Psychiatry 144:1207–1209, 1987.

Higgins ST, Budney AJ, Bickel WK, et al: Achieving cocaine abstinence with a behavior approach. Am J Psychiatry 150:763–769, 1993.

Hong R, Matsuyama E, Nur K: Cardiomyopathy associated with the smoking of crystal methamphetamine. JAMA 265:1152–1154, 1991.

Judson BA, Goldstein A, Inturrisi CE: Methadyl acetate (LAAM) in the treatment of heroin addicts. Arch Gen Psychiatry 40:834–840, 1983.

Kang SK, Kleinman PH, Woody GE, et al: Outcomes for cocaine abusers after once-a-week psychosocial therapy. Am J Psychiatry 148:630–635, 1991.

Khantzian EJ: The self–medication hypothesis of addictive disorders. Am J Psychiatry 142:1259–1264, 1985.

Liester MB, Grob CS, Bravo GL, et al: Phenomenology and sequelae of 3,4-methylenedioxymethamphetamine use. J Nerv Ment Dis 180:345–352, 1992.

O'Brien CP, Woody GE, McLellan AT: Psychiatric disorders in opioid-dependent patients. J Clin Psychiatry 45:9–13, 1984.

Peroutka SJ: Ecstasy: The Clinical, Pharmacological and Neurotoxicological Effects. Dordrecht, The Netherlands, Kluwer Academic, 1989.

Pope HG, Katz DL: Psychiatric and medical effects of anabolic androgenic steroid use. Arch Gen Psychiatry 51:375–382, 1994.

Ragan FA, Hite SA, Samuels MS, et al: Extended EMIT-DAU phencyclidine screen. J Clin Psychiat 47:194–195, 1986.

Satel SL, Southwick SM, Gawin FH: Clinical features of cocaine induced paranoia. Am J Psychiatry 148:495–498, 1991.

Schnoll SH, Daghestani AN: Treatment of marijuana abuse. Psychiatr Ann 16:249–254, 1986.

Sramek JJ, Baumgartner WA, Tallos JA, et al: Hair analysis for detection of phencyclidine in newly admitted psychiatric patients. Am J Psychiatry 142:950–953, 1985.

Sujata U, Gossop M, Strang J: Factors associated with relapse among opiate addicts in an outpatient detoxification programme. Br J Psychiatry 161:654–657, 1992.

Tennant FS: The clinical syndrome of marijuana dependence. Psychiatr Ann 16:225–234, 1986.

Thomas SH: Psychiatric symptoms in cannabis users. Br J Psychiatry 163:141–149, 1993.

Verebey K, Gold MS, Mule SJ: Laboratory testing in the diagnosis of marijuana intoxication and withdrawal. Psychiatr Ann 16:235 241, 1986.

Westermeyer J: The psychiatrist and solvent-inhalant abuse. Am J Psychiatry 144:903–907, 1987.

Woody GE, McLellan AT, Luborsky L, O'Brien CP: Twelve-month followup of psychotherapy for opiate dependence. Am J Psychiatry 144:590–596, 1987.

Yesavage JA, Leirer VO, Denari M, Hollister LE: Carryover effects of marijuana intoxication on aircraft pilot performance. Am J Psychiatry 142:1325–1329, 1985.

# Chapter 18

# Psychosexual Disorders

These disorders are often first brought to the attention of the general physician. The three distinct categories are:

— Psychosexual dysfunction—inhibition in sexual desire and/or psychophysiological performance.
— Paraphilia—sexual arousal to deviant stimuli.
— Gender identity disorders—patient feels like the opposite sex.

## PSYCHOSEXUAL DYSFUNCTION

Clinically observable features of the normal human sexual response cycle consist of:

Stage I: Excitement (minutes to hours)
  Males—psychological arousal and penile erection.
  Females—psychological arousal, vaginal lubrication, nipple erection, and vasocongestion of the external genitalia.
Stage II: Plateau (seconds to 3 min)
  Males—several drops of fluid appear at head of penis (from Cowper's gland).
  Females—tightening of outer third of vagina, breast engorgement.
Stage III: Orgasm (5–15 sec)
  Males—ejaculation, involuntary muscular contraction (eg, pelvis); followed by a refractory period.
  Females—contractions of outer third of vagina, some involuntary pelvic thrusting; may be multiple.
Stage IV: Resolution
  Males—relaxation, detumescence, sense of well-being.
  Females—relaxation, detumescence, sense of well-being.

Patients (or their partners) may complain of decreased sexual desire and/or of one or more specific abnormalities of the response cycle. The dysfunctions may be situational, partial rather than complete, and primary or acquired. The phases usually occur in a stepwise fashion, but that is not mandatory— identify the stage involved. Often there are marital problems, unrealistic expectations, long-standing personal "hangups," chronic difficulty establishing and maintaining intimate inter-personal relations, etc. Identify these through history and psychiatric evaluation. Always evaluate carefully for organic causes (particularly with impotence and dyspareunia). Organic conditions tend to be chronic and independent of the situation.

Treatment should be global with an emphasis on intimacy and relationship—not just technique. Identify and treat psychosocial causes with dynamic psychotherapy, marital therapy, hypnotherapy, and group therapy. Sedatives may help temporarily if anxiety is prominent. Even purely physical causes often have significant associated secondary interpersonal problems that must be addressed once the medical condition has been corrected. A good prognosis is associated with acute, recent dysfunction in a psychologically healthy patient with good past sexual functioning and strong sexual interests. Some relationships between partners are sufficiently hostile and destructive that, unless other matters are resolved, prognosis is very poor for a correction of the psychosexual dysfunction.

The "new sex therapy" (Masters and Johnson) uses individual psychotherapy, couples therapy, education, behavior modification techniques, and often a male-female therapist pair (dual-sex therapy). Their numerous techniques have wide applicability with sexual dysfunctions and should be considered for use. Many of these methods center on decreasing a patient's (or couple's) anxiety about making love. Essential principles include:

— Good communication with full exploration of sexual feelings.
— Training in specific stimulation and coital techniques (through "pleasuring sessions").
— Emphasis on the couple as a pleasure-giving team.
— Prohibition of intercourse early in therapy (to reduce performance anxiety).
— Emphasis on multimodal sensory pleasure (touch, sight, sound) and sensory awareness exercises.
— Insistence that physiological responses be ignored (erection, etc.— "Don't worry about it; it will happen").

## Male Erectile Disorder; Female Sexual Arousal Disorder (DSM-IV p 502 & 504, 302.72):

<u>Males (Impotence)</u>: A persistent or recurrent failure to reach or maintain a complete erection. Two forms exist:

— <u>Primary impotence</u>—Patient has never maintained an erection.
— <u>Secondary impotence</u>—Patient has lost the ability: may be person or situation specific (selective impotence).

Impotence is a common sexual complaint of men—predominantly the secondary form. It is <u>not</u> a "natural consequence" of aging. Some believe 90% of cases are psychogenic, but recent studies emphasize the frequency of an organic etiology. This is the most common sexual dysfunction caused by SEXUAL DYSFUNCTION DUE TO A GENERAL MEDICAL CONDITION (DSM-IV p 518) or SUBSTANCE-INDUCED SEXUAL DYSFUNCTION (DSM-IV p 521), although several other sexual problems can have an organic etiology as well. Organic causes include:

— <u>Disorders of the hypothalamic-pituitary-gonadal axis:</u> Low serum testosterone level due to primary testicular hypofunction, pituitary tumors, etc.
— <u>Endocrine:</u> Hyperthyroidism (may have elevated testosterone), hyperprolactinemia, diabetes mellitus, acromegaly, Addison's disease, myxedema.
— <u>Medication:</u> Tricyclic antidepressants, MAOIs, major tranquilizers (particularly thioridazine), cholinergic blockers, antihypertensive drugs (particularly adrenergic blockers and false sympathetic neurotransmitters), estrogens, ethyl alcohol (alcoholism), addictive drugs (particularly narcotics and amphetamines), anticholinergic drugs.
— <u>Illness:</u> Any illness may cause impotence temporarily but particularly chronic debilitating disease, chronic renal disease, peripheral vascular disease, and local physical and neurological disorders.

Psychogenic causes include depression, anxiety (over cardiac status, performance, etc.), hostility and marital conflict, etc.

First identify any physical cause—do a complete medical evaluation (look for physical illness, absent beard and body hair, small testes, gynecomastia), get serum testosterone (then further hormonal studies if low). Early morning sleeping erection or occasional successful intercourse does not rule <u>out</u> an organic etiology, nor does a normal pattern of nocturnal penile tumescence (NPT—erections during REM sleep) rule in a psychogenic etiology, although most (all?) psychogenic cases have normal NPT. Treat medical causes (often curative). Follow with global therapy, if needed. Therapy includes allowing the female to play the dominant role and insisting on a gradual shift from foreplay to intercourse. Perhaps 30–40% will not improve.

Females: An inadequate genital sexual response (failure to reach the excitement or plateau stages) although the woman may find sexual activity pleasurable. It often reflects personality or marital problems, but other specific causes include poor physical health, alcoholism, fatigue, depression, fear of pregnancy, and a postpartum state. Treat the couple.

## Premature Ejaculation
### (DSM-IV p 511, 302.75)

The ejaculation occurs before the patient wishes it to, and usually before his partner reaches orgasm (40% of all patients with sexual complaints; 30% of all males). Cause is usually functional and secondary to anxiety (determine the source of the anxiety). It is much more common in stressful marriages. "Squeeze technique" effective—just prior to ejaculation, woman squeezes head of glans. This is coupled with the man practicing imagery control. The young and vigorous male may benefit from 1% Nupercaine ointment applied to the coronal ridge and frenulum. Recently, SSRIs (eg, fluoxetine 20–40 mg/day) have been found effective in many patients.

## Male Orgasmic Disorder
### (DSM-IV p 509, 302.74)

The patient fails to ejaculate. Differentiate from retrograde ejaculation ("ejaculation" into the bladder—due to organic factors, eg, anticholinergic drugs, prostatectomy). Some patients can have an orgasm only under certain conditions (eg, with masturbation, with a stranger)—identify the circumstances in which orgasm can take place. Psychological causes include lack of interest (eg, primary sexual deviation), anxiety, compulsive personality, marriage stresses, and sexual "hangups." Physical causes include medication (guanethidine, methyldopa, phenothiazines—particularly thioridazine, MAOIs), GU surgery, and lower spinal cord impairment (eg, parkinsonism, syringomyelia). First train the patient to ejaculate by himself, then treat the interpersonal relationship—individual psychotherapy is often needed. The technique of the female self-inserting her partner's penis may be effective.

## Female Orgasmic Disorder
### (DSM-IV p 506, 302.73)

The patient persistently fails to reach orgasm during intercourse. There are primary (the majority) and secondary forms, although be aware that many women become orgasmic as they get older (peak at age 35). There may be a hormonal basis in some, but most causes are psychological. This condition is very situation specific—some women never have orgasm despite ample excitement; others have orgasm only with masturbation; still others require clitoral manipulation during intercourse; and a minority of women can have an orgasm with intercourse alone. Psychotherapy often involves first training the woman to have an orgasm by herself, then treating the couple.

## Dyspareunia
### (DSM-IV p 513, 302.76)

Pain with intercourse. It often is related to a physical condition (50%): cervical or vaginal infection or anatomic abnormality, endometriosis, tumor, or other pelvic pathology. Anxiety about sexual activity (for a variety of reasons) can produce pelvic muscle tightening and pain but, remember, pain from organic causes can produce anxiety that exacerbates the pain. Also, dyspareunia can produce vaginismus, and vaginismus can produce dyspareunia.

## Vaginismus
### (DSM-IV p 515, 306.51)

The patient has an involuntary spasm during coitus of the muscles surrounding the outer third of the vagina which prevents penile entrance. It may be related to physical causes producing pain—dyspareunia. Psychological causes include past sexual trauma (eg, rape), a hostile marital relationship (perhaps from a vicious cycle), or sexual "hangups." Individual therapy and relaxation techniques are usually required. Hegar dilators (size increased over 3–5 days) rarely may be useful.

### Hypoactive Sexual Desire Disorder (DSM-IV p 498, 302.71):

Common (20% of population, more F than M) and difficult to treat. It may present as inhibited excitement or inhibited orgasm—don't be misled. Causes usually are functional. It varies with time, the sexual partner, depression, anxiety, and the stresses of the relationship. It may reflect a fear of intimacy or pregnancy, a passive-aggressive personality style, strong religious orthodoxy, or homosexuality, among others. Individual or couple therapy is useful.

### Sexual Aversion Disorder (DSM-IV p 500, 302.79):

Similar to hypoactive sexual desire disorder but represents an active avoidance of sexual activity. Patient has often been sensitized by past (unpleasant) experiences.

### PARAPHILIA (SEXUAL DEVIATION)

These patients become sexually excited only by unusual or bizarre stimuli (practices or fantasies). The particular type of arousing stimulus determines the diagnosis. Orgastic release usually occurs by masturbation during or after the event. Etiology is uncertain—possibly biological, learned, and/or dynamic-instinctual. Most types are rare (courts see them most frequently), although physicians will occasionally encounter them. Men predominate although women may display sadomasochism, voyeurism, and exhibitionism.

These patients may not be troubled by their desires (ego syntonic) and thus are difficult to treat, although depression, anxiety, and guilt do occasionally occur. These conditions frequently coexist with personality disorders, alcohol and drug abuse, and other psychiatric disorders—treat them. The patients often have impaired interpersonal relationships, particularly heterosexual relations.

Psychotherapy is frequently unsuccessful. Specific behavior modification techniques to eliminate the deviation are most successful (eg, aversion covert conditioning) although these must be paired with a more global retraining program. Hypersexual states and some other sexual deviations may benefit from medroxyprogesterone acetate (Depo-Provera) or cyproterone acetate, while some recent research suggests a possible use for fluoxetine and other antidepressants in decreasing aberrant drive.

### Pedophilia
### (DSM-IV p 528, 302.2):

These patients repeatedly approach prepubertal children sexually (touch, explore, mutually masturbate; occasionally intercourse). They are usually anxious, depressed, inadequate males who know the child involved (a neighbor, relative). Three general types are recognized: heterosexual pedophilia (prefers preadolescent girls), homosexual pedophilia (prefers early teenage boys—very resistant to therapy), and mixed pedophilia (younger children, either sex). Pedophiliacs derive sexual arousal primarily from children: don't confuse with child molestation due to decreased impulse control (eg, organic conditions, intoxication, retardation, psychosis) or a onetime event (eg, due to loneliness or after a marital crisis). There may be biological, familial roots. Behavior modification is the treatment of choice.

### Exhibitionism
### (DSM-IV p 526, 302.4)

Usually timid males (onset usually in teen years) who become sexually aroused by exposing their genitals to an unsuspecting female (adult or child). They are only rarely aggressive. They may masturbate during the exposure and need a shock reaction from the female for satisfaction. Very resistant to treatment, although "compulsive" exhibitionism may respond to SSRIs.

Less frequent paraphilias include:

FETISHISM (DSM-IV p 526, 302.81): Sexual arousal to inanimate objects. May be combined with other sexual preferences.

FROTTEURISM (DSM-IV p 527, 302.89): Arousal from touching or fondling a nonconsenting person, usually in a crowded place where escape is possible. Usually teenage or young adult males.

TRANSVESTIC FETISHISM (DSM-IV p 531, 302.3): Aroused by female clothing and cross-dressing. Don't confuse with transsexualism (the wish to become a female) or effeminate homosexuality (cross-dressing to attract others—not to produce arousal itself).

VOYEURISM (DSM-IV p 532, 302.82): Sexual arousal by watching unsuspecting people who are naked or sexually active. Masturbation usually takes place concurrently.

SEXUAL MASOCHISM (DSM-IV p 529, 302.83): Arousal from being sexually bound, beaten, humiliated, etc. Chronic.

SEXUAL SADISM (DSM-IV p 530, 302.84): Sexual excitement after inflicting psychological or physical (sexual or nonsexual) harm on a consenting or nonconsenting partner. The severity of the harm required to produce excitement may increase with time, making the person a potential killer. Some rapists deserve this diagnosis.

## GENDER IDENTITY DISORDER
### (DSM-IV p 537)

These adults have experienced prolonged discomfort about their anatomic sex and identify with and wish they were the opposite sex. A few actively want to change their sex (transsexuals). Males predominate, and their clinical characteristics are more variable. They may have experienced the discomfort since childhood or only recently. They may be homosexual, heterosexual, or have little sexual interest. Many have an effeminate appearance and cross-dress. Females with this disorder are usually homosexual and masculine appearing. Many display discomfort with their sex, cross-dressing, no desire for a sex change, and a diversity of additional psychiatric symptomatology.

Etiology is unclear—it may be predominantly biological and/or psychological, although the mother/child bond always appears disturbed (often too close). Check karyotype and sex hormone levels. These patients are very likely to have personality disorders, particularly of the borderline type. The course is chronic, and there is significant risk for depression, suicide, anxiety, and genital self-mutilation. Rule out effeminate homosexuality (patient does not want to be the other sex), schizophrenia, and hermaphroditism.

Treat with supportive psychotherapy and feminizing-masculinizing hormones. Sex change surgery (castration, penectomy, vaginoplasty, phalloplasty) is falling out of fashion: it is irreversible and the results appear no better (perhaps worse) than psychotherapy alone. There have been isolated reports of gender identity changes with intensive behavior modification.

## HOMOSEXUALITY

Homosexuality (an arousal to and preference for sexual relations with adults of the same sex) is not currently considered to be a mental disorder, except if the patient is "persistently and markedly" distressed by it (classed as SEXUAL DISORDER NOS; DSM-IV p 538, 302.9). It may be a temporary phase during adolescence.

Homosexuality is common in the US; possibly 5–10% of males and 2–4% of females. Despite numerous theoretical explanations, the cause(s) is unknown. There may be congenital, prenatal, familial, biological, and/or genetic (eg, a gene on the X chromosome) etiologies for some; environmental factors may dominate in the choice of sexual orientation in others.

These distressed homosexuals often have internalized a negative attitude toward homosexual behavior and chronically and consistently want to change. They suffer from depression, anxiety, and shame. Most psychotherapy is of little value. However, specialized behavior modification techniques (concentrating on decreasing deviant arousal, stimulating heterosexual arousal, and teaching heterosocial skills) may facilitate change in some.

### Suggested Readings

Abel GG, Osborn C: The paraphilias: The extent and nature of sexually deviant and criminal behavior. Psychiatr Clin North Am 15:675–687, 1992.

Araoz DL: Uses of hypnosis in the treatment of psychogenic sexual dysfunctions. Psychiatr Ann 16:102–105, 1986.

Bancroft J, Wu FC: Erectile impotence. Br Med J 290:1566–1568, 1985.

Bancroft J: Homosexual orientation. Br J Psychiatry 164:437–440, 1994.

Barlow DH: The treatment of sexual deviation: Toward a comprehensive behavioral approach, in Calhoun K, Adams H, Mitchell K: Innovative Treatment Methods in Psychopathology. New York, John Wiley & Sons, 1974.

Barlow DH, Abel GG, Blanchard EB: Gender identity change in transsexuals. Arch Gen Psychiatry 36:1001–1007, 1979.

Berlin FS, Meinecke CF: Treatment of sex offenders with antiandrogenic medication. Am J Psychiat 138:601–607, 1981.

Brown GR: A review of clinical approaches to gender dysphoria. J Clin Psychiatry 51:57–64, 1990.

Chantry K, Craig RJ: Psychological screening of sexually violent offenders with the MCMI. J Clin Psychol 50:430–435, 1994.

Cole M: Sex therapy—A critical appraisal. Br J Psychiatry 147:337–351, 1985.

Gaffney GR, Lurie SF, Berlin FS: Is there familial transmission of pedophilia? J Nerv Ment Dis 172:546–548, 1984.

Green R. Gender identity in childhood and later sexual orientation. Am J Psychiatry 142:339–341, 1985.

Hamer DH, Hu S, Magnuson VS, et al: A linkage between DNA markers on the X chromosome and male sexual orientation. Science 261:321–327, 1993.

Kafka MP: Successful antidepressant treatment of nonparaphilic sexual addictions and paraphilias in men. J Clin Psychiatry 52:60–65, 1991.

Karacan I: Nocturnal penile tumescence as a biologic marker in assessing erectile dysfunction. Psychosomatics 23:349–360, 1982.

Langevin R: Biological factors contributing to paraphilic behavior. Psychiatr Ann 22:307–314, 1992.

LeVay S: A difference in hypothalamic structure between heterosexual and homosexual men. Science 253:1034–1037, 1991.

LeVay S: The Sexual Brain. Cambridge, MA, The MIT Press, 1993.

Perilstein RD, Lipper S, Friedman LJ: Three cases of paraphilias responsive to fluoxetine treatment. J Clin Psychiatry 52:169–170, 1991.

Pillard RC, Weinrich JDL: Evidence of familial nature of male homosexuality. Arch Gen Psychiatry 43:808–812, 1986.

Seidman SN, Rieder RO: A review of sexual behavior in the United States. Am J Psychiatry 151:330–341, 1994.

Snaith P, Tarsh MJ, Reid R: Sex reassignment surgery. Br J Psychiatry 162:681–685, 1993.

Stein DJ, Hollander E, Anthony DT, et al: Serotonergic medications for sexual obsessions, sexual addictions, and paraphilias. J Clin Psychiatry 53:267–271, 1992.

Zohar J, Kaplan Z, Benjamin J: Compulsive exhibitionism successfully treated with fluvoxamine. J Clin Psychiatry 55:86–88, 1994.

# Chapter 19

# Sleep Disturbances

Sleep disorders are extremely common—10–20% of the population have had trouble sleeping within the past year; 3–4% have had hypersomnia.

Current classification and understanding of sleep problems rests on recent advances in knowledge of normal sleep. Much of this has been obtained through physiological (sleep, EEG, EMG, etc.) measures of patients in sleep laboratories.

## NORMAL SLEEP

Normal sleep is cyclical (45 cycles/night) and active, not passive. Distinct stages (measured by EEG) occur, and a person passes stepwise through them. Patients enter stage 1, descend by steps over approximately 30 min to stage 4, plateau there for 30–40 min, and then ascend to lighter stages (12) in order to enter REM sleep 90–100 minutes after falling asleep. Then the cycle repeats. As the night progresses, the REM periods lengthen, stage 4 disappears, and the sleep is generally lighter. The length of time spent in any one stage varies in a characteristic fashion with age. The significance of each stage is not known.

Waking—alpha waves (8–12 cps)

NREM Sleep (Nonrapid eye movement)—low level of activity: lowered BP, heart rate, temperature, and respiratory rate. Good muscle tone and slow, drifting eye movements.

Stage 1—lightest sleep, a transition stage; low voltage, desynchronized waves.

Stage 2—sleep spindles (13–15 cps) and high spikes (K complexes).

Stage 3—some delta waves (high voltage at 0.5–2.5 cps).

Stage 4—deepest sleep, mostly in first half of night; mostly delta waves.

REM Sleep—active sleep characterized by rapid synchronous eye movement, twitching of facial and extremity muscles, penile erections, and variation in pulse, BP, and respiratory rate. Muscular paralysis (absent tone) is present. Depth is similar to stage 2. Dreaming can occur in several stages but is most common in REM sleep.

For clinical purposes, patients with sleep disorders can be divided into those presenting with complaints of insomnia or hypersomnia. In each category, there are several distinct syndromes which must be ruled out.

### INSOMNIA (PRIMARY INSOMNIA, DSM-IV p 557, 307.42)

Sleep laboratory studies usually are not needed for diagnosis and treatment. Take a good history of the sleep problem, including the 24-hour sleep-wake cycle. Identify the pattern: trouble falling asleep, trouble staying asleep (frequent awakenings), early morning awakenings. Inquire about life stresses, drug and alcohol use, marital and family problems. Consider the following:

— Is the insomnia simply normal sleep?
  a. Some "insomniacs" get ample sleep (pseudoinsomnia). The problems are psychological and lie elsewhere—use psychotherapy and reassurance about the adequacy of the sleep.
  b. Sleep time lessens with age—explain to concerned elderly. Help them avoid a complicating "worry over sleeplessness" cycle.
  c. Some patients are substance abusers seeking drugs.
— Is the insomnia transient (situational insomnia)? Patient usually has trouble falling asleep. Identify the stress. Help the patient correct and deal with it. Consider the time-limited (1–2 wk) use of sleeping medication (eg, flurazepam, 15–30 mg, PO, HS; temazepam, 15–30 mg, PO, HS).
— Is there a chronic, minor psychiatric illness? Insomnia is due most frequently to chronic depression and/or anxiety. Antisocial and obsessive-compulsive features are also common among these patients. They often self-medicate, producing more insomnia. Insomniacs often have trouble expressing aggressive feelings, internalize their problems, and/or have a fear of losing control. The resulting problem is usually sleep onset in type with decreased stage 4 sleep. These patients must be differentiated from those with conditioned insomnia, in which the patient has inadvertently trained himself to stay awake at bedtime.
— Is there a major psychiatric illness? (INSOMNIA RELATED TO ANOTHER MENTAL DISORDER, DSM-IV p 596, 307.42)

a. Acute psychosis: Often produces major sleep disruption—treat with antipsychotics.
b. Mania or hypomania: Very short sleep time—use antipsychotics or lithium.
c. Major depression: Usually there is early morning awakening, but frequent awakenings during the night are also common. REM sleep begins very quickly. Treat the depression (tricyclics decrease REM sleep).

— Is there a medical problem? (SLEEP DISORDER DUE TO A GENERAL MEDICAL CONDITION, INSOMNIA TYPE, DSM-IV p 600, 780.52)

a. Chronic pain and related anxiety and depression, eg, back pain, headache, arthritis, asthma, nocturnal angina (increased pains during REM sleep), duodenal ulcer.
b. Hyperthyroidism, epilepsy, general paresis.
c. Is the patient simply worried about a medical problem?

— Is there substance use or abuse (SUBSTANCE-INDUCED SLEEP DISORDER; DSM-IV p 606)? Very common so always inquire.

a. Alcohol—The most common self-prescribed hypnotic. Chronic use produces fragmented sleep.
b. Hypnotic medication—Often prescribed by physicians for insomnia. Tolerance develops to each of them with, ironically, sleep disruption ("sleeping-pill insomnia"). Severe rebound insomnia usually occurs with withdrawal—least with the long-acting benzodiazepines (eg, flurazepam). Treatment must begin with withdrawal of the medication—at the rate of one therapeutic dose/wk.
c. Caffeine—patients often overlook. Ask.
d. Cigarettes (nicotine) can stimulate.
e. Amphetamines, methylphenidate, hallucinogens, aminophylline, ephedrine, thyroid, and corticosteroids all can interrupt sleep.

— Is there sleep cycle disruption? (CIRCADIAN RHYTHM SLEEP DISORDER; DSM-IV p 578, 307.45) Sleepiness may become out of phase if there is "jet lag" or night shift work. Usually self-limited.

— Is there DYSSOMNIA NOS (DSM-IV p 579, 307.47)? Could it be Nocturnal Myoclonus: restless sleep with frequent awakenings secondary to muscle contractions (jerks) in the legs? Ask the bed partner. However, recent evidence suggests that nocturnal myoclonus plays little role in producing insomnia. There is no assured treatment but consider a trial of a small dose of clonazepam (0.5–2 mg) or nitrazepam not in us at bedtime. Or could it be caused by the Restless Legs Syndrome? Legs feel "uncomfortable." Relieved by moving; clonazepam may help.

— Are there frequent nightmares (NIGHTMARE DISORDER, DSM-IV p 583, 307.47), night terrors (pavor nocturnus—SLEEP TERROR DISORDER; DSM-IV p 583, 307.46), or sleepwalking (somnambulism—SLEEPWALKING DISORDER; DSM-IV p 591, 307.46)?

   a. Nightmares (REM sleep) can be chronic and disruptive—psychotherapy may help.

   b. Night terrors (stage 4 sleep) occur early in the night in children, are terrifying to observers, but are not remembered by the patient. They usually disappear with adulthood. Some respond to low doses of minor tranquilizers (eg, diazepam) or SSRIs.

   c. Somnambulism (stage 4 sleep) can persist into adulthood. The patient's behavior appears strange to an observer—there is marked clouding of consciousness. Protect the patient from his actions. Diazepam 15 mg HS, imipramine 50 mg HS, or SSRIs may help.

### General Treatment of Insomnia

1. Rule out, or treat, specific syndromes.
2. Maintain a regular bedtime. Keep room dark and quiet. Develop a "sleeping ritual." Arise promptly in the morning.
3. Regular exercise during the day helps. Avoid vigorous mental activities late in the evening. Try a bedtime snack but don't drink alcohol after supper.
4. Provide support and reassurance. Psychotherapy may be essential.
5. Try relaxation techniques: progressive relaxation, biofeedback, self-hypnosis, meditation, etc.
6. Use sedative-hypnotics for a limited time only (see Chapter 23). Most hypnotic medications (exception is flurazepam) become ineffective within 2 weeks if used nightly. Try initially for 1 week in an effort to establish a successful sleep pattern (eg, flurazepam 15–30 mg, PO, HS but be aware that flurazepam can produce a gradual worsening of psychomotor performance). If used longer than a week, introduce drug holidays and don't exceed recommended dosage. L-tryptophan (a serotonin precursor in food) may relieve insomnia in a few patients.

### HYPERSOMNIA
### (PRIMARY HYPERSOMNIA; DSM-IV p 562, 307.44)

1. Hypersomnia is associated more commonly with purely psychological causes (HYPERSOMNIA RELATED TO ANOTHER MENTAL DISORDER; DSM-IV p 597, 307.44): depression (particularly in younger

patients), anxiety, and withdrawal. It is a means of escape from stress. These patients usually sleep excessively at night rather than during the day.

2. Does the patient have NARCOLEPSY (DSM-IV p 567, 347)? Narcolepsy is a lifelong disorder which usually begins at puberty, is more common in males, probably has a genetic component, occurs with a frequency of about 1/2000, and is characterized by the narcoleptic tetrad:

   a. Daytime sleep attacks—The patient falls abruptly asleep (REM activity on EEG) during the day, despite efforts to stay awake. He usually sleeps for several minutes and wakes refreshed but may have from several to more than 100 episodes during a day. The attacks are likely to occur while he is active and engaged and can be embarrassing or dangerous (during a speech, driving a car).

   b. Cataplexy—A sudden loss of muscle tone that may result in a fall to the ground or just a feeling of weakness. It usually is precipitated by a strong emotion (eg, anger, laughter) and can last from seconds to many minutes. The patient is conscious throughout.

   c. Hypnagogic hallucinations—Dream-like and often frightening auditory and/or visual hallucinations that occur as the patient falls asleep or as he awakens (hypnopompic).

   d. Sleep paralysis—A flaccid, generalized paralysis lasting for several seconds in a fully conscious patient, either while waking or falling asleep, and accompanied by a strong sense of fear. It resolves spontaneously or when the patient is touched or his name is called.

Some patients suffer only sleep attacks, many also have cataplexy (more than two-thirds), and less than 50% also display hallucinations or sleep paralysis. Ten to 20% of patients have the complete tetrad. Most patients with narcolepsy also have disturbed nighttime sleep with frequent awakenings and nightmares.

### Treatment

— Train the patient to avoid dangerous occupations and precipitating stimuli. Planned daytime naps can help.

— Sleep attacks—methylphenidate (Ritalin), 5–10 mg, PO, tid. Insist on occasional drug holidays. This treatment is unsatisfactory, but psychopharmacological advances are on the horizon.

— Narcolepsy with cataplexy—add imipramine, 10–25 mg, PO, tid (suppresses REM sleep).

— Consider sedation for insomnia (ie, benzodiazepines).

3. Does the patient have sleep apnea (BREATHING-RELATED SLEEP DISORDER; DSM-IV p 573, 780.59)? This serious abnormality of nighttime respiratory function can cause long-standing daytime sleepiness, particularly during quiet times (unlike narcolepsy), but is not a likely cause of insomnia. It occurs in three types: (1) a few patients briefly cease nighttime breathing efforts (Central Sleep Apnea), (2) the majority struggle to draw air through nose and mouth passageways which have markedly increased sleep-induced resistance (Obstructive Sleep Apnea), and (3) some suffer both phenomena (Mixed S.A.). There may be from 30 to several hundred episodes each night lasting from 10 seconds to more than 2 min. Males are affected 20:1 (look for obese men over 50 with short, thick necks). The patients may experience a variety of symptoms, including frequent awakenings, impaired libido, loud snoring, sleepwalking, hypertension, headaches, depression, and intellectual and personality changes. Only a few cases will demonstrate anatomical abnormalities of upper airway structures. In serious chronic cases pulmonary hypertension, right heart failure, and/or cardiac arrhythmias may occur.

No treatment has been clearly effective for Central Sleep Apnea. A permanent tracheostomy may be dramatically successful in Obstructive Sleep Apnea, but try weight loss, continuous positive airway pressure (CPAP), and antidepressants first. Hypnotics can further compromise nighttime breathing—avoid them. This diagnosis is significantly underrecognized and mimics depression, anxiety, panic disorder, and early dementia.

4. Rule out current use of sedative drugs or rebound in chronic amphetamine users.

5. Rule out medical conditions (SLEEP DISORDER DUE TO A GENERAL MEDICAL CONDITION, HYPERSOMNIA TYPE; DSM-IV p 600, 780.54): eg, myxedema, hypercapnia, any brain tumor but particularly those involving the mesencephalon and walls of the third ventricle, seizures, cerebrovascular disease, hypoglycemia. Severe hypersomnia with marked postawakening confusion occurs with both the Pickwickian syndrome (obesity and respiratory insufficiency) and the Kleine-Levin syndrome (attacks of hyperphagia, hypersomnia, and hypersexuality).

## Suggested Readings

Ancoli-Israel S, Kripke DF, Mason W: Characteristics of obstructive and central sleep apnea in the elderly. Biol Psychiatry 22:741–750, 1987.

Berlin RM: Psychotherapeutic treatment of chronic insomnia. Am J Psychother 39:68–74, 1985.

Berlin RM, Qayyum U: Sleepwalking: Diagnosis and treatment through the life cycle. Psychosomatics 27:755–760, 1986.

Gillin JC, Byerley WF: The diagnosis and management of insomnia. N Engl J Med 322:239–248, 1990.

Kales A, Kales JD: Evaluation and Treatment of Insomnia. New York, Oxford University Press, 1984.

Kales JD, Kales A, Bixler EO, et al: Biopsychobehavioral correlates of insomnia. Am J Psychiatry 141:1371–1376, 1984.

Kryger MH, Roth T, Dement WC: Principles and Practice of Sleep Medicine, ed 2. Philadelphia, W.B. Saunders, 1993.

Kwentus J, Schulz SC, Fairman P, Isrow L: Sleep apnea: A review. Psychosomatics 26:713–724, 1985.

Lillywhite AR, Wilson SJ, Nutt DJ: Successful treatment of night terrors and somnambulism with paroxetine. Br J Psychiatry 164:551–554, 1994.

Manfredi RL, Cadieux RJ: Sleep disorders of organic origin: Narcolepsy and sleep apnea. Psychiatr Ann 17:470–478, 1987.

McClusky HY, Milby JB, Switzer PK, et al: Efficacy of behavioral versus triazolam treatment in persistent sleep-onset insomnia. Am J Psychiatry 148:121–126, 1991.

Mendelson WB, James SP, Garnett D, et al: A psychophysiological study of insomnia. Psychiatry Res 19:267–284, 1986.

Moldofsky H, Tullis C, Quance G, Lue FA: Nitrazepam for periodic movements in sleep. Can J Neurol Sci 13:52–54, 1986.

Montplaisu J, Lapierre O, Warnes H, et al: The treatment of restless legs syndrome with or without periodic leg movements of sleep. Sleep 15:391–395, 1992.

Salin-Pascual R, Ruente J, Fernandez-Guardiola A: Effects of clonidine in narcolepsy. J Clin Psychiatry 46:528–531, 1985.

Scharf MB, Brown D, Woods M, et al: The effects and effectiveness of gammahydroxybutyrate in patients with narcolepsy. J Clin Psychiatry 46:222–225, 1985.

VelaBueno A, Soldatos CR, Julius DA: Parasomnias: Sleepwalking, night terrors, and nightmares. Psychiatr Ann 17:465–469, 1987.

Young T, Palta M, Dempsey J, et al: The occurrence of sleep disordered breathing among middle-aged adults. N Engl J Med 328:1230–1235, 1993.

# Chapter 20

# Personality Disorders

**Personality** is a consistent style of behavior uniquely recognizable in each individual. **Personality disorders** (Axis II of DSM-IV p. 633) refers to personality characteristics of a form or magnitude that are unchanging, chronic, occur in most settings, deviate significantly from cultural norms, and are maladaptive and cause poor life functioning. Many patients display a mixture of several different maladaptive traits. These long-term traits feel "natural" (ego syntonic), even though a person may be bothered by the results of his behavior. There are elements of the personality disorders in all of us, and the difference between health and pathology may be one of degree. Moreover, many patients only display their pathology clearly when under stress.

Most personality disorders develop in childhood and become fixed by the early 20s, yet some occur after organic insults to the brain. Some may have a biologic, and even a genetic, component (eg, schizotypal and borderline personality disorders). Psychological testing may facilitate diagnosis: WAIS, MMPI, Bender Gestalt, and Rorschach. Atypical and mixed types are common, and some may grade into or be confused with similar appearing Axis I disorders (eg, Paranoid P.D.: paranoid schizophrenia). These patients often resist treatment and change slowly, but occasionally respond to a variety of treatment modalities, including individual or group therapy, and short-term use of antianxiety agents or low doses of major tranquilizers. Some may require inpatient treatment during periods of decompensation. Adolescents (under 18), and even children, may receive a personality disorder diagnosis (except Antisocial P.D.) if the pattern is stable, clear, and incompatible with an Axis I childhood disorder.

## PARANOID P.D. (DSM-IV P. 634, 301.0)

These aloof, emotionally cold people typically display unjustified suspiciousness, hostility, hypersensitivity to slights, jealousy, and a fear of intimacy. They tend to be grandiose, rigid, unforgiving, sarcastic, contentious, and litigious and are thus isolated and disliked. They accept criticism poorly, blaming others instead. This disorder may be associated with chronic CNS impairment, drug use (eg, amphetamines), depression, obsessive-compulsive states, or as a precursor to Schizophrenia. Psychotic decompensation sometimes occurs, requiring major tranquilizers. They rarely seek treatment and therapy, including medication, is of little value.

## SCHIZOID P.D. (DSM-IV P. 638, 301.20)

These are seclusive people who have little wish or capacity to form interpersonal relations, are indifferent to and derive little pleasure from social and sexual contacts, and yet prefer and can perform well at solitary activities (eg, night watchman). They have a limited emotional range, experience little pleasure, daydream excessively, and are humorless and detached. They do not seem to have an increased risk of developing Schizophrenia as was previously thought. "Loners" are not necessarily schizoid unless they have impaired functioning. Treatment seems of little help.

## SCHIZOTYPAL P.D. (DSM-IV P. 641, 301.22)

In addition to having features of the schizoid (isolated, anhedonic, aloof), these people are "peculiar." They relate strange intrapsychic experiences, display odd and magical beliefs as well as strange speech, reason in odd ways (eg, ideas of reference), are frequently anxious, and are difficult to "get to know"; yet none of these features reach psychotic proportions. It is found in 3% of the population, commonly occurs with Major Depression, and is associated with an increased incidence of Schizophrenia in family members (suggesting that this condition is part of the "schizophrenic spectrum" of disorders). Biological measures found in schizophrenia also occur (eg, impaired eye tracking, increased CSF homovanillic acid). Low dose antipsychotic medication may reduce the more flamboyant of symptoms.

## ANTISOCIAL P.D. (DSM-IV P. 645, 301.7)

Antisocial behavior begins in childhood or early adolescence: aggressiveness, fighting, "hyperactivity," poor peer relationships, irresponsibility, lying, theft, truancy, poor school performance, runaway, inappropriate sexual activity, drug and alcohol use. As adults there is criminality, assaultiveness, self-defeating impulsivity, hedonism, promiscuity, unreliability, and crippling drug and alcohol abuse. They fail at work, change jobs frequently, go AWOL and receive dishonorable discharges from the service, are abusing parents and neglectful mates, can't maintain intimate interpersonal relationships, and spend time in jails and prisons ($50\%^+$ of prisoners). These patients are frequently, if temporarily, anxious and depressed (suicide, often impulsive, in as many as 5%) and are second only to patients with hysteria in the production of conversions symptoms. The behavior peaks in late adolescence and the early 20s with improvement in the 30s; however, the patients usually continue their antisocial patterns and they rarely recover from the "lost years." Males are involved more severely, earlier, and more frequently (3% of population) — M:F = 3–5:1.

Their rearing is generally impaired by rejection, neglect, desertion, poverty, and inconsistent discipline—they are frequently illegitimate and unwanted. The parents are often criminals (30% of fathers), alcoholics (50% of fathers), and chronically unemployed. Male first degree relatives have an increased incidence of antisocial personality disorder, alcoholism, and drug abuse, and female relatives have associated Somatization Disorder. A genetic component is likely.

No tests are diagnostic, although a 4–9 MMPI profile is common and there is an increased incidence of nonspecific EEG abnormalities (increased slow-wave activity, etc.). It is necessary to rule out primary drug and alcohol abuse (difficult, look for normal childhood behavior), Schizophrenia (thought disorder present), OBS (disorientation, memory impairment), early mania, explosive disorder, and ADULT ANTISOCIAL BEHAVIOR (DSM-IV p. 683, V71.01). Several very specialized disorders of impulse control can also mimic this disorder: PATHOLOGICAL GAMBLING (DSM-IV p. 615, 312.31), KLEPTOMANIA (DSM-IV p. 612.32), and PYROMANIA (DSM-IV, p. 614, 312.33). The patients are resistant and manipulative—don't rely on the patient's report; check your data. They rarely seek help for personality change, and treatment is difficult and often unsuccessful. Best results follow closely supervised inpatient care: utilize strong, frequent, and accurate confrontation of interpersonal behavior, particularly by peers. Individual outpatient psychotherapy is of little value. The terms Antisocial P.D., sociopathy, and psychopathy generally are used synonymously.

### BORDERLINE P.D. (DSM-IV P. 650, 301.83)

These usually socially adapted patients have complex clinical presentations, including diverse combinations of anger and sarcasm, anxiety, intense and labile affect, brief disturbances in consciousness (eg, depersonalization, dissociation), chronic loneliness, boredom, a chronic sense of emptiness, unstable and volatile interpersonal relations, identity confusion, impulsive behavior (including self-injury—cutting and self-mutilation; recurrent suicide attempts; and death by suicide in 8%$^+$), and a hypersensitivity to abandonment. Stress can precipitate a transient psychosis. Many other diagnoses are often suggested or can also be made: depression, Brief Psychotic Disorder, other personality disorders, Cyclothymic Disorder, and Substance-Related Disorders. Some of this common (2% in general population; F:M = 3:1), heterogeneous group may be related genetically to affective disorders or schizophrenia and others to subtle organic deficits, while specific symptoms may be related to specific neurotransmitters (eg, impulsivity and low CNS serotonin). There is often, but not always, a history of early childhood abuse. Psychological testing is useful. Be sure to rule out organic states such as mild delirium, psychomotor epilepsy, or drug use in the acute presentation. Long-term, intermittent, supportive psychotherapy is often beneficial although numerous other psychotherapies have their supporters. Low-dose antipsychotic agents (thioridazine 100-300 mg hs, haloperidol 4–6 mg hs) for short periods, antidepressants (SSRIs, MAOIs), or lithium carbonate may help selected individuals. These patients tend to stabilize in their 40s and 50s.

### HISTRIONIC P.D. (DSM-IV P. 655, 301.50)

Histrionic patients initially seem charming, likable, lively, and seductive but gradually become seen as emotionally unstable, egocentric, immature, dependent, manipulative, excitement-seeking, and shallow. They demand attention, are exhibitionistic and suggestible, and present a "caricature of femininity," yet have a limited ability to maintain stable, intimate interpersonal relationships with either sex. This common disorder ($2\%^+$ in general population) is associated with depression, substance abuse, and Conversion and (particularly) Somatization Disorders. Suicidal gestures and attempts are common. Lesser impaired patients respond to psychotherapy.

### NARCISSISTIC P.D. (DSM-IV P. 658, 301.81)

Although often symptom-free and well functioning, these patients are chronically dissatisfied due to a constant need for admiration and habitually unrealistic self-expectations. They are impulsive and anxious, are arrogant, envious, and lacking in empathy, have ideas of omnipotence and of being a "special person," become quickly dissatisfied with others, and maintain superficial, exploitative interpersonal relationships. Under stress and when others are not adequately admiring, they may become depressed, develop somatic complaints, have brief psychotic episodes, or display extreme rage. Mixtures with other personality disorders are common. Long-term psychotherapy helps.

### AVOIDANT P.D. (DSM-IV P. 662, 301.82)

The classic presentation is of an exceedingly shy, lonely, hypersensitive individual with low self-esteem who would rather avoid personal contact than face any potential social disapproval, even though desperate for interpersonal involvement (as opposed to the schizoid person). They assume others will be critical: this affects performance in school, work, and life. These patients are troubled by anxiety (especially Social Phobia) and depression. Group therapy may help.

## DEPENDENT P.D. (DSM-IV P. 665, 301.6)

These are excessively passive, unsure, pessimistic, isolated people who are hypersensitive to criticism and who become abnormally dependent on one or more people. Initially acceptable, the behavior can become subtly controlling of others. Anxiety and depression are common, particularly if the dependent relationship is threatened.

## OBSESSIVE-COMPULSIVE P.D. (DSM-IV P. 669, 301.4)

These patients, frequently successful men (M:F = 2:1), are inhibited, stubborn, perfectionistic, judgmental, overly conscientious, rigid, and chronically anxious individuals who avoid intimacy and experience little pleasure from life. They are indecisive, yet demanding, and are often perceived as cold and reserved. They are at risk to develop depression and perhaps obsessive-compulsive disorder. Psychotherapy can effect changes over time.

---

## ATTENTION-DEFICIT/HYPERACTIVITY DISORDER (DSM-IV P. 78, 314.01)

ADHD is a disorder of early childhood which can continue to produce problems well into adulthood and which has many features of, and is frequently mistaken for, a personality disorder. These patients have been distractible, inattentive, impulsive, quick-tempered, unable to tolerate stress, and restless since childhood. They often have learning disabilities. Their lability impairs interpersonal relations and job stability and may produce depression. They are at risk for drug abuse and alcoholism. Frequently, with age, the full criteria cannot be met (usually the hyperactivity disappears) and the diagnosis becomes "ADHD, In Partial Remission." Differentiate from personality disorders, cyclothymic disorder (more recent onset), intermittent explosive disorder (normal between episodes), and primary depression. ADHD is most effectively treated with stimulants (eg, methylphenidate 10 mg PO tid), but use them very cautiously due to abuse potential. (Propranolol, the TCAs, and bupropion may be alternatives.) Combine with supportive psychotherapy.

## Suggested Readings

Alden L: Short-term structured treatment for avoidant personality disorder. J Consult Clin Psychol 57:756–764, 1989.

Bellak L, Black RB: Attention-deficit hyperactivity disorder in adults. Clin Ther 14:138–147, 1992.

Bornstein RF: The dependent personality: Developmental, social, and clinical perspectives. Psychol Bull 112:3–23, 1992.

Flick SN, Roy-Byrne PP, Cowley DS, et al: DSM-IIIR personality disorders in a mood and anxiety disorders clinic: prevalence, comorbidity, and clinical correlates. J Affect Disord 27:71–79, 1993.

Gitlin MJ: Pharmacotherapy of personality disorders: conceptual framework and clinical strategies. J Clin Psychopharmacol 13:343–353, 1993.

Karterud S, Vaglum S, Friis S, et al: Day hospital therapeutic community treatment for patients with personality disorders. J Nerv Ment Dis 180:238–243, 1992.

Korzekwa M, Links P, Steiner M: Biological markers in borderline personality disorder: new perspectives. Can J Psychiatry 38(suppl 1):S11–15, 1993.

Lencz T, Raine A, Scerbo A, et al: Impaired eye tracking in undergraduates with schizotypal personality disorder. Am J Psychiatry 150:152–154, 1993.

Levitt AJ, Joffe RT, Ennis J, et al: The prevalence of cyclothymia in borderline personality disorder. J Clin Psychiatry 51:335–339, 1990.

Mannuzza S, Klein RG, Bonagura N, et al: Hyperactive boys almost grown up. Arch Gen Psychiatry 48:77–83, 1991.

McGuffin P, Thapar A: The genetics of personality disorder. Br J Psychiatry 160:12–23, 1992.

Nehls N, Diamond RJ: Developing a systems approach to caring for persons with borderline personality disorder. Commun Ment Health J 29:161–172, 1993.

Paris J: The treatment of borderline personality disorder in light of the research on its long term outcome. Can J Psychiatry 38(suppl 1):S28–34, 1993.

Paris J, Zweig FH: A critical review of the role of childhood sexual abuse in the etiology of borderline personality disorder. Can J Psychiatry 37:125–128, 1992.

Ronningstam E, Gunderson J: Identifying criteria for narcissistic personality disorder. Am J Psychiatry 147:918–922, 1990.

Rost KM, Akins RN, Brown FW, et al: The comorbidity of DSM-IIIR personality disorders in somatization disorder. Gen Hosp Psychiatry 14:322–326, 1992.

Salzman JP, Salzman C, Wolfson AN, et al: Association between borderline personality structure and history of childhood abuse in adult volunteers. Compr Psychiatry 34:254–257, 1993.

Shaffer D: Attention deficit hyperactivity disorder in adults. Am J Psychiatry 151:633–638, 1994.

Siever LJ, Amin F, Coccaro EF, et al: CSF homovanillic acid in schizotypal personality disorder. Am J Psychiatry 150:149–151, 1993.

Siever LJ, Coccaro ER, et al: Psychobiology of personality disorders: pharmacologic implications. Psychopharmacol Bull 23:333–336, 1987.

Stone MH: Long-term outcome in personality disorders. Br J Psychiatry 162:299–313, 1993.

Thompson DJ, Goldberg D: Hysterical personality disorder. Br J Psychiatry 150:241–245, 1987.

van Reekum R, Conway CA, Gansler D, et al: Neurobehavioral study of borderline personality disorder. J Psychiatry Neurosci 18:121–129, 1993.

Ward MF, Wender PH, Reimherr FW: The Wender Utah rating scale: An aid in the retrospective diagnosis of childhood attention deficit hyperactivity disorder. Am J Psychiatry 150:885–890, 1993.

Wender PH, Reimherr FW: Bupropion treatment of attention-deficit hyperactivity disorder in adults. Am J Psychiatry 147:1018–1020, 1990.

Widiger RA: Generalized social phobia versus avoidant personality disorder: a commentary on three studies. J Abnorm Psychol 101:340–343, 1992.

Winston A, Laikin M, Pollack J, et al: Short-term psychotherapy of personality disorders. Am J Psychiatry 151:190–194, 1994.

Zanarini MC, Gunderson, JG, Frankenburg FR, et al: Discriminating borderline personality from other Axis II disorders. Am J Psychiatry 147:161–167, 1990.

# Chapter 21

# Mental Retardation

There are 2–2.5,000,000 mentally retarded persons in the US (1%$^+$ of population; M:F = 1.5:1) of whom 80–85% are only mildly retarded. Retardation requires a decreased intellectual functioning (as measured by standard IQ tests) as well as impaired general functioning, but its presentation is modified by social and occupational adaptation, age and maturation, and the environmental and cultural setting. Adults with intellectual impairment which developed before age 18 have **retardation,** and those developing it after age 18 have **dementia.**

## CLASSIFICATION

**MILD MENTAL RETARDATION** (DSM-IV p. 41, 317)—IQ 50–70. Usually recognized when they enter school—require special education. Constitutes 85% of the retarded (but its prevalence decreases markedly with adulthood). The majority become self-supporting, with help.

    **MODERATE MENTAL RETARDATION** (DSM-IV p. 41, 318)—IQ 35–50. Ten percent of all retarded. They are trainable, can learn simple work skills, and can be partly self-supporting in sheltered settings.

    **SEVERE MENTAL RETARDATION** (DSM-IV p. 41, 318.1)—IQ 20–35. Four percent of all retarded. They are capable of simple speech but require institutional or other intensely supportive care.

    **PROFOUND MENTAL RETARDATION** (DSM-IV p. 41, 318.2)—IQ below 20. One percent of all retarded. They are totally dependent upon others for survival and usually have significant neurological damage.

A presumably retarded patient who is untestable is considered to have MENTAL RETARDATION, SEVERITY UNSPECIFIED (DSM-IV p. 42, 319).

## CAUSES

Distinct causes (usually biological) are identified in about 50% of patients; these are more likely in the moderately-to-profoundly retarded patients. Other causes include environmental factors (eg, pre- and perinatal problems, infant illness, psychosocial neglect, malnutrition), with an uncertain polygenic contribution in some cases. Moderate-to-profound retardation is distributed uniformly across social classes, while mild retardation is weighted toward the lower classes.

**Biological causes** include:

Chromosomal abnormalities—numerous types including Down's syndrome (mongolism, trisomy 21; the most common abnormality), Fragile X syndrome (males, 1-2000 live births, 2nd most common abnormality), Cri–du–chat syndrome, Klinefelter's syndrome (XXY), Turner's syndrome (XO/XX).

Dominant genetic inheritance—Neurofibromatosis (Von Recklinghausen's disease), Huntington's Chorea (with childhood onset), Sturge-Weber syndrome, tuberous sclerosis.

Metabolic disorders—Phenylketonuria (PKU), Hartnup disease, fructose intolerance, galactosemia, Wilson's disease, a variety of lipid disorders, hypothyroidism, hypoglycemia.

Prenatal disorders—maternal rubella (particularly in the 1st trimester), syphilis, toxoplasmosis, or diabetes; maternal alcohol abuse (fetal alcohol syndrome) and use of some drugs (eg, thalidomide); toxemia of pregnancy; erythroblastosis fetalis; maternal malnutrition.

Birth trauma—difficult delivery with physical trauma and/or anoxia, prematurity.

Brain trauma—tumors, infection (particularly encephalitis, neonatal meningitis), accidents, poisons (eg, lead, mercury), hydrocephalus, numerous types of cranial abnormalities.

**Social causes** include substandard education, environmental deprivation, childhood abuse and neglect, restricted activity.

Rule out Pervasive Developmental Disorders, dementia, and Residual Schizophrenia. Rule out BORDERLINE INTELLECTUAL FUNCTIONING (DSM-IV p. 684, V62.89). Look for associated psychiatric or neurological syndromes.

## TREATMENT AND PROGNOSIS

Formal cognitive testing at 1–2 years of age is predictive of global outcome in many cases. However, mildly retarded individuals do develop further, often at an unpredictable but slower rate, with education and a supportive environment. They are at risk for adjustment reaction, depression, psychotic reactions, and behavioral disturbances 2° to a negative self-image. Treat the patient with supportive, reality-oriented psychotherapy. Determine the patient's coping style and temperamental strengths and encourage them but don't demand too much. Simple behavior modification techniques may be very effective and should be part of any treatment program.

Severely retarded persons may require some form of institutionalization, yet training in sheltered settings should be considered if possible. If the patient lives with his family, treat the family. Parents and siblings frequently display anger, rejection, overprotection and overcontrol, denial, and/or guilt—all of which should be recognized and dealt with by the physician. Provide genetic counseling. Coordinate with outside agencies and specialists, when available.

Psychiatric syndromes are 3–4 times more common among the retarded. Consider psychopharmacology in patients with typical syndromes when appropriate. Low doses of minor or major tranquilizers may help behavior problems (eg, aggressiveness): don't overuse (it's easy to do). Lithium or propranolol may moderate self-abuse and aggression in some cases.

The majority of mildly retarded adults, when no longer in school, are indistinguishable from the general population—and no longer receive the diagnosis of mental retardation (ie, they develop skills, adapt, and "grow out of it"). Prognosis is good for a productive, self-sufficient life.

### Suggested Readings

Baroff GS: Mental Retardation Nature, Cause and Management. New York, Hemisphere Pub, 1986.

Boshes RA: Pharmacotherapy for patients with mental retardation and mental illness. Psychiatr Ann 17:627–632, 1987.

Bregman JD: Current developments in the understanding of mental retardation, Part II: psychopathology. J Am Acad Child Adolesc Psychiatry 30:861–872, 1991.

Bregman JD, Hodapp RM: Current developments in the understanding of mental retardation, Part I: Biological and phenomenological perspectives. J Am Acad Child Adolesc Psychiatry 30:707–719, 1991.

Largo RH, Graf S, Kundu S, et al: Predicting developmental outcome at school age from infant tests of normal, at-risk and retarded infants. Dev Med Child Neurol 32:30–45, 1990.

Ratey JJ, Mikkelsen EJ, Smith B, et al: Beta-blockers in the severely and profoundly mentally retarded. J Clin Psychopharmacol 6:103–107, 1986.

Reiss AL, Freund L: Fragile X syndrome. Biol Psychiatry 27:223–240, 1990.

Thapar A, Gottesman II, Owen MJ, et al: The genetics of mental retardation. Br J Psychiatry 164:747–758, 1994.

Torrey WC: Psychiatric care of adults with developmental disabilities and mental illness in the community. Commun Ment Health J 29:461–481, 1993.

Vitiello B, Behar D: Mental retardation and psychiatric illness. Hosp Community Psychiatry 43:494–499, 1992.

# Chapter 22

# The Psychotherapies

There are dozens of different psychotherapies addressing innumerable different patient problems. With the possible exception of a few specific behavioral methods applied to several very limited and discrete problems, rigorous proof of psychotherapy's effectiveness doesn't exist. However, there is much nonrigorous but very compelling experience which indicates that various psychotherapies can help many patients. Unfortunately, specific indications for specific therapies generally are not available. Some experts argue that many supposedly different psychotherapeutic methods are actually quite similar in practice. Others suggest that trained therapists utilizing specific techniques may be less important for the patient's improvement than the therapist's personal characteristics of accurate empathy, nonpossessive warmth, and genuineness.

There remain more questions than answers about the utility of and indications for psychotherapy. It is a field that has yet to reach a high level of scientific objectivity. However, it is clear that some patients benefit from such care and that an essential ingredient to that care is a good patient-therapist relationship built on trust and genuine interest. Psychotherapy is an art, and a good therapist does make a difference.

## INDIVIDUAL THERAPY

Individual treatment is the most common form of psychotherapy and comes in almost endless variations. Three of the most common types practiced in the US are:

### Supportive Therapy

This is the most typical form of individual therapy provided to inpatients and outpatients. Therapists skilled in this method include psychiatrists, clinical psychologists, and social workers. The goal is to evaluate the patient's current life situation and his strengths and weaknesses and then to help him make whatever realistic changes will allow him to be more functional. Patients usually are seen weekly (or more often) for several weeks or months (although some patients are followed infrequently for years). Also included is brief (13 session) crisis intervention.

The therapist deals with the patient's symptoms but works very little with the patient's unconscious processes and does not attempt major personality change. Psychological defenses are reinforced—techniques used include reassurance, suggestion, ventilation, abreaction, and environmental manipulation. The therapist must be active, interested, empathic, and warm—listen to the patient, understand his concerns, and help him find direction. Medication may be used.

Patients who are failing to cope successfully with present stress are good candidates, whether or not they have underlying psychiatric problems. Patients with serious psychiatric illnesses (e.g., schizophrenia, major affective disorder) often benefit from concurrent use of biological methods and supportive psychotherapy.

### Psychoanalytic Psychotherapy

**Psychoanalysis** is the classic, long-term insight-oriented therapy. The goal is to make major personality changes by identifying and modifying ("working through") unconscious conflicts by means of free association, analysis of transference and resistance, and dream interpretation. An "analysis" typically takes several hundred hours. "Neurotics" and those with personality disorders are the preferred patients.

**Psychoanalytic psychotherapy** is similar to supportive therapy in that the goal is removal of symptoms, yet is similar to psychoanalysis in requiring a dynamic understanding of the patient's unconscious conflicts (insight) and in utilizing analysis of the transference and dream interpretation. It is briefer than psychoanalysis and used more often.

Recently, **brief psychotherapy** has been explored as a way to impact a patient's problems while at the same time limiting both the number of therapy sessions (12–25$^+$) and the number of issues addressed. Usually a single conflict or interpersonal issue is chosen for therapy and explored in depth. Early results appear promising.

## Cognitive Therapy

Cognitive therapy attributes emotional difficulties to faulty thinking or beliefs. Psychiatric conditions presumably improve when the patient's thinking is more accurate. Thus, the cognitive therapist works with the patient to identify and correct misperceptions, one by one. Therapy is very reality based and encourages the patient to think about his thinking. Cognitive therapy has been used most successfully in the treatment of mild-moderate depression, but is of value in a variety of other psychiatric conditions: e.g., anxiety disorders, substance abuse.

## BEHAVIOR THERAPY

Behavior therapy is based on learning theory, which postulates that problem behaviors (ie, almost any of the manifestations of psychiatric conditions) are involuntarily acquired due to inappropriate learning. Therapy concentrates on changing behavior (behavior modification) rather than on changing unconscious or conscious thought patterns and, to that end, it is very directive (ie, patient receives much instruction and direction). Specific techniques to facilitate those changes include the following:

**Operant conditioning**—These therapeutic techniques are based on careful evaluation and modification of the antecedents and consequences of a patient's behavior. Desired behavior is encouraged by positive reinforcement and discouraged by negative reinforcement. These new ways of responding to the patient can be taught to the people who live with the patient or, for inpatients, may take the form of a token economy.

**Aversion therapy**—A patient is given an unpleasant, aversive stimulus (eg, electric shock, loud sound) when his behavior is undesirable. Some of these procedures have been legally discouraged. An alternate technique, covert sensitization, is less objectionable since it uses unpleasant thoughts as the aversive stimulus.

**Implosive therapy**—The patient with a situation-caused anxiety is directly exposed for a length of time to that situation (flooding) or exposed in imagination (implosion).

**Systematic desensitization**—The anxious or phobic patient is exposed to a gradual hierarchy of frightening situations or objects, beginning with the least worrisome. He eventually learns to handle the more frightening ones. If this is paired with relaxation (ie, an antagonistic response pattern—relaxation is incompatible with anxiety), the technique is reciprocal inhibition.

Common to these methods (and numerous others) is rigorous data collection. Behavior therapy relies on careful measurement of behavior. A technique is considered useful only if it is successful, and its success is determined by whether it eliminates measurable undesired behavior or increases desired behavior.

Although behavior modification has been successful in treating some kinds of conditions (eg, phobias, sexual deviance, regressed behavior), it has been criticized for not considering thought processes. This has led to broader conceptualizations including cognitive-behavioral therapy and multimodal behavior therapy.

## GROUP THERAPY

Group therapy comes in many different forms—most of them derived from types of individual therapy.

**Interpersonal exploration groups**—The goal is to develop self-awareness of interpersonal styles through corrective feedback from other group members. The patient is accepted and supported, thus promoting self-esteem. It is the most common type of group therapy.

**Guidance-inspirational groups**—Highly structured, cohesive, supportive groups that minimize the importance of insight and maximize the value of ventilation and camaraderie. Groups may be large, eg, Alcoholics Anonymous (AA), Synanon. Members often are chosen because they "have the same problem."

**Psychoanalytically oriented therapy**—A loosely structured group technique in which the therapist makes interpretations about a patient's unconscious conflicts and processes from observed group interactions.

Numerous other types of group therapies include behavioral therapy, Gestalt, encounter, psychodrama, transactional analysis (TA), marathon, EST, etc.

Groups may run for weeks, months, or years, and usually

meet weekly. They usually have 5–12 members (depending on type). Therapists from many different disciplines conduct groups—many groups run with cotherapists.

Some groups have patients with only one diagnosis (eg, schizophrenia, alcoholism) while others are mixed. It is not clear which patients will benefit (or will be harmed) by group therapy but most patients can be treated safely in groups. Most of the success of a group appears to depend more on the experience, sensitivity, warmth, and charisma of the leader than on the group's theoretical orientation.

A group experience that is too intense or confrontative can produce anxiety, depression, or psychotic reactions in susceptible patients. Acutely psychotic patients should not be included. Paranoid individuals make poor group members.

## FAMILY THERAPY

Family therapy can be conceptualized as a variant of group therapy. There are numerous types of family therapy but no "one right way." Although a family often enters therapy because one of the family members is "having problems," it is the implicit or explicit assumption of many family therapists that the family system is sick, not the patient. The expectation is that improvement in unhealthy interpersonal interactions and communications will result in improvement of the identified patient.

Most (but not all) family therapists recognize that some patients bring problems to family therapy that are not due to family malfunctioning, but most therapists argue that those problems are frequently worsened by any untreated malfunctioning.

## MARITAL THERAPY

Therapy of a married couple is often called for if that relationship is at risk. It is particularly common if there is a psychosexual problem present. Theoretical orientations and treatment techniques are diverse—none has been clearly shown to be superior. There are no clear guidelines for choosing couples likely to improve with marital therapy. Therapists may come from one of several professional disciplines (eg, psychiatry, psychology, social work, marriage and family counseling).

## MILIEU THERAPY

Milieu therapy usually takes place in an inpatient "therapeutic community." Often the entire community is geared toward support for the patient and toward helping him develop more adaptive coping skills. In a sense, all the staff members are therapists and all the patients are similarly concerned with facilitating each other's well-being. It is a useful adjunct to other forms of therapy (eg, pharmacotherapy).

## Suggested Readings

Buckley P: A neglected treatment. Psychiatr Ann 16:515–521, 1986.

Conte HR, Plutchik R: Controlled research in supportive psychotherapy. Psychiatr Ann 16:530–533, 1986.

Frances A, Sweeney J, Clarkin J: Do psychotherapies have specific effects? Am J Psychother 39:159–174, 1985.

Frank JD, Frank JB: Persuasion and Healing, 3rd ed. Baltimore, Johns Hopkins University Press, 1991.

Horowitz MJ, Marmar CR, Weiss DS, et al: Comprehensive analysis of change after brief dynamic psychotherapy. Am J Psychiatry 143:582–589, 1986.

Jones EE, Pulos SM: Comparing the process in psychodynamic and cognitive-behavioral therapies. J Consult Clin Psychol 61:306–316, 1993.

Jarrett RB, Rush AJ: Short-term psychotherapy of depressive disorders. Psychiatry 57:115–132, 1994.

Karasu TB: The psychotherapies: Benefits and limitations. Am J Psychother 40:324–342, 1986.

Luborsky L, Crits-Christoph P, Mintz J, et al: Who Will Benefit from Psychotherapy? New York, Basic Books, 1988.

Luborsky L, Crits-Christoph P, McLellan T, et al: Do therapists vary much in their success? Am J Orthopsychiatry 56:501–512, 1986.

Mackenzie KR: Principles of brief intensive psychotherapy. Psychiatr Ann 21:398–404, 1991.

Mackenzie KR, Livesley WJ: Outcome and process measures in brief group psychotherapy. Psychiatr Ann 16:715–720, 1986.

Reich J, Neenan P: Principles common to different short-term psychotherapies. Am J Psychother 40:62–69, 1986.

Rockland LH: A review of supportive psychotherapy, 1986-1992. Hosp Comm Psychiatry 44:1053–1060, 1993.

Sotsky SM, Glass DR, Shea MT, et al: Patient predictors of response to psychotherapy and pharmacotherapy: Findings in the NIMH treatment of depression collaborative research program. Am J Psychiatry 148:997–1008, 1991.

Strupp HH: The nonspecific hypothesis of therapeutic effectiveness. Am J Orthopsychiatry 56:513–520, 1986.

Ursano RJ, Hales RE: A review of brief individual psychotherapies. Am J Psychiatry 143:1507–1517, 1986.

Vinogradov S, Yalom ID: Group Psychotherapy. Washington, D.C., American Psychiatric Press, 1989.

Wallerstein RS: The psychotherapy research project of the Menninger foundation. J Consult Clin Psychology 57:195–204, 1989.

Winston A, Pinsker H, McCullough L: A review of supportive psychotherapy. Hosp Community Psychiatry 37:1105–1114, 1986.

Wolpe J: Misrepresentation and underemployment of behavior therapy. Comp Psychiatry 27:192–200, 1986.

Yalom ID: The Theory and Practice of Group Psychotherapy. New York, Basic Books, 1983.

# Chapter 23

# Biological Therapy

### ANTIPSYCHOTICS (NEUROLEPTICS)

These are the "major tranquilizers" which revolutionized psychiatry by providing an effective treatment for large numbers of psychotic patients. Their antipsychotic effect is <u>not</u> due to sedation but to a specific action on thought and mood disorder.

### Drugs Available

There are many different antipsychotics available which are divided among seven chemical classes. Common examples of each class are listed in Table 23.1 along with relative dosages (with reference to chlorpromazine).

### Indications for Use

Recommended for:

1. Acute schizophrenia and other acute psychoses (eg, amphetamine psychosis, organic psychoses). Should be used in conjunction with lithium in the acute manic attacks of bipolar disorder.
2. Chronic schizophrenia.
3. Major depression with significant psychotic features—used in conjunction with an antidepressant.
4. Tourette's Syndrome—haloperidol is the drug most commonly used.

Other uses:

— Antipsychotics can be of temporary use in several conditions, eg, acute agitation of a nonpsychotic nature, antiemesis, etc.

### Mechanisms of Action

The dopamine hypothesis postulates that schizophrenia is secondary to increased central dopamine activity. Antipsychotic

**208**

**Table 23.1**
**Seven Chemical Classes of Major Tranquilizers**

| | Equivalent doses (mg) |
|---|---|
| **TRICYCLICS** | |
| 1. *PHENOTHIAZINES* | |
| *Dimethylamino-alkyl Derivatives* | |
| chlorpromazine (Thorazine) | 100 |
| *Piperidine-alkyl Derivatives* | |
| thioridazine (Mellaril) | 100 |
| mesoridazine (Serentil) | 50 |
| *Piperazine-alkyl Derivatives* | |
| fluphenazine (Prolixin, Permitil) | 1–2 |
| fluphenazine decanoate (long-acting) | |
| trifluoperazine (Stelazine) | 8 |
| perphenazine (Trilafon) | 10 |
| 2. *THIOXANTHENES* | |
| thiothixene (Navane) | 4 |
| 3. *DIBENZOXAZEPINES* | |
| loxapine (Loxitane) | 15 |
| clozapine (Clozaril) | 50 |
| **NON-TRICYCLICS** | |
| 4. *DIHYDROINDOLONES* | |
| molindone (Moban) | 15 |
| 5. *BUTYROPHENONES* | |
| haloperidol (Haldol) | 1–2 |
| haloperidol decanoate (long-acting) | |
| 6. *DIPHENYLBUTYLPIPERIDINES* | |
| pimozide (Orap) | 1–2 |
| 7. *BENZISOXAZOLES* | |
| risperidone (Risperdal) | 2–10 |

drugs are believed to act by postsynaptic blockade of the $D_2$ (and possibly the newly discovered $D_3$ and $D_4$) receptors. (Clozapine may primarily affect $D_1$.) The three major CNS dopamine pathways with their putative activities are:

Nigrostriatal—extrapyramidal actions
Tuberoinfundibular—endocrine actions (increased prolactin)
Mesolimbic—antipsychotic actions (probably)

The different side effect patterns of the various antipsychotic drugs are believed to be due to their different locations of primary activity. However, antipsychotics also block central noradrenergic (NE) receptors, thus we can't yet determine whether DA or NE blockage (or another mechanism entirely) is responsible for the antipsychotic effect.

## Pharmacokinetics

Chlorpromazine is variably absorbed from the intestine and is probably partly degraded in the mucosal wall. It is approximately 95% protein bound. Much higher blood levels are attained after IM or IV than PO administration. The half-life is 1–2$^+$ days but variable, with the majority of the drug stored in body fat. There are marked interindividual differences in blood levels (reasons are unclear).

Metabolism is complex (eg, chlorpromazine is degraded by sulfoxidation, hydroxylation, deamination, demethylation, etc, to form well over 100 metabolites). Some of the metabolites are active, some inactive—not completely worked out. In part because of this complexity, measured plasma levels of many antipsychotics are not clinically useful. In contrast, certain other antipsychotics (eg, Haldol, Navane) have a simple metabolism; however, their measurement as a guide to outcome is of uncertain value.

## Side Effects

Side effects are common and are almost unavoidable at higher drug dosages. The particular pattern of side effects is in part determined by the chemical class of any given antipsychotic (see Table 23.2).

These side effects also have marked interindividual variability. The most common side effects of these medications include sedation, extrapyramidal and anticholinergic symptoms, hypotension, weight gain, and reduced libido, but many other side effects occur as well. (NOTE: clozapine is unique in several ways, including side effects, and will be discussed later.)

— Sedation: Common; use a QD schedule, if possible.
— **Anticholinergic symptoms**
  Dry mouth—Common. May lead to moniliasis, parotitis, and an increase in cavities. Consider treatment with oral water and ice, sugarless gum; also neostigmine 7.5–15 mg PO or pilocarpine 2.5 mg PO qid.

**Table 23.2**
**Most Common Side Effects**

| Drug | Sedation | Extrapyramidal | Hypotension |
|------|----------|----------------|-------------|
| Phenothiazines | | | |
|   Aliphatic | 3 + | 2 + | 3 + |
|   Piperidine | 2 + | 1 + | 2 + |
|   Piperazine | 1 + | 3 + | 1 + |
| Dibenzoxazepines | 2 + | 3 + | 2 + |
| Butyrophenones | 2 + | 3 + | 1 + |
| Dihydroindolones | 1 + | 2 + | 1 + |

Constipation—Treat with stool softeners.

Blurred vision—Near vision. Treat with physostigmine drops, 0.25% solution, 1 drop Q6H, if a major problem.

Urinary hesitancy and retention—Consider using Urecholine 10–25 mg PO tid.

Exacerbation of glaucoma

Central anticholinergic syndrome—Occurs particularly in those patients simultaneously taking several drugs with anticholinergic properties (eg, an OD or a patient taking an antipsychotic, an antidepressant, and an antiparkinsonian). The syndrome can vary from mild anxiety and vasodilation to a toxic delirium or even coma. It is much more common in the elderly. Symptoms and signs to be looked for include:

Anxiety, restlessness, agitation grading into confusion, incoherence, disorientation, memory impairment, visual and auditory hallucinations—grading into seizures, stupor, and coma.

Warm and dry skin, flushed face, dry mouth, hyperpyrexia.

Blurred vision, dilated pupils.

Absent bowel sounds.

Treat an acute delirium with withdrawal of the causative agent, close medical supervision (eg, cardiac monitor), and physostigmine 1–2 mg IM or slowly IV (eg, 1 mg/min). Repeat in 15–30 min and then every 12 hours, if needed. Avoid physostigmine in patients with bowel or bladder obstruction, peptic ulcer, asthma, glaucoma, heart disease, diabetes, or hypothyroidism. Watch for cholinergic overdosage (salivation, sweating, etc.) and treat with atropine (0.5 mg for each mg of physostigmine).

—**Extrapyramidal symptoms:** These reactions are common, get worse with stress, disappear during sleep, and wax and wane over time.

Acute dystonic reaction—An involuntary sustained contraction of a skeletal muscle which usually appears suddenly (over 5–60 minutes). The jaw muscles are most frequently involved (ie, "lock jaw") but other muscle systems may also be disturbed (eg, torticollis, carpopedal spasm, oculogyric crisis, even opisthotonos). Usually occurs during the first 2 days of treatment (in 2–10% of patients—more common in younger patients).

Parkinson-like syndrome—The three primary symptoms occur individually or together, usually during weeks 1–4 of treatment. They are more common in older patients.

"Tremor"—An irregular tremor of the upper extremities, tongue, and jaw. It occurs with both movement and rest and is slower than the tremors produced by TCAs and lithium.

"Rigidity"—A cogwheel rigidity which starts with the shoulders and spreads to the upper extremities and then throughout the body.

"Akinesia"—A "zombie-like" effect with slowness, fatigue, micrographia, and little facial expression. It may occur alone and at anytime during the course of treatment and is easily mistaken for social withdrawal or depression.

Akathisia: Common. Patients are fidgety, constantly move their hands and feet, rock from the waist, and shift from foot to foot. Easily mistaken for anxiety or agitation. The patients are typically dysphoric. Treat with anticholinergics, propranolol (10 mg tid—90–120 mg/day), or lorazepam.

Rabbit Syndrome: Involuntary chewing movements.

Tardive dyskinesia: Slow choreiform or tic-like movements, usually of the tongue and facial muscles, but occasionally of the upper extremities or the whole body. Risk is increased in the aged, those with OBS, females, high doses of medication, simultaneous use of several antipsychotics, and possibly long duration of treatment. Develops over months or years of antipsychotic use, a few severe cases may be irreversible, but it usually follows a stable, benign, long-term course. Symptoms disappear with an increased dosage of antipsychotic: don't "misread" the movements as a worsening psychosis, raise the dose of medication, remove the symptom, and thus begin a vicious cycle. "Drug holidays" don't seem to prevent, and may even worsen, the development of TD. There is no acceptable treatment. Try to discontinue the antipsychotic, if possible.

**Treatment of Extrapyramidal Symptoms**—Treat with the anticholinergic antiparkinsonism drugs listed in Table 23.3.

**Table 23.3**
**Antiparkinsonism Drugs**

| Drug | Typical Dosage |
|------|----------------|
| benztropine (Cogentin) | 1–4 mg, QD-BID, PO |
| biperiden (Akineton) | 1–2 mg, TID, QID, PO |
| procyclidine (Kemadrin) | 2–5 mg, TID-QID, PO |
| trihexyphenidyl (Artane, Tremin) | 2–5 mg, TID-QID, PO |
| diphenhydramine (Benadryl) | 25–50 mg, TID-QID, PO |
| amantadine (Symmetral) | 100 mg, QD-TID, PO |

Begin at a lower dosage and raise over several days. Use for several weeks, then discontinue if possible. Try not to use for more than 2–3 months (although they may be necessary long-term in a few patients). They probably should not be used prophylactically (begun when antipsychotics are started) except in those patients very likely to be resistant to taking meds. Treat acute dystonic reactions immediately (IM or IV) with, for example, Cogentin 1 mg, Benadryl 25–50 mg, or Valium 5–10 mg—then begin regular oral dose for several weeks. These drugs often worsen sxs of TD; they may also be abused.

— Alpha-adrenergic blocking symptoms: Orthostatic hypotension, inhibition of ejaculation (particularly thioridazine).

— Cholestatic jaundice: Probably a sensitivity reaction. Fever and eosinophilia, usually during the first 2 months of treatment (in 1% of patients taking chlorpromazine). Little cross-sensitivity with other antipsychotics.

— Agranulocytosis: Usually in elderly females during the first 4 months of treatment but can occur anytime. Train patients to report persistent sore throats, infections, or fever. Rare.

— Neuroleptic Malignant Syndrome (NMS): Rapidly developing (hrs to 1–2 days) muscular rigidity and cogwheeling, fever, confusion, hypertension, sweating, tachycardia. Look for rhabdomyolysis with myoglobinemia and very elevated CPK. In 1%[+] of pts, particularly (but not exclusively) following high dose, high potency depot meds. Often fatal if untreated. Stop meds immediately; provide medical support; consider treatment with dantrolene or bromocriptine (7.5–45 mg/day, tid (uncertain Rx; check first)). Patient may recover over 5–15 days. It typically does not recur upon later reexposure to antipsychotics.

— Hypothermia; hyperthermia: Watch out for hot seclusion rooms.

— Weight gain, obesity.

— Pigmentary changes in skin: Particularly with chlorpromazine. A tan, gray, or blue color.
— Retinitis Pigmentosa—Possible blindness. Occurs with dosages of thioridazine of more than 800 mg/day.
— Photosensitivity: Bad sunburns with Thorazine.
— Grand mal seizures: Particularly with rapid increases in dose.
— Nonspecific skin rashes: In 5%.
— Reduced libido in males and females.
— Increased prolactin levels: Produces galactorrhea, amenorrhea, and lactation.
— EKG changes: Particularly with thioridazine—T-wave inversions, occasionally arrhythmias.
— Appears safe during pregnancy: no known congenital abnormalities. Slight hypertonicity among newborns, but little effect on nursing infant.

Suicide is difficult but possible with the antipsychotics—requires very large doses.

### Drug Interactions

Antacids—May inhibit absorption of oral antipsychotics.
Tricyclic antidepressants—May inhibit antipsychotic metabolism and raise plasma levels, and vice versa.

### Treatment Principles

— Drug choice:
  The primary reason to choose one drug over another is the side effect spectrum—they are all equally capable of controlling psychosis when used appropriately. If a patient or a similarly affected family member has responded well to one medication, try it. If a patient has a seizure disorder, use a high potency drug (eg, fluphenazine, haloperidol).
— Treatment of acute psychosis:
  Sedating antipsychotics which can be given IM usually provide the best control initially (eg, Haldol, Thorazine), although they have no long-term advantages. Give orally if the patient is cooperative—IM if he is not.
  1. If possible, give a small test dose (eg, Haldol 5 mg) and wait 1 hour to see if it is tolerated.
  2. Then begin Haldol 10–15 mg/day, Thorazine 300–400 mg/day, or the equivalent. Use tid or qid schedule initially, then switch

to bid or qd after 12 wks. A qd schedule is usually well tolerated and helps insomnia. It may be necessary to increase to 500 mg/day of chlorpromazine, 15–20 mg/day of Haldol, or the equivalent. Rarely go higher. If side effects become a problem, begin antiparkinsonism drugs and/or reduce the dosage and increase more slowly.

3. If the patient is wild and needs immediate control and effective physical control is not readily available, consider more rapid tranquilization: eg, Haldol 5 mg IM every hour ×3–4 (or, perhaps more effective, Haldol, 5 mg + Ativan 2–4 mg, IM—in the same syringe). (Droperidol, 5 mg IM, may be the most effective acute tranquilizer (not FDA approved for that purpose, but it is used.)) Monitor carefully for hypotension or oversedation. Once the patient is under control, switch to the preceding daily schedule.

— Disease control is cognitive as well as behavioral—the goal is not just to "quiet" the patient. Improvement is slow and often partial. Increasing socialization is an early sign of a drug response. Agitated, disruptive behavior usually improves in the first several days. The thought disorder disappears over weeks or months. Antipsychotics improve the positive symptoms of psychosis (eg, hallucinations, delusions, bizarre behavior) but, unfortunately, they usually don't change the negative symptoms (eg, flat affect, social impairment)— a major problem. (Early reports suggest that pimozide, clozapine, and risperidone may be exceptions.) Patients who are "acutely crazy" are most likely to respond well, as are those with good premorbid functioning who are having their first psychotic episode.

— If a patient does not respond, switch to another drug of a different class. However, the unimproved patient needs at least one 2–3 week trial at a higher dose of an antipsychotic before you conclude that he doesn't respond to medication. There is rarely any reason to use two different antipsychotics simultaneously. The most common cause for lack of response is underdosage (and noncompliance), but always be wary that the patient may have an organic psychosis.

— Clozapine, a new and different antipsychotic, should be used with schizophrenic patients who can't tolerate or are refractory to traditional meds. Marked improvement occurs in almost 30% of chronic patients; modest improvement in another 10–20%. Unlike other antipsychotics, clozapine may improve sxs of apathy, withdrawal, anhedonia, and flat affect—a "significant cure" in a few patients.

After a thorough medical (lab) exam, begin dosage at 25 mg and increase to 300–400, bid-tid, over 2–4 weeks. (It is very expensive—the median daily dosage of 400 mg costs $4000+/yr.) A response may take weeks or even months. Upper limit is 900 mg/day but be very cautious above 600 mg because some side effects are related to dose and speed of increase: eg, sedation, GM seizures (unusual under 300 mg; 5% of patients over 600 mg; don't use in patients with a history of a seizure disorder). Other SEs include sialorrhea, weight gain, tachycardia, hypotension, fever, and elevated liver enzymes.

The life-threatening side effect is **agranulocytosis:** 1–2% of patients; usually during months 1–6 (but possible anytime); requires weekly WBC with diff "forever" (stop meds if the WBC<3000 or granulocytes<1500); apparently not dose related. If WBCs drop below 2000, never rechallenge the patient with clozapine. Don't use in patients with known blood dyscrasias or who are taking drugs with similar effects on the WBCs (eg, carbamazepine). TAKE THESE GUIDELINES SERIOUSLY.

— Risperidone (Risperdal) is a second new and different antipsychotic that has few side effects (see Chapter 3), is safe in overdose, and seems to affect both positive and negative symptoms. The ideal dose for most patients may be in the 6–8 mg/day range—effective and well tolerated at that level. Although untried, this drug looks very promising (and there are more on the way).

— Once improvement has occurred, maintain drug levels over 1–2 months and then consider reducing to maintenance levels. If this is the first episode of an acute psychosis in a previously well-functioning patient, consider discontinuing the medication over another 1–2 months. If this episode is one of many, place the patient on maintenance.

— Antipsychotic maintenance therapy:

Decrease dosage slowly (over weeks—months) to one-third or one-quarter of the acute dose. Depending on past history, try discontinuing after 6–12 months, although some patients may need meds for many years. If a relapse develops, increase the dose. Eighty to 90% of patients relapse (during first 24 months) without meds, 40%+ relapse while taking them. Teach the patient to recognize his own developing relapse so it can be caught early.

Antipsychotics are often unpleasant to take, so compliance is a major problem with outpatients (particularly in those patients who are suspicious and paranoid). Pay attention to and work aggressively to control side effects (particularly akathisia). A major recent advance has been the development of long-acting depot forms of two antipsychotics: prolixin decanoate and haloperidol decanoate, given IM every 2–4 weeks. Although still being researched, the best and safest maintenance may be with low dose depot meds: eg, prolixin decanoate (12.5–25 mg IM every 2 weeks) or haloperidol decanoate (50–100$^+$ mg IM every month). The relapse rate may be slightly increased at these doses, but side effects and compliance are improved as well. (In fact, depot meds may be preferable, whether or not the patient is noncompliant, particularly in the med refractory patient.)

## LITHIUM CARBONATE

### Drugs Available

Lithium carbonate (Li$^+$—atomic #3)
  Slow-release lithium (Eskalith CR)

### Indications for Use

Recommended for:

1. Acute bipolar disorder, manic. Lithium is the drug of choice for stabilization after an acute manic attack (80% of patients return to normal) although, due to the usual 7–10 day delay in onset of clinical effect, a major tranquilizer may be needed initially as well.
2. Used with an antidepressant in acute depression in a bipolar patient to prevent "manic overshoot."
3. Long-term prophylaxis of mania in a bipolar patient. It is moderately effective at preventing recurrences. Be careful of chronic renal toxicity.

Possible uses:

— Prophylaxis for bipolar disorder, depressed and for major depression.
— May be an effective antidepressant for some patients with an acute bipolar depression. It may act synergistically with other antidepressants.
— May assist or replace antipsychotics in treatment of some patients with schizophrenia or schizoaffective disorder (but lithium can make a few schizophrenics worse).
— May help control mood swings and explosive outbursts in patients with intermittent explosive disorder and emotionally unstable character disorder.
— Retarded patients with aggressiveness and/or self-mutilation.

### Mechanisms of Action

The reasons for the clinical effects are unknown although it does increase central NE reuptake and decrease its release.

## Pharmacokinetics

Lithium is quickly absorbed from the GI tract (completely absorbed in 8 hours) and develops a peak plasma level in 1–3 hr. It is not protein bound or metabolized and is excreted by the kidney. The CSF concentration is 30–60% of that in plasma and equivalent to that in RBCs. It is concentrated by bone and by thyroid (4–5× that in plasma).

Lithium can only be used safely if blood concentrations are monitored carefully (oral dosage is not an adequate measure). To obtain consistent levels, blood is routinely drawn 12 hr after the last dose (usually before breakfast). The lithium half-life is 18–36 hr (fastest in youth, slowest in elderly)—a constant oral dosage requires 5–8 days to reach steady state. Once a steady state is reached, the lithium level is proportional to the daily oral dose (and determined by the renal clearance).

## Side Effects

The number and severity of side effects increase with increasing or rapidly changing blood levels. A slight change in blood level (0.1–0.2 mEq/l) may dramatically alter the number or intensity of the side effects. Minor side effects (tremor, thirst, anorexia, and GI distress) commonly occur at therapeutic levels (0.8–1.5 mEq/l), and fatal effects (seizures, coma) may occur at only slightly higher levels (eg, as low as 2.0–2.5 mEq/l but more commonly at 3–5 mEq/l). Lithium has a very narrow margin of safety and is a dangerous drug in overdosage. It should be given cautiously (or not given at all) in patients who are dehydrated, febrile, have sodium depletion (kidney reabsorbs more lithium), or have major renal or cardiovascular disease. Brain damaged patients and the elderly are at risk for side effects at low blood levels.

Normal subjects administered lithium report irritability and emotional lability, anxiety, mild depression, tiredness and malaise, weakness, inability to concentrate, impaired memory, and slowed reaction time. Patients taking lithium often experience a "lithium-induced dysphoria"—25–50% stop lithium AMA. Unlike other psychoactive medication, sedation is not a side effect.

**Neurological:**

EEG—Usually shows increased amplitude and generalized slowing (in 50% of patients at therapeutic blood levels).

Headaches, occasional slurred speech.

Toxicity:

> Confusion, poor concentration, and clouding of consciousness; leads to delirium; leads to coma; leads to death.
>
> Cerebellar effects—dysarthria, ataxia, nystagmus, severe incoordination.

Basal ganglia effects—parkinsonian symptoms, choreiform movements.

Seizures—grand mal; status epilepticus.

**Neuromuscular:**

Hand tremor (fine, fast) which does not respond to anticholinergics. Occurs in 50% of the patients started on lithium but the incidence decreases with time (5% of long-term patients). Treat with $\beta$-blockers; eg, 30–80 mg propranolol PO/day.

Muscular weakness—one-third of patients during the first week of treatment; transient.

Neuromuscular toxicity—hyperactive reflexes, fasciculations, paralysis.

**Kidney:**

Polyuria and polydipsia—secondary to a vasopressin resistant, diabetes insipidus-like syndrome. Reversible and occurs in 50% of all new patients (5% of all chronics).

Reversible oliguric renal failure with acute lithium intoxication.

Possible irreversible nephrotoxic effect in a few chronic patients—focal interstitial cortical fibrosis with tubular atrophy and sclerotic glomeruli. Look for a gradually increasing blood lithium in patients taking a constant oral dose. There is increased serum creatinine and an increased 24-hr urine volume. Poorly characterized currently, this serious effect of chronic lithium administration may limit the ability to use lithium prophylactically in some.

**Blood:**

Leukocytosis (10,000–14,000 WBCs—neutrophilia with lymphocytopenia). Common and reversible, it is persistent but periodic while the patient is taking lithium.

Occasional increased ESR.

**GI:**

Thirty percent of patients have GI symptoms in the early weeks of treatment—gastric irritation, nausea, anorexia, diarrhea, bloating, abdominal pain (a switch to lithium citrate may relieve symptoms).

**Heart:**

T-wave flattening or inversion (common but reversible).

Unusual—myocarditis, SA block, primary AV block; ventricular irritability and perhaps sudden death (particularly in older males with cardiac pathology; more common at toxic levels).

**Thyroid:**

Lithium may produce hypothyroidism with (10% of chronic patients) or without a goiter. Measure TSH. Low dose thyroxine may help but consult an endocrinologist.

**Other:**

Impaired memory

Lithium accumulates in bone—no known harmful effects.

Occasional maculopapular rash, acne—also (rarely) alopecia, ulceration, and exacerbation of psoriasis.

Weight gain in 10% of patients. Partly related to a Li-induced reactive hypoglycemia.

Occasional benign, reversible exophthalmos.

Hyperparathyroidism—increased serum calcium and parathyroid hormone, usually without other symptoms.

Most of the side effects disappear with chronic lithium administration. Persistent side effects include tremor, polyuria, leukocytosis, goiter, and elevated blood sugar.

In pregnancy:

1. Lithium crosses the placenta freely and can produce cardiac malformations (Ebstein's anomaly and others), although they seem to be infrequent. Pregnant women should avoid lithium unless the risks of a "manic pregnancy" outweigh the small risk of fetal malformations. Such infants are also at risk for nephrogenic diabetes insipidus, hypoglycemia, and euthyroid goiter.
2. Lithium in milk is 30–100% of the maternal blood level—thus, these mothers should not breast feed.
3. Lithium clearance increases 50–100% early in pregnancy and returns to normal at delivery; so a dosage which had been raised during pregnancy must be immediately reduced, or the mother will become toxic.

## Drug Interactions

Diuretics—Thiazides decrease lithium clearance and increase blood levels. Furosemide, ethacrynic acid, spironolactone, and triamterene may also. Mannitol, urea, and acetazolamide decrease blood levels. Tetracyclines, indomethacin, phenylbuta-zone, and methyldopa may increase lithium blood levels.

Haloperidol (and other high potency neuroleptics)—a (usu-ally) reversible neurotoxicity may occur in some patients at higher doses of antipsychotic (confusion, disorientation, etc). Potentially life-threatening—watch for it.

Chlorpromazine may increase the rate of lithium excretion.

Tricyclic antidepressants may act synergistically with lithium.

Aminophylline increases lithium excretion.

Lithium probably prolongs the neuromuscular blocking effect of succinylcholine.

### Treatment Principles

—Select appropriate patients. Screen for serious medical ill-ness. Preadministration laboratory evaluation should include: CBC, BUN, UA

Serum creatinine.

$T_3$, $T_4$; examine thyroid.

Serum Na if there is reason to question the patient's electro-lyte status.

EKG if the physical or history suggest cardiac disease.

If chronic use of lithium is expected, obtain 24–hour urine volume, creatinine clearance, and protein excretion.

—Treatment of acute mania:

The goal is to produce a therapeutic blood level (1.2–1.4 mEq/l) and maintain it until a clinical effect is seen (usually 7–10 days after an appropriate level is attained). Begin lithium 300 mg PO bid-tid. Always give in divided doses (usually tid-qid; bid-tid with slow-release form). Increase by 300 mg every 2–3 days (typical effective oral dose is 1200–2400 mg/day). Slow-release total oral dosage should be the same as that of regular Li required.

Methods to determine the appropriate steady state dose of Li based on blood levels after a single initial test dose of Li have been developed. As yet, none can be considered standard, but some appear promising—they would help speed up the treat-ment of manic patients.

Since the mania is not controlled by lithium for 2–3 weeks, usually also begin an antipsychotic on the first day of treatment (equivalent of chlorpromazine, 300–1200 mg/day or more, in divided doses). (Watch for <u>possible</u> neurotoxicity.) The antipsychotic provides rapid control of the psychomotor activity while the lithium acts more gradually but is more specific for control of the affect and ideation of mania.

Once the mania begins to remit, the blood Li level <u>may</u> increase—keep watch. Maintain a therapeutic level until the mania is completely controlled (measure blood levels every 1–2 wk).

— Maintenance treatment of mania:

If a patient has a history of recurrent mania, continue lithium after the acute attack. An effective maintenance blood level is 0.8 mEQ/l (range = 0.6–1.0). When stable, measure the blood level every 2–3 months (be aware, a crash diet or strenuous exercise program may change the patient's level). Unfortunately, noncompliance is common, so work with the patient.

Teach the patient to be alert to side effects that suggest toxicity—measure lithium level if they occur. Lithium level increases with sodium loss so advise the patient to be aware of changes in dietary salt intake, sweating, and hot climates (although Li <u>may</u> be lost more rapidly than sodium, causing the Li level to <u>fall</u>).

Concern about gradual lithium-induced renal toxicity is decreasing: standard measures of serum creatinine, UA, BUN, protein excretion, and 24-hour urine volume every 6–12 months may not be necessary. Monitor thyroid function—$T_3$, $T_4$, and physical exam every 6 months.

—Lithium prophylaxis of mania/depression is only partial. If a patient on maintenance lithium shows signs of developing mania, raise the lithium to an acute therapeutic level ($50\%^+$ respond). If the patient develops a severe depression, begin a tricyclic antidepressant (although a few patients will have developed subclinical hypothyroidism $2°$ to Li, so consider thyroid supplementation instead). However, equally effective meds for prophylaxis may include carbamazepine, valproate, and clonazepam—consider them in difficult patients.

## OTHER MOOD STABILIZERS

Carbamazepine (Tegretol) is an anticonvulsant which seems to be as effective as lithium for treating acute mania and for mania prophylaxis. Moreover, it may be of use as an antidepressant and in treating certain violent individuals. Doses are typically $800^+$ mg/day (blood level = 6–8 mg/l)—begin slowly, raise over 2–3 weeks, and check blood level five-six times during first month since level changes because the drug induces its own metabolism. Toxic doses produce marked sedation, ataxia, and diplopia. Allergic rashes are common (5–15%), as are dose-related side effects like sedation and dizziness. Initial, mild, benign leukopenia is common (10%) but watch for more serious problems of aplastic anemia, agranulocytosis, and hepatic toxicity which develops over months or years. Get a CBC and diff at least with every drug blood level.

Another anticonvulsant, valproic acid (Depakene), has a similar spectrum of utility (rapid cycling bipolars, particularly for mania and mania prophylaxis but also depression) but with a different and safer side effect spectrum (sedation, tremor, rare hepatotoxicity). Half-life is $12^+$ hrs: maintain a blood level just above 50 ng/ml (start at 250 mg bid, but may require $1000^+$ mg/day).

## ANTIDEPRESSANT DRUGS

Three groups of antidepressant drugs are in common use: tricyclic antidepressants (TCAs), newer antidepressants, and monoamine oxidase inhibitors (MAOIs) (see Table 23.4). Combinations of these drugs are also occasionally helpful. The TCAs have been the first choice in treating depressions but newer antidepressants (particularly the SSRIs) may be just as effective with dysthymia and major depression as well as having fewer side effects and some specific indications (see below). Lithium carbonate can improve some major depressions, and the antipsychotic drugs are essential in psychotic depression.

**Table 23.4**
**Antidepressant Drugs in Common Use**

| Drugs Available (in USA) | Anticho-linergic | Sedation | Dose (mg/day) |
|---|---|---|---|
| TCAs | | | |
| imipramine (Tofranil) | 4 + | 3 + | 75–300 |
| amitriptyline (Elavil, Endep) | 5 + | 5 + | 75–300 |
| clomipramine (Anafranil) | 4 + | 3 + | 75–250 |
| doxepin (Sinequan, Adapin) | 4 + | 5 + | 75–300 |
| desipramine (Norpramin) | 1 + | 1 + | 75–300 |
| nortriptyline (Pamelor) | 3 + | 2 + | 40–150 |
| protriptyline (Vivactil) | 3 + | 1 + | 20–60 |
| trimipramine (Surmontil) | 3 + | 4 + | 75–200 |
| NEWER ANTIDEPRESSANTS | | | |
| Alprazolam (Xanax) | 1 + | 5 + | 2–6 |
| amoxapine (Asendin) | 2 + | 3 + | 200–300 |
| bupropion (Wellbutrin) | 0–1 + | 0–1 + | 200–450 |
| maprotiline (Ludiomil) | 2 + | 2 + | 50–225 |
| trazodone (Desyrel) | 1 + | 3 + | 100–600 |
| venlafaxine (Effexor) | 1 + | 1 + | 75–375 |
| fluoxetine (Prozac) | 0–1 + | 0–1 + | 10–40 + |
| paroxetine (Paxil) | 0–1 + | 0–1 + | 20–50 |
| sertraline (Zoloft) | 0–1 + | 0–1 + | 50–200 |
| MAOIs | | | |
| phenelzine (Nardil) | 1 + | 1 + | 30–90 |
| isocarboxazid (Marplan) | 1 + | 1 + | 10–30 |
| tranylcypromine (Parnate) | 1 + | 0 | 20–60 |

## TRICYCLIC ANTIDEPRESSANTS (TCAs)

### Indications for Use

**Recommended for:**

1. Major depression—particularly with vegetative symptoms and a diurnal variation (70–75% of patients respond).
2. Bipolar disorder, depressed or mixed—particularly if there are vegetative symptoms. Lithium may be useful as well.
3. Short-term maintenance therapy in patients with resolved major depression or bipolar disease.
4. Prophylaxis in patients with severe, recurrent major depression.

5. Psychotic depression (hallucinations, delusions, paranoia, etc.)—must be combined with antipsychotics (although ECT may be preferable for some).
6. Postpartum depressions that are severe.

**Other uses:**

— Dysthymic disorder—mild chronic depressions deserve a trial of TCAs (or SSRIs).
— Atypical depression—patients with significant anxiety, hypochondriasis, and "neurotic" complaints—as an alternative to MAOIs.
— Panic disorder—one among several choices.
— Agoraphobia, with panic attacks.
— Obsessive compulsive disorder—particularly those patients who also have a depressed mood.
— Selected patients with chronic pain (with, and without, depression).
— Childhood conditions—both enuresis and school phobia may respond to low doses of a TCA.

TCAs should <u>not</u> be used routinely in the various minor depressive syndromes.

## Mechanisms of Action

The effects of TCAs on CNS neurotransmitters are complex and vary from one tricyclic to another. Therapeutic impact is <u>thought</u> to be related to some combination of CNS interneuronal norepinephrine increase due to presynaptic NE reuptake blockade and to the sensitization of postsynaptic neurons to serotonin. Although affecting both systems, <u>secondary amines</u> (desipramine, protriptyline, and nortriptyline) may preferentially raise NE levels while <u>tertiary amines</u> (amitriptyline, imipramine, and doxepin) have a greater effect on serotonin—a fact used to account for some interpatient response differences. In summary, however, knowledge is incomplete and we use these drugs based on "clinical wisdom."

## Pharmacokinetics

TCAs are absorbed rapidly and completely from the GI tract, undergo an enterohepatic cycle, and develop peak plasma levels in 2–8 hr. TCAs are highly bound to plasma and tissue proteins and are fat-soluble—free TCA is only about 1% of the total body load. They are metabolized by the liver and are excreted by the kidney. The half-life ranges from several hours to more than 2 days.

Well-studied plasma blood levels are available for imipramine, nortriptyline, desipramine, and amitriptyline. Do not measure them routinely—indications include:

1. Treatment failure—Interindividual plasma levels vary markedly following the same oral dose (up to 30–fold differences), so always consider an ineffective plasma level when explaining a treatment failure. Therapeutic range is 150–300 ng/ml for imipramine ( + its metabolite, desipramine), amitriptyline ( + nortriptyline), or desipramine, and 50–160 ng/ml for nortriptyline.
2. Therapeutic window—Some TCAs may have a therapeutic window (eg, nortriptyline and possibly desipramine)—the drugs are ineffective outside this range—while others seem to have no therapeutic upper limit (eg, imipramine—range limited only by side effects).
3. Suspected patient noncompliance.
4. Patients with significant side effects on a usual oral dose—they may have an excessively high plasma level.
5. Patients with cardiac disease—attempt to maintain a low (but effective) plasma level.
6. The medically unstable patient (particularly the elderly).
7. Overdose—plasma levels are mandatory.

## Side Effects

Side effects are frequent and usually mild but they can be serious or fatal (particularly cardiac effects in TCA overdoses) and are more common in the elderly.

Anticholinergic:
  Dry mouth
  Blurred vision (near vision)
  Constipation, urinary hesitancy
Autonomic:
  Sweating
  Impotence, ejaculatory dysfunction
Cardiac:
  In normal dosages:
    Tachycardia
    EKG changes (T-wave flattening, increased PR and QT interval)
  In overdose:
    PVCs, ventricular arrhythmias
    AV block and BBB
    CHF and cardiac arrest

Other:
  Orthostatic hypotension (can be severe)
  Sedation
  Restlessness, insomnia
  Rashes, allergic reactions
  Weight gain (a common cause of patient noncompliance)
  Anorexia, nausea and vomiting
  EEG changes
  Tremor (fine, rapid, usually hands and fingers)
  Confusion (in elderly)
  Seizures in patients who are predisposed

Tolerance usually develops to the anticholinergic and sedative side effects. Use cautiously in the elderly and in patients with BPH—avoid in patients with narrow-angle glaucoma. Pregnancy is not an absolute contraindication for TCA use, although there is suggestive (but not convincing) evidence of teratogenicity: avoid use in the first trimester if possible. Severe hypotension occasionally can limit drug use (it is least with nortriptyline and doxepin).

Most worrisome are the cardiac effects. There have been a few reports of sudden death from presumed arrhythmias—patients with preexisting heart disease (particularly bundle-branch disease) and/or hypertension (eg, the elderly) are at risk for any of the cardiac side effects. Do not use following an acute MI or while in CHF. The danger is greatest with higher doses, eg, following an OD with a TCA.

There are wide differences between agents in their ability to produce some side effects, and these should be considered when choosing a drug. The presence of side effects is not a good indication that a therapeutic plasma level has been reached.

Certain psychiatric conditions may be adversely affected by TCAs.

— Schizophrenia may be made worse.
— A depressed bipolar patient may become manic (10%+; "may" be lower with other antidepressants).

A withdrawal syndrome occurs in some patients who have been taking high doses of TCAs (eg, imipramine 150–300 mg/day) for weeks or months. If medication is stopped abruptly, symptoms begin in 1–2 days and include anxiety, headache, myalgia, chills, malaise, and nausea. Withdraw the medication gradually (eg, 25–50 mg/wk).

### Drug Interactions

— TCA plasma level is increased (at times dangerously) by methylphenidate, Antabuse, MAOIs, antipsychotics, exogenous thyroid, cimetidine, and guanethidine.
— TCA plasma level is decreased (frequently below therapeutic range) by barbiturates, alcohol, carbamazepine, phenytoin, doxycycline, and smoking (may need to monitor level in heavy smokers).
— CNS depression occurs with antipsychotics, anticonvulsants, hypnotic-sedatives, and alcohol.
— TCAs impair the antihypertensive effect of methyldopa, guanethidine, and bethanidine.
— There is a synergistic anticholinergic effect with other central anticholinergics—may produce a toxic psychosis.
— Marked hypertension can be caused by administration of TCAs with sympathomimetic drugs (eg, isoproterenol, epinephrine, phenylephrine, amphetamines).
— TCAs may dangerously increase the half-life of anticoagulants (eg, Dicumarol)—monitor prothrombin time.

### Treatment Principles

— Identify the patient likely to benefit from a TCA (remember: for many patients the starting drug of choice may be one of the newer antidepressants).
    1. Appropriate clinical presentation (eg, major depression).
    2. Past personal history of good TCA response.
    3. Past family history of good TCA response.
— Unless side effects are likely to be a problem, begin with a tertiary TCA. They are metabolized in the liver to 2° TCAs (imipramine to desipramine; amitriptyline to nortriptyline) and thus both the 3° and 2° TCAs are present in the body.
— Side effects may be useful (eg, consider amitriptyline or doxepin in the agitated depressive, desipramine in the elderly with anticholinergic intolerance, protriptyline if sedation is a problem, and nortriptyline if hypotension is excessive).
— One technique for treating depression with TCAs is:
    Begin imipramine 50 mg PO HS (or equivalent—less in elderly; more in the obese) and increase by 25–50 mg every 2–3 days until 150 mg is reached. If side effects interfere, slow down.

Hold dosage at 150 mg for 1 week. If depression remains, increase to 200 mg (50 mg during the day, 150 at HS).

Hold dosage at 200 mg for 1 week, then increase in 50 mg steps to 300 mg (150 mg in divided doses during the day, 150 mg at HS). Consider hospitalizing the patient for trials above 200 mg/day. Maintain at 300 mg for 2–3 weeks. It is important to do complete trials, if side effect problems allow. If depression remains:

1. Has patient been taking medication?
2. Has a therapeutic window been passed?
3. Measure plasma level.

If the patient is unimproved, consider:

1. A newer antidepressant or a different TCA.
2. ECT.
3. An MAOI. Allow 1–2 wks for transfer.
4. After 2–3 unsuccessful trials, reevaluate the diagnosis.

With a good response, sleep and appetite usually return first, then an improved mood. There is usually a 1–3 wk delay in the therapeutic effect, so don't stop meds prematurely.

— Never give a worrisomely depressed or seriously suicidal patient a prescription for more than 1000 mg of imipramine (or equivalent).
— If treating a psychotic depression, use a TCA and an antipsychotic simultaneously.
— If treating a depression in a bipolar patient taking lithium, continue the lithium if it has been effective prophylactically. The lithium <u>may</u> help prevent a manic overshoot.
— If treating a phobic-anxiety disorder, expect improvement with a lower dosage (eg, 100 mg).
— Simultaneous use of a TCA and an MAOI is currently discouraged by the FDA but is often useful.

— Maintenance care: In a successfully treated patient, maintain the medication at acute levels for 6 months. If the patient has had a recurrence of a major depression, consider long-term TCA maintenance at full dosage (reduces likelihood of a relapse by 50%). Consider lithium maintenance in a recurrent bipolar illness. If there is no previous history of illness, gradually withdraw the medication.
— Recognize (1) as many as one-quarter of the improved patients relapse during the first 4 months and (2) a significant number of patients (30%+) maintain a chronic, low-level depression, even though treated successfully for the acute illness ("double depression"). Depression, all too often, is a chronic illness.

— Clomipramine (Anafranil) is a little special: approved for OCD but an effective TCA antidepressant with a significant serotonin effect.

Range of effectiveness is closer to some of the new antidepressants (although it has all the TCA side effects).

— TCA overdose is life-threatening and should be treated in a medical inpatient unit. Recognize that dangerously high plasma levels may continue for more than 1 week.

— Although generally not considered drugs of abuse, illicit use of amitriptyline to produce anticholinergic intoxication has been reported. Watch for it.

## NEWER ANTIDEPRESSANTS

The primary reason for using "newer antidepressants" is their different side effect spectrums and toxicity: they differ little from TCAs in effectiveness, disorders treated, or speed of onset. Generally, use these drugs if a TCA trial fails or if the depression is less severe. Their mechanisms of action are diverse and poorly understood (most effect 5–HT, NE, and/or DA) although one group, the "pure serotonin reuptake inhibitors" (fluoxetine, paroxetine, and sertraline), have a more focused action. The key drugs include:

**alprazolam:** a benzodiazepine that may be antidepressant at higher doses; few side effects except sedation and risk of addiction; safe in overdose. (Probably a "second-string" antidepressant.)

**amoxapine:** a metabolite of the antipsychotic loxapine; side effects similar to TCAs; may be of particular use in psychotic depressions.

**bupropion:** an effective drug with few side effects and safe in overdose; can produce insomnia and sweating; may be more likely to produce seizures, so go slow and avoid patients at risk. Probably one of the better new drugs. Aim for 300–400 mg/day in divided doses. Mechanism of action is unknown.

**maprotiline:** like TCAs; less cardiotoxicity in overdose.

**serotonin reuptake blockers:** Fluoxetine—little sedation or anticholinergic effects (perhaps daytime sedation in a few); does produce GI upset, rashes, sexual inhibition, insomnia, and restlessness. Clearly effective in mild/moderate depressions and may be the med to start with, rather than a TCA. Try 20 mg daily (one dose—long half-life (days)), although a few patients require 40 mg while some benefit from 20 mg every other day.

Sertraline is similar to fluoxetine; safe and mild side effects—nausea, diarrhea, tremor, insomnia, somnolence, dry mouth, ejaculatory delay; one dose/day of 50–200 mg.

Paroxetine is also similar; daily dose is 20–50 mg. Two more SSRIs are on the way: fluvoxamine (Luvox; approved for OCD) and nefazodone (Serzone). Eventually the price to the patient of these essential but expensive medications should drop (I hope).

Three drug-drug combinations are of concern. (1) Fluoxetine plus an MAOI produces a dangerous **serotonin syndrome:** restlessness, tremor and myoclonus, hyperreflexia, diarrhea, and diaphoresis leading possibly to confusion and death. Wait 5 weeks to begin an MAOI after stopping fluoxetine or several weeks after sertraline; wait 2–3 weeks going from an MAOI to an SSRI. (2) SSRIs raise (sometimes dramatically) blood levels of TCAs, trazodone, maprotiline, carbamazepine, the benzodiazepines, as well as (probably) others, so be careful. (3) L-tryptophan plus SSRIs can produce myoclonic jerks. Finally, marked concern has been expressed by a few about the possibility that these medications may produce (or worsen) suicidal and/ or aggressive impulses—this may be a "red herring"; much evidence refutes this but the evidence is not definitive in individual cases.

**trazodone:** free of anticholinergic and most cardiac effects; produces orthostatic hypotension, sedation (useful if insomnia is a major problem), GI distress, headaches, and (rarely) priapism. Start low (eg, 50 mg) and raise to the 200–300 mg range. Is it less effective than others?

**venlafaxine:** a "serotonin-like" antidepressant with NE effects. It has a short half-life (less than 1 day rather than days), few side effects (nausea, sleepiness, dizziness and nervousness, sexual inhibition), and appears safe. Looks like another good one. Aim for about 150 mg in divided doses.

## MONOAMINE OXIDASE INHIBITORS (MAOIs)
### Indications for Use

Recommended for:

1. Atypical depression—MAOIs should probably be the drug of choice for "atypical, neurotic depressions" (50–60% improve), ie, patients with varying degrees of depressive and anxious affect, rejection sensitivity, irritability, emotional lability, hyperphagia, hypersomnolence, reversed diurnal variation (worse in evening), and hypochondriasis (all with the vegetative symptoms of a major depression). If a TCA is tried first and fails, follow with a trial of an MAOI. ECT is notoriously unsuccessful with these patients.

Other uses:

— Patients with major depression or dysthymic disorder who have not improved with a trial of one or more TCAs and for whom ECT is not the obvious next choice. Has the patient or a family member responded to an MAOI in the past?

— MAOIs appear useful in panic disorder and in agoraphobia with panic attacks (particularly phenelzine).

## Mechanisms of Action

MAOIs block MAO (and other enzymes) throughout the body (eg, blood, platelets, gut, CNS). MAO catalyzes the oxidation of the biogenic amines tyramine, 5–HT, DA, and NE. The therapeutic effect of MAOIs is probably related to the increase in CNS NE and 5–HT which result from the ability of MAOI to block this oxidation of intracellular catecholamines.

MAO exists in two forms: MAO-A (in brain, liver, gut, and sympathetic nerves) which acts primarily on 5–HT and NE, and MAO-B (in brain, liver, and platelets) which acts on phenylethylamine. They both act on DA and tyramine. The MAOIs phenelzine, isocarboxazid, and tranylcypromine inhibit both types of MAO; clorgyline (not on the market) inhibits MAO-A; while pargyline (Eutonyl—used as an antihypertensive, not an antidepressant) and selegiline (Eldepryl—available for Parkinson's disease) inhibit MAO-B. MAO-A inhibitors may be more effective antidepressants, while MAO-B inhibitors are less prone to produce hypertensive reactions. More work remains to be done.

## Pharmacokinetics

MAOIs are rapidly absorbed and are metabolized into inactive products by several means including acetylation (hydrazide MAOIs only). There may be patients who are "rapid acetylators" and who require increased oral doses of MAOI for improvement to occur. There is usually a delay of 1–4 weeks before a clinical response is seen. Measured inhibition of platelet MAO in blood samples (80–90% inhibition appears necessary) provides some indication that an effective level of CNS MAOI has been reached, although this procedure is currently primarily a research technique.

## Side Effects

MAOIs have numerous side effects. However, they do not have the range of cardiotoxic effects of the TCAs, although some experts believe that they should be contraindicated in the elderly because of the risk of hypertensive crisis (see below) with its potentially fatal outcome in the older patient.

The most common side effects include drowsiness or stimulation (short-lived), insomnia, giddiness, dizziness, dry mouth, impotence, orthostatic hypotension, constipation, and weight gain. They also can precipitate a manic or schizoaffective attack. Since occasional patients develop hepatotoxicity, patients using MAOIs long-term should have periodic examinations of liver function. They are contraindicated in patients with liver disease, CHF, or pheochromocytoma.

The most serious (but infrequent) side effect is hypertension (hypertensive crisis, cerebrovascular bleeding) and hyperpyrexia in response to ingested tyramine (or other pressor amines). The MAO in the gut wall which usually prevents entrance of large quantities of ingested pressor amines is inhibited by MAOIs, thus allowing a generalized sympathetic effect when tyramine-containing foods are eaten. The first sign of an impending crisis is usually a sudden, severe occipital or temporal headache (also sweating, fever, neck stiffness, photophobia). Patients taking MAOIs should avoid:

Protein-containing foods which are cultured or spoiled:
Strong cheeses (cottage, ricotta, or cream cheese are OK).
Pickled or kippered herring; dried, salted fish.
Chicken livers or liver pate; any slightly spoiled meat; ripened sausages.
Old yogurt, chocolate.
Nondistilled alcohol—red or Chianti wine; beer.
Broad beans (Fava, Italian green, and lima beans).

A number of adrenergic drugs (see below) may also produce a hypertensive crisis. If one occurs, treat with slow administration of phentolamine (Regitine, 5 mg IV). It usually resolves in a few hours. The responsible patient may carry a 10 mg capsule of nifedipine with him to take sublingually for rapid relief when signs of a crisis appear (then visit an ER).

### Drug Interactions

Hypertensive crisis—can be produced by amphetamines, cocaine, and anorectics (stimulate NE release from adrenergic neurons), catecholamines (epinephrine, NE), sympathomimetic precursors (dopamine, methyldopa, levodopa), and sympathomimetic amines (ephedrine, phenylephrine, phenylpropanolamine, pseudoephedrine, metaraminol, over-the-counter cold and hay fever medication).

Meperidine (Demerol)—A few patients develop severe, immediate hypertension and sweating or hypotension and coma. Narcotics may act similarly.

CNS depression—potentiated by alcohol, major tranquilizers, and hypnotic-sedatives.

## Treatment Principles

— Instruct the patient carefully about the potential side effects and the drugs and foods to avoid.
— Begin phenelzine 15 mg PO bid-tid and increase by 15 mg weekly to 60–90 mg/day. Maintain that dosage for 4 weeks before assuming a failure.
— Maintenance is at acute treatment doses. In some patients, for unknown reasons, both the antidepressant and antiphobic effects become ineffective after 6 months to 1 year of use.
— Allow for a 1–2 week washout before starting another drug.
— If insomnia becomes a major problem, give all doses before midafternoon.
— Tranylcypromine has significant stimulant properties.
— Don't give impulsive, potentially suicidal outpatients large prescriptions.

## ANTIDEPRESSANT DRUG COMBINATIONS

Combined drug therapy may help a patient who has failed trials with single antidepressants. Such treatment is empirical (almost every conceivable combination has been tried by someone at some time): proceed carefully and watch out for side effects (do not combine SSRIs with the MAOIs). Potentially useful combinations include:

**Antidepressant** and **lithium**—an effective mix for both unipolar and bipolar depression; adding lithium to a TCA or a MAOI occasionally may produce a rapid (days) improvement. Effective Li blood level varies from 0.6–1.2.

**Antidepressant** and **antipsychotic**—for psychotic depressions.

**Antidepressant** and **thyroid**—occasional patients improve (Did they have a subclinical thyroid dysfunction?). Choose triiodothyronine

($T_3$), 25–50 $\mu$g/day—if ineffective, stop.

**TCA or SSRIs** and low-dose **buspirone** (10 mg tid)

**TCA** and an **MAOI**—particularly nortriptyline or amitriptyline with phenelzine; avoid imipramine and serotonin reuptake inhibitors; do not add a TCA to an MAOI; use lower doses than if you were using each drug alone.

**MAOI** and low-dose **trazodone** (50–75 mg)

**Lithium** and **bupropion**—for rapid cycling bipolars?

## ANTIANXIETY AGENTS

### Drugs Available

There are numerous drugs available for sedation, of which only the benzodiazepines and the new and unique agent, buspirone, can be recommended (see Table 23.5).

### Indications for Use

1. Short-term treatment of restlessness and anxiety (eg, after life crises). They are sedative at low dosage and hypnotic at higher doses.

**Table 23.5**
**Sedative-Hypnotic Agents**

| Drug | Half-life (hrs) | Dose (mg/day) |
|------|-----------------|---------------|
| alprazolam (Xanax) | 11–14 | .5–4 |
| chlordiazepoxide (Librium) | 15–60 | 15–60 |
| clorazepate (Tranxene) | 50–100 | 15–45 |
| diazepam (Valium) | 30–60 | 5–40 |
| halazepam (Paxipam) | 50–100 | 60–160 |
| lorazepam (Ativan) | 10–20 | 2–6 |
| oxazepam (Serax) | 5–10 | 30–120 |
| prazepam (Centrax) | 60–70 | 20–60 |
| [clonazepam (Klonopin)] | 30–40 | 1–15 |
| estazolam (ProSom) | 10–24 | 1–2 (HS) |
| flurazepam (Dalmane) | 50 + | 15–30 (HS) |
| quazepam (Doral) | 40 + | 7.5–15 (HS) |
| temazepam (Restoril) | 8–18 | 15–30 (HS) |
| triazolam (Halcion) | 2–3 | 0.125–0.25 (HS) |
| zolpidem (Ambien) | 2–3 | 5–10 (HS) |
| buspirone (Buspar) | 2–3 | 15–60 |

They have no antipsychotic activity and thus should not be used as the exclusive treatment for psychotic disorders.

2. Generalized anxiety disorder and mild panic symptoms. Panic disorder (alprazolam, clonazepam).
3. Alcohol withdrawal (see Chapter 16); hypnotic-sedative withdrawal; psychosis due to hallucinogens.
4. Various seizure disorders.
5. Muscle relaxant (diazepam).

### Mechanisms of Action and Pharmacokinetics

They enhance the inhibitory neurotransmitters (eg, GABA, glycine) and they have a specific depressant effect on the limbic system. As the dosage rises, there is generalized CNS depression. Buspirone, on the other hand, affects dopamine and serotonin receptors.

They are well absorbed orally, are all both water and lipid soluble, and are usually metabolized by the liver but may also be excreted by the kidney. They are slowly and variably absorbed IM (faster by PO route). There is very little hepatic enzyme induction. Peak blood levels usually occur 1–4 hr after the oral dose (1 hr for diazepam).

### Side Effects

In comparison to other classes of psychoactive drugs, side effects are few.

— Most common problem is CNS depression manifested by daytime sedation, decreased concentration, and poor coordination in some patients at therapeutic doses. They are very safe drugs, although a massive OD or combination with alcohol or other drugs will produce life-threatening CNS depression.
— Anterograde amnesia can occur after hypnotic-induced sleep with short-acting drugs (eg, lorazepam, triazolam). Patients may lose memory for events which occurred during the night or during the next day.
— Tolerance and physical addiction occur, particularly with short-acting drugs or when taken at high doses for several months. The withdrawal syndrome is usually mild (but may be severe: rebound anxiety, nausea, sweating, hyperalertness, and occasionally seizures) and typically occurs 2–14 days after stopping the drug (most rapid with the shorter-acting drugs). Discontinuing alprazolam may be particu-

larly difficult (withdrawal sxs can include paranoia, marked anxiety and agitation, psychosis, hallucinations, and seizures)—go very slowly (eg, decrease 0.5 mg weekly at first, then 0.25 mg weekly below a total daily dose of 2 mg).
— Untoward but infrequent psychiatric manifestations include exacerbation of schizophrenia and depression.
— There appear to be no autonomic side effects.
— Benzodiazepines seem to be safe in pregnancy.

## Drug Interactions

— There is an increased sedative effect when combined with CNS depressants (eg, alcohol). Moreover, the combination with alcohol at times actually may be anxiogenic.
— Disulfiram (Antabuse) and cimetidine impair the metabolism of the long-acting benzodiazepines and thus raise the plasma levels. The shorter-acting drugs appear less affected.
— Food, antacids, and anticholinergic drugs appear to decrease the rate, but not the extent, of drug absorption.

## Treatment Principles

— Use the long-acting benzodiazepines (chlordiazepoxide, diazepam, clorazepate) on an HS or bid schedule. Use a tid-qid schedule for the shorter-acting ones (oxazepam, lorazepam).
— Recognize that the longer-acting drugs (and their active metabolites) may accumulate over days or weeks, producing increasing symptoms of sedation, etc. Lorazepam and oxazepam have a simple metabolism and do not accumulate.
— Try to avoid use for longer than 1–3 weeks in most patients either as a sedative or a hypnotic. Some patients may be able to use them less frequently but long-term on an "as needed" basis, but be alert for those patients prone to abuse. Reevaluate if you find that you have used meds for longer than 2–4 months (however, a few patients seem to do well on low doses for long periods—not recommended if it can be avoided). Addiction can occur (particularly among alcoholics) but is uncommon.
— Use by PO route, if possible.
— Encourage the patient to avoid the simultaneous use of a benzodiazepine and alcohol or another sedative-hypnotic drug.
— Be very careful when giving to the elderly—confusion is common. Dosage may need to be 20% or less of the usual young adult dose.
— If the patient has been taking benzodiazepines for several months, stop meds over 2–3 weeks (particularly the long-acting drugs).

— The more sedative benzodiazepines and those with shorter half-lives are used primarily as hypnotics although, in adequate dosage, any drug in this class can be hypnotic. Flurazepam is rapidly absorbed and is useful for sleep onset problems; temazepam and flurazepam may help frequent awakening. Flurazepam, particularly because of its long-acting metabolite N-desalkylflurazepam (quazepam has the same major active metabolite), accumulates and produces a hangover in a few (often older) patients. Triazolam is very short-acting and does not accumulate but has been associated in a number of patients with "withdrawal-like" symptoms after each dose: eg, early morning insomnia, irritability, daytime anxiety and dysphoria (and even (rare) confusion and paranoia). [It has been "accused" of producing rage attacks in some patients—the issue remains unsettled but the drug looks suspicious.]

   Zolpidem (Ambien; rapidly absorbed, short half-life, minimal rebound insomnia or daytime somnolence) is a new nonbenzodiazepine hypnotic that may be an improvement but may have the usual problems of tolerance with extended use and addiction at higher doses.

— **Buspirone** represents a new class of anxiolytics (a serotonin (5-HT$_{1A}$) agonist). It has few side effects, produces less sedation and cognitive and psychomotor impairment than the benzodiazepines, is not likely to be abused, but may be less effective as well. It is a reasonable alternative drug, particularly for chronic anxiety states and in the elderly. Begin at 5 mg tid (5 mg QD in the elderly) and increase over 10 days to the average daily dose of 20–30 mg, bid-tid. Unlike the benzodiazepines, expect 2–3 wks before it begins to work. It "may" also augment the antidepressant effects of the SSRIs and decrease agitation in the demented elderly.

## ELECTROCONVULSIVE THERAPY (ECT)

Despite its unjustified notoriety, ECT is legitimate. Although its mechanism of action is unknown, it is effective, painless, and safe (mortality rate less than competing therapies or the untreated state: 0.01–0.03% of patients treated—mostly cardiovascular deaths). However, before administration always obtain:

1. Informed consent from a voluntary, competent patient.
2. Informed consent from a relative or guardian of a voluntary, incompetent patient and an independent psychiatric opinion of therapeutic need.
3. Court approval for administration to a resisting, involuntary patient who is a danger to himself or others.

Discuss the risks of amnesia, confusion, and headache with the patient and his family. Also discuss the risks of not receiving ECT.

## INDICATIONS FOR USE

ECT is a serious procedure—use only in those conditions for which it is recommended. It is tempting to give ECT to any patient who is not improving—don't!

MAJOR AFFECTIVE ILLNESS: Patients with Major Depression or Bipolar disorder, depressed respond well to ECT (80–90% recover vs 70%+ treated with antidepressants). Patients with marked vegetative symptoms (eg, insomnia, constipation, suicidal rumination, obsessions with guilt, anorexia and weight loss, psychomotor retardation) are particularly responsive. ECT is much more effective than antidepressants for psychotically depressed patients—ie, vegetative symptoms and paranoid or somatic delusions. Give antidepressants a full trial (eg, imipramine 200–300 mg/day for 4 wk), then consider ECT if there is no improvement.

Mania (Bipolar Disorder, manic) also responds to ECT: typically used only if lithium carbonate ( + antipsychotic) fails to control the acute phase.

SCHIZOPHRENIC DISORDERS: Catatonic Schizophrenia of either stuporous or excited type responds well to ECT. Try antipsychotic medication first but, if the condition is life threatening (eg, hyperexcited delirium), go quickly to ECT. Occasional acutely psychotic patients (particularly of the schizoaffective type) who do not respond to medication alone may improve if ECT is added, but for most schizophrenics (eg, chronics) it is of little value.

ECT is the treatment of choice for:

1. Actively suicidal depressed patients who may not live until antidepressants begin to work.
2. Depressed patients (particularly the elderly) whose medical condition makes administration of antidepressants risky. Patients with both depression and organic brain impairment may do better with ECT. ECT can be safely performed during pregnancy.
3. Seriously depressed patients who have had an adequate trial of antidepressants (60–70% recovers with ECT).

**CONTRAINDICATIONS FOR USE**

There are no <u>absolute</u> contraindications. Always weigh the risk of the procedure against the danger incurred if the patient is untreated. Neurological disease is not a contraindication. Response improves with age—patients under 30 respond more poorly.

<u>Very high risk:</u>

Increased intracranial pressure (eg, brain tumor, CNS infection): ECT briefly increases CSF pressure and risks tentorial herniation. Always check for papilledema before administration.

Recent MI: ECT frequently causes arrhythmias (vagal arrhythmias producing postictal PVCs and extravagal arrhythmias producing PVCs anytime during the procedure) which can be fatal if there has been recent muscle damage. Wait until enzymes and EKG have stabilized.

<u>Moderate risk</u>

Severe osteoarthritis, osteoporosis, or recent fracture: Prepare thoroughly for treatment (ie, with muscle relaxants); retinal detachment.

Cardiovascular disease (eg, hypertension, angina, aneurysm, arrhythmias): Premedicate carefully; have a cardiologist available.

Major infections, recent CVA, chronic respiratory difficulty, acute peptic ulcer, pheochromocytoma.

**TECHNIQUE OF ADMINISTRATION**

**Pre-ECT Medical Workup**

Complete history and physical, concentrating on cardiac and neurological status, CBC, chemistry, UA, VDRL, chest and spine X-rays, EKG. Get EEG (and/or CT scan) if neurological is abnormal.

**A Typical Technique**

ECT routines vary—there is no "one right way." Usually perform in a hospital and with the aid of an anesthesiologist.

1. Prepare the patient with information and psychological support. Have him void and defecate beforehand. NPO after midnight. If

markedly anxious, give 5 mg of diazepam IM 1–2 hr before treatment. Antidepressants, antipsychotics, sedative-hypnotics, and anticonvulsants (among others) should be stopped the day before treatment. Lithium usually should be stopped several days beforehand: risk is organicity.

2. Make patient comfortable. Remove dentures. Hyperextend the back with a pillow.

3. When ready, premedicate with atropine (0.6–1.2 mg SC, IM, or IV). This anticholinergic controls vagal arrhythmias and reduces GI secretions.

4. Provide 90–100% oxygen by bag when respirations are not spontaneous.

5. Give sodium methohexital (Brevital) (40–100 mg IV, rapidly). This short-acting barbiturate anesthetic is used to produce a light coma.

6. Next quickly give enough of the muscle relaxant succinylcholine (Anectine) (30–80 mg IV, rapidly—monitor depth of relaxation by the muscle fasciculations produced) to remove all but very minor evidences of a generalized seizure (eg, plantar flexion).

7. Once relaxed, place a bite-block in the mouth and then give electroconvulsive stimulus. Two methods are common and acceptable today:

   Unilateral: One electrode placed in the frontotemporal area and the other 7–10 cm away in the parietal region—both on the nondominant hemisphere (right side for right-handed persons, 60% R and 40% L for left-handers). Unilateral ECT is commonly used because it produces less postictal confusion and amnesia but it seems to be less effective than bilateral ECT.

   Bilateral: Bifrontotemporal electrode placement. This is the traditional technique—effective but produces more side effects (eg, amnesia, headache).

   Effectiveness of either method depends on producing a central generalized seizure (peripheral effects are not necessary) lasting at least 25 seconds. A "brief-pulse" abrupt electrical stimulus rather than a sign wave seems to work better. Monitor this with EEG, peripheral EMG, or the tonic/clonic movement of the hand on the same side as the electrode (unilateral) which has been freed of muscle relaxant by a tight cuff applied before the administration of the succinylcholine. If a seizure is not produced, increase the stimulus and repeat ("missed" or unilateral seizures are usually of little therapeutic value—they occur more frequently with unilateral shock, perhaps accounting for its lesser effectiveness).

8. Monitor patient carefully until stable—there is usually 15–30 minutes of postictal confusion. These patients are at risk for prolonged apnea and a postictal delirium (5–10 mg of IV diazepam may help).

## COMPLICATIONS OF ECT

— Amnesia (retrograde and anterograde)—variable; beginning after 3–4 treatments; lasting weeks to 2–3 months (but occasionally much longer); more severe with bilateral placement, increased number of treatments, increased current strength, and prior presence of organicity.
— Headache, muscle aches, nausea.
— Dizziness, confusion—The persistence and severity of the confusion increases with an increasing number of treatments.
— Reserpine and ECT given concurrently have resulted in fatalities.
— Fractures—rare with good muscle relaxation.
— ECT anesthesia risks:
Atropine worsens narrow angle glaucoma.
Succinylcholine's action is prolonged in pseudocholinesterase deficiency states. These conditions (malnutrition, liver disease, chronic renal dialysis, use of echothiophate for glaucoma) can lead to potentially fatal hypotonia.
Procainamide, lidocaine, and quinidine can potentiate succinylcholine.
Methohexital can precipitate an attack of acute intermittent porphyria.

## TREATMENT PRINCIPLES

1. Usually give one treatment/day—on alternate days.
2. Depressions usually require 6–12 treatments. Mania and catatonia require 10–20 treatments. Expect to see improved behavior after 2–6 treatments if it is going to be effective. Allow the clinical response to determine the treatment endpoint. Be <u>very cautious</u> (and seek a second opinion) about exceeding 20 treatments during one period of illness.
3. Maintenance ECT (single treatments every 1–3 months during the months or years after recovery) <u>may</u> be useful, particularly with elderly depressed patients, or in those who relapse on medication or in whom it is contraindicated.
4. Maintenance antidepressants, antipsychotics, and lithium (begin after a successful course of ECT) definitely forestall relapse. Without medication, the relapse rate is high.

## PSYCHOSURGERY

Little psychosurgery is currently performed in the US. Modern psychosurgeons make one of several possible small cuts in the brain (usually in the limbic system) which can improve a variety of psychiatric conditions and which have few side effects unlike the widely destructive prefrontal lobotomy of the past).

All candidates for surgery must have an intractable and devastating condition unrelieved by any other therapy. Conditions likely to respond include chronic pain with depression and severe depression alone. Improvement occurs in some patients who have severe obsessive-compulsive and anxiety states and in a few schizophrenics. The mechanism for the improvement is uncertain and a variety of different surgical cuts yield similar results. Despite the lack of theoretical sophistication, there are patients for whom psychosurgery is a valid "last resort."

## Suggested Readings

Abrams R: Electroconvulsive Therapy, 2nd ed. New York, Oxford University Press, 1992.

Beasley CM, Dornseif BE, Bosomworth JC, et al: Fluoxetine and suicide: A meta-analysis of controlled trials of treatment for depression. Br Med J 303:685–692, 1991.

Blackwell B: Monoamine oxidase inhibitor interactions with other drugs. J Clin Psychopharmacol 11:55–58, 1991.

Bollini P, Pampallona S, Orza MJ, et al: Antipsychotic drugs: is more worse? Psychological Med 24:307–316, 1994.

Bowden CL, Schatzberg AF, Rosenbaum A, et al: Fluoxetine and desipramine in major depressive disorder. J Clin Psychopharmacol 13:305–310, 1993.

Breier A, Buchanon RW, Irish D, et al: Clozapine treatment of outpatients with schizophrenia. Hosp Community Psychiatry 44:1145–1149, 1993.

Calabrese JR, Delucchi GA: Spectrum of efficacy of valproate in 55 patients with rapid-cycling bipolar disorder. Am J Psychiatry 147:431–434, 1990.

Caroff SN, Mann SC, Lazarus A, et al: Neuroleptic malignant syndrome: Diagnostic issues. Psychiatric Ann 21:130–147, 1991.

Carroll JA, Jefferson JW, Greist JH: Treating tremor induced by lithium. Hosp Community Psychiatry 38:1280–1288, 1987.

Cohen LS, Friedman JM, Jefferson JW, et al: A reevaluation of risk of in utero exposure to lithium. JAMA 271:146–150, 1994.

Cole JO: New directions in antidepressant therapy: A review of sertraline, a unique serotonin reuptake inhibitor. J Clin Psychiatry 53:333–340, 1992.

Cole JO, Bodkin JA: Antidepressant drug side effects. J Clin Psychiatry 51(1, suppl):21–26, 1990.

Davis JM, Wang Z, Janicak PG: A quantitative analysis of clinical drug trials for the treatment of affective disorders. Psychopharmacol Bull 29:175–181, 1993.

DePaulo JR, Correa EI, Sapir DG: Renal function and lithium. Am J Psychiatry 143:892–895, 1986.

Doddi S, Rifkin A, Karajgi B, et al: Blood levels of haloperidol and clinical outcome in schizophrenia. J Clin Psychopharmacol 14:187–195, 1994.

Dominguez RA, Goldstein BJ: 25 years of benzodiazepine experience: Clinical commentary on use, abuse, and withdrawal. Hosp Formul 20:1000–1014, 1985.

Dubin WR, Jaffe R, Roemor R, et al: The efficacy and safety of maintenance ECT in geriatric patients. J Am Geriatr Soc 40:706–709, 1992.

Feighner JP, Boyer WF: Selective Serotonin Reuptake Inhibitors, 2nd ed. New York, John Wiley & Sons, 1995.

Fein S, Paz V, Rao N, LaGrassa J: The combination of lithium carbonate and an MAOI in refractory depressions. Am J Psychiatry 145:249–250, 1988.

Fier M: Safer use of MAOIs (letter). Am J Psychiatry 148:391–392, 1991.

Frank E, Kupfer DJ, Perel JM, et al: Three-year outcomes for maintenance therapies in recurrent depression. Arch Gen Psychiatry 47:1093–1099, 1990.

Gardos G, Casey DE, Cole JO, et al: Ten-year outcome of tardive dyskinesia. Am J Psychiatry 151:836–841, 1994.

GarzaTrevino ES, Hollister LE, Overall JE, et al: Efficacy of combinations in intramuscular antipsychotics and sedative hypnotics for control of psychotic-agitation. Am J Psychiatry 146:1598–1601, 1989.

Glazer WM, Kane JM: Depot neuroleptic therapy: An underutilized treatment option. J Clin Psychiatry 53:426–433, 1992.

Goff DC, Baldessarini RJ: Drug interactions with antipsychotic agents. J Clin Psychopharmacol 13:57–67, 1993.

Goldney RD, Spence ND: Safety of the combination of lithium and neuroleptic drugs. Am J Psychiatry 143:882–884, 1986.

Halstead SM, Barnes TRE, Speller JC: Akathesia: Prevalence and associated dysphoria in an inpatient population with chronic schizophrenia. Br J Psychiatry 164:177–183, 1994.

Haykal RF, Akiskal HS: Bupropion as a promising approach to rapid cycling bipolar II patients. J Clin Psychiatry 51:450–455, 1990.

Joffe RT, Singer W, Levitt AJ, et al: A placebo-controlled comparison of lithium and triiodothyronine augmentation of tricyclic antidepressants in unipolar refractory depression. Arch Gen Psychiatry 50:387–393, 1993.

Kane JM: Dosage strategies with long-acting injectable neuroleptics, including haloperidol decanoate. J Clin Psychopharmacol 6:20S–23S, 1986.

Keller MB, Lavori PW, Kane JM, et al: Subsyndromal symptoms in bipolar disorder. Arch Gen Psychiatry 49:371–376, 1992.

Lieberman JA, Kane JM, Johns CA: Clozapine: Guidelines for clinical management. J Clin Psychiatry 50:329–338, 1989.

Lydiard RB: Tricyclic-resistant depression: Treatment resistance or inadequate treatment. J Clin Psychiatry 46:412–417, 1985

Marder SR, Meibach RC: Risperidone in the treatment of schizophrenia. Am J Psychiatry 151:825–835, 1994.

Marinkovic D, Timotijevic I, Babinski T, et al: The side-effects of clozapine. Prog Neuro-Psychopharmacol Biol Psychiatry 18:537–544, 1994.

McEvoy JP: Efficacy of risperidone on positive features of schizophrenia. J Clin Psychiatry 55(5, suppl):18–21, 1994.

Miller DD, Perry PJ, Kelly MW, et al: Pharmacokinetic protocol for predicting plasma haloperidol concentrations. J Clin Psychopharmacol 10:207–212, 1990.

Olajide D, Lader M: A comparison of buspirone, diazepam, and placebo in patients with chronic anxiety states. J Clin Psychopharmacol 7:148–152, 1987.

Pearlman C: Electroconvulsive therapy. Gen Hosp Psychiatry 13:128–137, 1991.

Peet M: Induction of mania with selective serotonin reuptake inhibitors and tricyclic antidepressants. Br J Psychiatry 164:549–550, 1994.

Phillips KA, Nierenberg AA: The assessment and treatment of refractory depression. J Clin Psychiatry 55(2, suppl):20–26, 1994.

Pickar D, Owen RR, Litman RE, et al: Clinical and biological response to clozapine in patients with schizophrenia: Cross-over comparison with fluphenazine. Arch Gen Psychiatry 49:345–353, 1992.

Pope HG, Aizley HG, Keck PE, et al: Neuroleptic malignant syndrome: Longterm followup of 20 cases. J Clin Psychiatry 52:208–212, 1991.

Preskorn SH: Tricyclic antidepressants: The whys and hows of therapeutic drug monitoring. J Clin Psychiatry 50:34–42, 1989.

Prien RF, Gelenberg AJ: Alternatives to lithium for preventive treatment of bipolar disorder. Am J Psychiatry 146:840–848, 1989.

Quitkin FM, Harrison W, Stewart JW, et al: Response to phenelzine and imipramine in placebo nonresponders with atypical depression. Arch Gen Psychiatry 48:319–323, 1991.

Ravindran AV, Bialik RJ, Lapierre YD: Therapeutic efficacy of specific serotonin reuptake inhibitors (SSRIs) in dysthymia. Can J Psychiatry 39:21–26, 1994.

Rosenberg JG, Binder RL, Berlant J: Prediction of therapeutic lithium dose. J Clin Psychiatry 48:284–286, 1987.

Sakkas P, Davis JM, Hua J, et al: Pharmacotherapy of neuroleptic malignant syndrome. Psychiatric Ann 21:157–164, 1991.

Scharf MG, Roth T, Vogel GW, et al: A multicenter, placebo controlled study evaluating zolpidem in the treatment of chronic insomnia. J Clin Psychiatry 55:192–199, 1994.

Schweizer E, Feighner J, Mandos LA, et al: Comparison of venlafaxine and imipramine in the treatment of major depression in outpatients. J Clin Psychiatry 55:104–108, 1994.

Schweizer E, Rickels K, Case G, et al: Longterm therapeutic use of benzodiazepines. Arch Gen Psychiatry 47:908–915, 1990.

Simpson GM, Yadalam K: Blood levels of neuroleptics. J Clin Psychiatry 46(5, suppl 2):22–28, 1985.

Small JG, Milstein V: Lithium interactions: Lithium and electroconvulsive therapy. J Clin Psychopharmacol 10:346–350, 1990.

Sokoloff P, Giros B, Martres M, et al: Molecular cloning and characterization of a novel dopamine receptor ($D_3$) as a target for neuroleptics. Nature 347:146–151, 1990.

Stein G, Bernadt M: Lithium augmentation therapy in tricyclic resistant depression. Br J Psychiatry 162:634–640, 1993.

Sternbach H: The serotonin syndrome. Am J Psychiatry 148:705–713, 1991.

Stuppaeck C, Barnas C, Miller C, et al: Carbamazepine in the prophylaxis of mood disorders. J Clin Psychopharmacol 10:39–42, 1990.

Sussman N: The uses of buspirone in psychiatry. J Clin Psychiatry 12(1, suppl):3–19, 1994.

Task Force on the Use of Laboratory Tests in Psychiatry: Tricyclic antidepressants—blood level measurements and clinical outcome. An APA Task Force Report. Am J Psychiatry 142:155–162, 1985.

Teicher MH, Glod C, Cole JO: Antidepressant drugs and the emergence of suicidal tendencies. Drug Safety 8:186–212, 1993.

Weiner RD, Hammersley D, Moench L, et al: Choice of stimulus electrode placement: Clarification by the APA Task Force on ECT. Convulsive Ther 6:319–321, 1990.

# Chapter 24

# The Elderly Patient

More than 25,000,000 Americans are over 65: 85% have a chronic illness (usually medical); 20–30% have a psychiatric illness (most common in the very old).

## EVALUATION OF THE ELDERLY

1. Assess each patient carefully—mental decline is <u>not</u> "normal" for the aged.
2. Always carefully evaluate physical condition. An impaired physical state can markedly alter the psychiatric evaluation. Make sure the patient can hear and see. Check for deficiency states (iron, folate, vitamin $B_{12}$ and D, calcium, serum proteins).
3. Interview technique—be respectful, use surname, sit near, speak slowly and clearly, allow time for answers, be friendly and personal, pat and hug, be supportive and issue oriented, keep interview short.
4. Collect history, do mental status—perhaps in more than one interview.
5. Identify premorbid personality—defense mechanisms and coping styles (eg, independent vs passive-dependent, rigid vs flexible, use of denial, etc.).
6. Assess the major <u>risk factors:</u>
   A. Loss—of spouse, friends, physical health, job, status, independence, etc.
   B. Poverty—many elderly are poor; some are victims of crime.
   C. Social isolation—impaired mobility, few friends, etc.
   D. Sensory deprivation—poor hearing, vision, etc.
   E. Sickness—chronic pain, forced inactivity, etc.
   F. Fears—of being dependent, of being alone, of being helpless.
7. See family—assess their strengths, dynamics, support for the patient, hidden agendas.

## COMMON PSYCHIATRIC DISORDERS

**Delirium:** Common. May be the primary presentation of:

1. CNS—Cerebral infarction (embolic or thrombotic), TIA, neoplasms.
2. Heart—MI (often without pain), arrhythmia, CHF.
3. Lungs—Pneumonia (without fever or leukocytosis), PE (without chest pain, dyspnea, tachycardia).
4. Blood—Anemia.
5. Metabolic—Diabetes, liver failure, hyper- or hypothyroidism, electrolyte abnormalities.
6. Psychogenic—strange surroundings, stress.
7. Infections—most kinds.
8. Other—Medication reaction, alcoholism, prescription drug misuse, dehydration, fecal impaction, "silent" appendicitis, urinary retention, UTIs, eye or ear disease, postoperative.

Treat the underlying disease process, if possible. Keep patient in a lighted room and with familiar surroundings and people. Restrain only if essential. If needed, use small doses of major tranquilizers (eg, thioridazine 25–50 mg, PO, often given as an HS dose; thiothixene 25 mg, PO, or 4 mg, IM). Mild delirium may continue (unnoticed) for months after the acute episode.

**Dementia:** Most elderly have unimpaired intellectual functioning. Dementia (20% of those 80 years old) is not "just a result of aging"—it needs an explanation. Dementia often presents first with agitation, anxiety, depression, and/or somatic complaints—always do a mental status exam on elderly patients with these complaints but remember that it can also be mimicked by depression, serious physical conditions, alcoholism, and malnutrition. Dementia in the elderly frequently occurs with and is made worse by depression or delirium. Treat the agitated demented patient with low-dose neuroleptics or benzodiazepines initially, then after several weeks, switch to SSRIs, buspirone, and/or trazadone; or later consider the $\beta$-blockers. The memory loss may be unrecognized by the patient but is of major concern to the family, who ultimately insist on evaluation and treatment for it.

Most patients with a progressive and nonreversible form of dementia can be maintained at home until the late stages of the disease process. The decision to institutionalize depends not only on what facilities are available locally (some may be very good) but also on the realistic strengths and limits of the family. Once the cause and prognosis of the dementia is determined, the physician may most profitably spend his time helping the family adjust.

**Depression:** Major Depression can develop in old age for the first time or be a recurrence of a major affective disorder. In the elderly it may at times closely mimic a dementia (pseudodementia)—or physical symptoms, apathy, or fatigue may dominate the clinical picture. It is common, frequently unrecognized, and potentially fatal (both from physical inanition and from suicide—remember, the highest suicide rate is among elderly males, particularly with alcoholism). When in doubt, hospitalize. Treat with psychotherapy and antidepressants (increase slowly; effective final daily oral dose may be as low as 10–50 mg of nortriptyline or 25–100 mg of desipramine). Consider a low-dose SSRI as an alternate first line medication. ECT may be the therapy of choice in patients with unstable cardiac status or in those patients with psychotic depression (eg, paranoia, hallucinations).

A less severe depression or depressive equivalent (listlessness, physical complaints, withdrawal) in a patient with long-standing depressive complaints may represent dysthymic disorder. Since stress and loss are so common among the elderly, adjustment disorder with depressed mood and bereavement occur frequently.

**Mania:** Does occur in old age but usually with a history of bipolar disorder. Extreme agitation or manic-like behavior can be caused by organic factors, dementia, schizophrenia, depression, or situational anxiety. Lithium is effective.

**Schizophrenia:** Usually there is a life-long history of schizophrenic illness but, rarely, the stresses of old age can precipitate a first episode in a predisposed individual (long-standing schizoid or borderline functioning). Occasionally there is associated intellectual deterioration. Treat with support and antipsychotics.

**Paranoia:** Mild suspiciousness among the elderly is very common. Bizarre forms or near psychotic levels may occur with:

1. Early dementia—always check for intellectual loss.
2. Delirium

3. Vision or hearing problems—may resolve promptly.
4. Social isolation; chronic illness.
5. Drugs—eg, steroids, antiparkinsonians, hypnotic withdrawal.

DELUSIONAL DISORDER (DSM-IV p 301, 297.1) often has an onset late in life (late paraphrenia). These patients have fixed paranoid delusions and occasionally auditory hallucinations but not the loose associations, grandiosity, major hallucinations, and autistic thought of paranoid schizophrenics (although the conditions may overlap). Treat with reality-oriented psychotherapy, behavior modification, maintenance antipsychotics, and possibly ECT.

**Hypochondriasis:** The elderly are frequently ill and may develop a preoccupation with exaggerated physical complaints and problems. This is particularly common among depressed and/or demented elderly. The physical symptoms may or may not improve with resolution of the depression.

The patient with severe hypochondriasis, whose life is dominated by ruminations about one or more physical problems, is very difficult to treat. Withdrawal and isolation are frequent. Don't expect a "cure." Develop an ongoing relationship with this patient. Be available. See every 2–3 wk for 10–20 min. Reassure that the problem may be persistent and incurable but not debilitating or fatal. Recognize that in some cases symptoms may continue because to lose them would mean to lose the reason for visiting the physician.

**Adjustment Disorders:** These are common in old age and are due to the numerous stresses (loss, physical illness, retirement, etc.) encountered. Symptoms include anxiety, depression, agitation, and physical complaints and most often occur in persons with past adjustment problems. Grief is common and may mimic a major depression but often has an obvious precipitant, is short-lived with therapy, and does not require antidepressants. Alcohol abuse is also a common response to stress in the elderly and is frequently unrecognized. Supportive psychotherapy, attention to concrete problems, and brief use of minor tranquilizers or low dose antipsychotics helps.

## PSYCHOPHARMACOLOGY OF OLD AGE

The elderly usually run higher blood levels (due to decreased hepatic metabolism and renal excretion, reduced plasma albumin and protein binding, and increased fat to lean tissue ratios), display increased receptor responsiveness, and thus require more gradual increases and lower doses of most psychoactive medication. They are also more susceptible to most side effects, eg, peripheral and central anticholinergic effects, sedation, hypotension, arrhythmias. They are at risk for bowel obstruction, urinary retention, BP problems (fainting, stroke), sudden death from fatal arrhythmias, glaucoma crises, delirium, and coma. Also, they are particularly likely to be taking multiple drugs, to misunderstand and fail to comply with prescribing instruction, and to have symptoms from such polypharmacy. Preferable medication may include:

Benzodiazepines: For anxiety, oxazepam (15–30 mg/day) and lorazepam (0.53–3 mg/day) are least likely to accumulate. In patients with insomnia, try relaxation or exercise first: if a medication is needed, try temazepam (7.5–15 mg HS; less likely to accumulate than flurazepam) or one of the sedating antihistamines (eg, diphenhydramine or hydroxyzine).

Tricyclics: Nortriptyline (less cardiotoxicity and hypotension) and desipramine (few anticholinergic effects). Begin as low as 10–25 mg daily and work up. Test for glaucoma and prostatic hypertrophy first. Monitor blood levels. The SSRIs are a reasonable first choice alternative.

MAOIs: All have little anticholinergic effect and cardiotoxicity but watch out for hypotension. They are effective antidepressants, but hypertensive crises are particularly worrisome in the elderly. Use low doses, eg, phenelzine 15 mg bid or tid.

Antipsychotics: Usually choose the more potent, least sedating types (eg, haloperidol, trifluoperazine), but be guided by patient's side effects. Thioridazine is well tolerated in low doses. Be particularly careful with IM meds—use U-100 insulin syringes to assure a small dose, if necessary.

Lithium: Toxicity occurs easily, so keep on a lower maintenance level (eg, 0.4–0.7 mEq/l).

## GENERAL TREATMENT PRINCIPLES

— Be supportive, respectful, sympathetic, and a "good listener." Touch the patient.
— Encourage patients to express themselves (about guilt, loneliness, helplessness) and unburden themselves (eg, grieve).

— Be directive and reality oriented. Help in a concrete way with problems (eg, who to see about rent assistance, calling "Meals-on-
Wheels," explanation of Medicare benefits). The quality of the patient's current environment is probably the single most important
factor promoting recovery and continued health.
— Strengthen defenses rather than restructure them.
— Encourage self-esteem. Helping patients "review their life" (to see it
as complete) can be enormously beneficial. Reminiscence is adaptive coping behavior and helps promote self-esteem.
— Encourage continued interests, friendships, socialization, activities,
and self-support. Identify those things still done well and keep the
patient doing them (if they can't fix the meal, maybe they can still
set the table).
— Be an ongoing presence. Be available—frequent, regular, short sessions. Be reachable by telephone.
— Involve and work with the family. Teach them appropriate skills and
expectation. Anger, frustrations, and resentment often develop—
help them deal with these feelings.
— A psychotherapy group of elderly patients is often very helpful—
locate one for the patient.
— Know and use community resources.

## Suggested Readings

Bienenfeld D: Clinical Geropsychiatry. Baltimore, Williams & Wilkins,
1990.

Brown JW, Chobor A, Zinn F: Dementia testing in the elderly. J Nerv
Ment Dis 181:695–698, 1993.

Cummings JL: Subcortical dementia. Br J Psychiatry 149:682–697,
1986.

Davidson M: Alzheimer's disease. Psychiatr Clin North Am 14:6, 1991.

Dietch JT, Fine M: The effect of nortriptyline in elderly patients with
cardiac conduction disease. J Clin Psychiatry 51:65–67, 1990.

Geller CJR, Stokes EJ, Levine DM, et al: Characteristics, diagnosis, and
treatment of alcoholism in elderly patients. J Am Geriatr Soc
37:310–316, 1989.

Hendrie HC, Crossett JHW: An overview of depression in the elderly.
Psychiatr Ann 20:64–70, 1990.

Holden NL: Late paraphrenia or the paraphrenias? Br J Psychiatry
150:635–639, 1987.

Jenike MA: Geriatric Psychiatry and Psychopharmacology. Chicago, Year
Book Medical Publications, 1989.

Jorgensen P, Munk-Jorgensen P: Paranoid psychosis in the elderly. Acta
Psychiatr Scand 72:358–363, 1985.

Lipowski ZJ: Transient cognitive disorders in the elderly. Am J Psychiatry 140:1426–1436, 1983.

Long PP: The elderly and drug interactions. J Am Geriatr Soc 34:586–592, 1986.

Leukoff SE, Evans DA, Liptzin B, et al: Delirium. Arch Intern Med 152:334–340, 1992.

Reisberg B: Dementia: A systematic approach to identifying reversible causes. Geriatrics 41:30–46, 1986.

Rovner BW, German PS, Brant LJ, et al: Depression and mortality in nursing homes. JAMA 265:993–996, 1991.

Sadavoy J, Lazarus LW, Jarvik LF: Comprehensive Review of Geriatric Psychiatry. Washington, D.C., American Psychiatric Press, 1991.

Small GW: Recognition and treatment of depression in the elderly. J Clin Psychiatry 52:(6, suppl):11–22, 1991.

Weiss KJ: Management of anxiety and depression syndromes in the elderly. J Clin Psychiatry 55(2, suppl):5–12, 1994.

Wieman HM: Avoiding common pitfalls of geriatric prescribing. Geriatrics 41:81–89, 1986.

Zisook S, Braff DL: Delirium: Recognition and management in the older patient. Geriatrics 41:67–78, 1986.

# Chapter 25

# Legal Issues

The interface between psychiatry and law is in flux, partly due to recent patient's rights legislation (based on the constitutional assurance that no person shall be deprived of his liberty without "due process of law"). A psychiatrist's dealings with his patients increasingly are constrained by case law and statute. It is essential that he learn the limits to his independence. Laws can differ markedly from state to state and may change with time—become familiar with those laws that apply to your area.

## CIVIL LAW

### Civil Commitment

All states permit civil commitment to inpatient (and, at times, outpatient) psychiatric care under specific, but differing, criteria. Know your local standards.

1. Mental Illness: All states require the presence of a mental illness, but definitions differ. Psychosis usually is included but personality disorder is not. Drug and/or alcohol abuse may be accepted. Mental illness alone is not sufficient for commitment but requires at least one of the following two additional conditions.
2. Dangerousness—to self or others: Most states require the patient to be dangerous but differ in the degree of urgency—an imminent danger (eg, likely to hurt himself in the next 24 hours) vs a relative danger (eg, physically deteriorating through depressive withdrawal). Two major problems with the dangerousness standard are: (1) psychiatrists have difficulty accurately predicting future dangerous behavior except in the most obvious cases, and (2) it has been uncertain what level of proof the law requires, ie, from the lowest civil standard of "preponderance of the evidence" (51% certainty) to the most strict criminal standard of "beyond a reasonable doubt" (95% certainty). This latter issue appears to have been resolved by a recent

US Supreme Court decision (Addington v Texas, 1979) favoring "clear and convincing evidence" (75% certainty).

3. Disabled and in need of treatment: Although diminished in number, some states allow commitment solely on the grounds that a person is significantly handicapped by a mental illness, is in need of treatment, and would benefit from that treatment.

Most states also have laws (usually less strict) allowing the patient to be briefly (1–14 days) held involuntarily. Committed patients who feel that they are being held illegally may obtain a hearing by a writ of habeas corpus.

Much of recent legislation defining these standards has redressed real past wrongs which occurred when commitment could result merely from a physician's OK, yet recent controversy has focused on associated losses to the patient and his family due to his exclusion from treatment because of complex, criminal-like commitment proceedings. As fewer patients have been treated involuntarily, some experts have noted a shift of mental patients from the civil to the criminal system, ie, the mental illness causes them to break a law they ordinarily would not have broken, and they are then arrested. The extent of this trend has not yet been determined.

An additional impact of the changing commitment laws has been to require the release of committed patients much earlier than in the past, resulting in a marked decline in the size of state mental hospitals. An unfortunate effect of this deinstitutionalization has been to release large numbers of marginally functioning persons into communities ill-equipped to deal with them—with the resultant formation of "psychiatric ghettos" in some large cities.

## The Right to Treatment

After the classic Alabama decision of Wyatt v Stickney (1972), it has become a general standard (amazingly, it had not been before) that an involuntarily committed person must receive a level of effective treatment adequate to encourage improvement. This concept was challenged, reviewed, and supported in another well-known case—Donaldson v O'Connor (1974). How to deal with the patient who is unlikely to improve with any treatment remains uncertain.

## The Right To Refuse Treatment

This is currently the most actively contested area of psychiatric law, and the results of the debate remain uncertain. Involuntary commitment is not prima facie evidence that the patient is incompetent to decide what treatment he is to receive. Federal court decisions set the tone but conflict: Rennie v Klein (1979) gives a patient a qualified right to refuse treatment and creates an appeal process, while Rogers v Okin (1981) allows absolute refusal but provides for treatment authorized by a guardian and Rogers v Commissioner insists the judge must make the treatment decision. Presumably the US Supreme Court ultimately will clarify these discrepancies, but has not yet done so. Meanwhile, be very cautious (and legal) when insisting that a patient receive ECT or medication against his will, even when he appears to need it badly. Know your local laws. The degree of a physician's liability in giving treatment to a resisting patient is likely to be clarified in the next few years.

## Abandonment

Refusing to treat a willing (although possibly difficult) and active patient is to risk the charge of "abandonment." When refusing continued care, always document the reasons (they should be sound, of course), attempt to transfer the patient to another therapist or institution if the patient is willing, make efforts to minimize any risk to the patient (and document), and arrange to care for the patient "in extremis" until the clinical situation has stabilized.

## Competency

Psychiatrists are sometimes asked to assess (the court decides) whether a patient is mentally competent to perform specific functions (eg, make a will, handle his finances, testify in court). There are rules for some of these decisions, eg, to be judged competent to make a will, a person must know (1) that he is making a will, (2) the extent and nature of his property, and (3) to whom he is leaving his possessions. To be found incompetent for one task does not necessarily imply incompetence for another; ie, competency is task-specific.

## CRIMINAL LAW

### Competency To Stand Trial

It is held in law that, to receive a fair trial, a person must be able to understand the nature of his charges, understand the possible penalties, understand legal issues and procedures, and work with his attorney and participate rationally in his own defense (Dusky v United States). If he can't do one or more of these, he is "incompetent to stand trial" and usually is transferred to a treatment facility until his competency is restored (eg, medication for a psychosis). Once found competent, the patient is usually returned to court to stand trial. Recently, some states have decided that if a patient's competency can't be restored in a "reasonable length of time" (eg, the length of time he probably would serve for the crime for which he has been charged), he must continue treatment in a civil facility if committable, or be released. Psychiatrists are most commonly the experts asked to help the court decide on competency (the decision is that of the court).

### Criminal Responsibility

The "not guilty by reason of insanity" plea is much debated by both the legal and psychiatric professions yet it continues to be used (infrequently). It is not widely abused. Part of the general dissatisfaction with this plea centers on whether psychiatrists (or anyone) can retrospectively determine a patient's mental functioning at the time of a crime. Just as an incompetency decision is concerned with the patient's mental state at the time of the trial, a responsibility decision involves the mental state at the time of the crime. Also in question are the criteria needed to make that judgment—several different ones are used in different states:

— The M'Naghten Rule: Did the person not know (1) the nature of his act and (2) that it was wrong? This is a common test (one-third of states).
— The Irresistible Impulse Test: Was he acting under an "irresistible impulse?" This test is invariably combined with other tests.
— The Durham Rule: Was his act the product of "a mental disease or defect?"
— The American Law Institute (ALI) Test: Does he have a mental dis-

ease or defect such that he "lacks substantial capacity either to appreciate the criminality of his conduct or to conform his conduct to the requirements of the law?" This test adds a "volitional" standard to the "cognitive" standard of the M'Naghten Rule. It is used in approximately one-half of the states and in all federal courts.

If one or more of the above conditions are met, the patient may be declared "not guilty by reason of insanity" and be freed of responsibility for his crime. If needing treatment at that point, he is usually placed in a psychiatric facility until his mental illness remits or until he is no longer believed to be a threat to the community because of mental illness.

Many states and the US Congress have considered restrictive modifications (or abolition) of the insanity defense in the wake of the public outcry after John Hinckley's "not guilty" verdict for his shooting of President Reagan. The form the insanity defense ultimately will take is not clear. Leading possibilities appear to be (1) a return to some form of the M'Naghten Rule by eliminating the "volitional" standard, and (2) a guilty but mentally ill verdict (thus, a person first would be judged and sentenced criminally, then treated in an appropriate setting for his mental illness).

## PERSONAL ISSUES

### Malpractice

The risk that a psychiatrist will be successfully sued for malpractice is low but climbing. Most suits involve use of ECT, improper or inadequately informed use of medication, unusual treatments, sexual involvement with patients, and successful patient suicide (suit brought by relatives). Although it sounds like a platitude, the best defense is a strong and respectful therapeutic alliance with the patient. (Yet even that is uncertain protection given a recent successful suit by a father arguing that the therapist had induced false memories of abuse by him in his daughter, the patient.)

### Confidentiality

Physicians are ethically obligated to maintain patient confidentiality, except when voluntarily waived by the patient. General knowledge by others of details of a patient's psychiatric treatment or even awareness of psychiatric care can be damaging socially and occupationally to a patient. Unfortunately, legal protection of the physician for maintaining that confidentiality is far from complete. In some cases (eg, Tarasoff v Regents of the University of California (1976) states that a therapist has a "duty to protect" a third party threatened harm by the patient), the psychiatrist may be liable if he does not break privacy. When uncertain, seek consultation from a colleague. Finally, utilization review groups and third-party payers are demanding more privileged information. Become familiar with your own state's laws.

## Informed Consent

Informed consent should be sought from all patients for all treatments, but formal (ie, written) consent should be obtained for physical procedures (eg, ECT, medication). The patient should be informed about the reasons for the treatment, its nature, the likelihood of success, the dangers and likelihood of side effects, and any alternative treatments.

A major problem arises if the patient is "incapable of being informed" (eg, due to retardation, OBS, psychosis). A guardian may need to be appointed whose duty would be to make the decision for the patient.

## Suggested References

AMA Committee on Medicolegal Problems: Insanity defense in criminal trials and limitation of psychiatric testimony. JAMA 251:2967–2981, 1984.

APA Committee on Confidentiality: Guidelines on confidentiality. Am J Psychiatry 144:1522–1526, 1987.

Appelbaum PS: Tarasoff and the clinician: Problems in fulfilling the duty to protect. Am J Psychiatry 142:425–429, 1985.

Appelbaum PS: Resurrecting the right to treatment. Hosp Community Psychiatry 38:703–704, 1987.

Bloom JD, Rogers JL: The duty to protect others from your patients. Tarasoff spreads to the northwest. West J Med 148:231–234, 1988.

Bromberg W: The perils of psychiatry. Psychiatr Ann 13:219–236, 1983.

Bursten B: Posthospital mandatory outpatient treatment. Am J Psychiatry 143:1255–1258, 1986.

Drane JF: Competency to give an informed consent. JAMA 252:925–927, 1984.

Gross BH, Southard MJ, Lamb HR, Weinberger LE: Assessing dangerousness and responding appropriately. J Clin Psychiatry 48:9–12, 1987.

Gutheil RG: Rogers v Commissioner: Denouement of an important right-to-refuse-treatment case. Am J Psychiatry 142:213–216, 1985.

Gutheil TG, Appelbaum PS: Clinical Handbook of Psychiatry and the Law. New York, McGraw-Hill Book Co., 1982.

Hipshman L: Assessing a patient's competence to make treatment decisions. Psychiatr Ann 17:279–283, 1987.

Kern SR: Issues of competency in the aged. Psychiatr Ann 17:336–339, 1987.

Lamb HR: Incompetency to stand trial. Arch Gen Psychiatr 44:754–758, 1987.

McNiel DE, Binder RL: Predictive validity of judgments of dangerousness in emergency civil commitment. Am J Psychiatry 144:197–200, 1987.

Miller RD: Need-for-treatment criteria for involuntary civil commitment: Impact in practice. Am J Psychiatry 149:1380–1384, 1992.

Mills MJ, Sullivan G, Eth S: Protecting third parties: A decade after Tarasoff. Am J Psychiatry 144:68–74, 1987.

Reid WH, Wise M, Sutton: The use and reliability of psychiatric diagnosis in forensic settings. Psychiatr Clin North Am 15:529–537, 1992.

Schwartz HI, Appelbaum PS, Kaplan RD: Clinical judgements in the decision to commit. Arch Gen Psychiatry 41:811–815, 1984.

Serban G: Multiple personality: An issue for forensic psychiatry. Am J Psychother 46:269–280, 1992.

Wettstein RM, Mulvey EP, Rogers R: A prospective comparison of four insanity defense standards. Am J Psychiatry 148:21–27, 1991.